# World Sea Fisheries

First published in 1956, *World Sea Fisheries* gives a general survey of the sea fisheries of the world. It assesses their relative importance at a time when the growing world population placed an increasing strain on food supplies. It examines the forces which mould the character of sea fisheries in any region. As the book attempts to explain the basic reasons for their varying characters, its regional section is preceded by sections dealing with the physical factors affecting fisheries, and with fishing techniques and craft. The author gives chief attention to certain essential features of an area by giving the reader a more accessible source of important figures and isolating most significant features and trends from the mass of detailed and complex statistics provided by many countries. The volume also contains several maps. It will be a fascinating read for students and researchers of economic geography and general readers interested in the topic as it gives a rare glimpse into the fishing industry that existed almost seventy years ago.

# World Sea Fisheries

Robert Morgan

Routledge
Taylor & Francis Group

First published in 1956
by Methuen & Co Ltd

This edition first published in 2024 by Routledge
4 Park Square, Milton Park, Abingdon, Oxon, OX14 4RN

and by Routledge
605 Third Avenue, New York, NY 10017

*Routledge is an imprint of the Taylor & Francis Group, an informa business*

**Publisher's Note**
The publisher has gone to great lengths to ensure the quality of this reprint but points out that some imperfections in the original copies may be apparent.

**Disclaimer**
The publisher has made every effort to trace copyright holders and welcomes correspondence from those they have been unable to contact.

A Library of Congress record exists under LCCN: a 56004431

ISBN: 978-1-032-88820-0 (hbk)
ISBN: 978-1-003-53984-1 (ebk)
ISBN: 978-1-032-88825-5 (pbk)

Book DOI 10.4324/9781003539841

LARGE TUNA BEING CAUGHT BY A CALIFORNIAN TUNA CLIPPER

# WORLD SEA FISHERIES

BY

ROBERT MORGAN

Ph.D.

METHUEN & CO LTD
36 ESSEX STREET, STRAND, LONDON WC 2

*First published in 1956*

I.I

CATALOGUE NO 5172/U

PRINTED AND BOUND IN GREAT BRITAIN BY
JARROLD AND SONS LTD, NORWICH

# FOREWORD

THE seas and their resources have attracted increasing world attention in recent years. There have been many scientific papers or books, each dealing with particular aspects of oceanography, marine biology and allied subjects, and with the techniques of fisheries. There have also been published a number of books directed at a wider readership, which have succeeded in stimulating much public interest in the life within the sea. Above all, the present rate of growth of world population calls for a closer concern with all sources of food.

At the time of writing, no book has been published aiming to give a general survey of the sea fisheries of the world as a whole. That is the intention of this book, which deals with the fisheries of all the world's major areas and assesses their relative importance. As it attempts to explain the basic reasons for their varying characters, its regional section is preceded by sections dealing with the physical factors affecting fisheries, and with fishing techniques and craft. In the treatment of these matters I have endeavoured to give a fair amount of information, while not commencing with the assumption that all readers are initially familiar with their background.

In covering so wide a field as the world in one volume, attention has necessarily to be given chiefly to certain essential features of an area. Many countries issue detailed and complex statistics, although there is sometimes a considerable time-lag in their preparation. One of the objects of this book is to give the reader a more accessible source of some important figures, and to isolate the most significant features and trends from the mass of detail in the official statistics. The book also contains a number of maps. These are intended to illustrate certain features, and it is assumed that for general background the reader is referring to a suitable atlas.

I should like to record my thanks to Professor R. O. Buchanan for his criticism and encouragement, and to Mr N. B. Marshall, of the British Museum of Natural History, for information on fish classification systems. My thanks are also due to the United States Information Service for Plates I, IV, VII, XIV and XV; the French Information Attaché for Plates II, VI, VIII, and XIII; the Norwegian Press and Foreign Information Office for

Plates XI and XII; the Shell Oil Company for Plate V; the Central Office of Information for Plates IIIa, IX, X, and XVI; the Iago Steam Trawler Company of Fleetwood for Plate IIIb; and to the British Transport Commission and the Mortensen publishing company of Oslo for the use of maps on which were based respectively Figs. 40 and 41.

*October 1955*                                    ROBERT MORGAN

# CONTENTS

# ILLUSTRATIONS

* *Photographs reproduced by permission of the Central Office of Information.*

xi

# INTRODUCTION

THE great growth of world population now occurring must place an increasing strain on food supplies. At the World Population Congress of 1954 in Rome, it was stated that the world's population was increasing at such a rate that, if it were maintained, the current total of 2,500 million would reach between 3,500 and 4,000 million as early as 1980. Apart from the demand for more food to maintain present levels of nutrition, there are large areas of the world where an increase in the level is essential to well-being. The need to find food for the world's great press of population is only one facet of the great twentieth-century problem, but failure to deal with it may ultimately have results as dire as failure to meet the more immediately dramatic dangers.

This situation brings fisheries into prominence. At present only about a tenth of the world's flesh foods is obtained from its waters. There seems little doubt that total world fisheries production could be doubled, even though some long important fisheries are capable of little further expansion. The possible rate of increase of output in a developing fishery is often decidedly greater than that usual in an agricultural area undergoing development or intensification, so that fisheries may prove particularly valuable in helping to meet the demands of the near future.

In this study the aim has been to examine the forces which mould the character of the sea fisheries of any region. Standards for comparison of fisheries in different areas are considered, and applied to the world's regions. Sea fisheries have immense extent and variety. There are strong contrasts in methods, vessels and types of product, and in the fishermen and kinds of community evolved. Yet the parts of this great loosely-knit world industry are linked by basic conditions common to them all. The factors which create a fishery, limit its extent, determine its methods, and locate the fishing settlements will be discussed.

No fishery develops haphazardly, but always in response, not always consciously ordered, to certain conditions. Changes in these conditions lead to repercussions, and then new tendencies towards equilibrium at a different stage. The fishery is the channel between the fish in the sea and in the inland market place, and it reacts sensitively to stimuli from both ends; to changes in conditions of supply in the sea, and to changes in conditions of demand in the shops. The geographical unit of a particular fishery, to be complete, must therefore embrace its fishing grounds, its fishing ports, and their hinterland markets with their lines of communication. The location and development of the large modern fishing port is often influenced more by its chief markets than by its fishing grounds. The exceptions are mainly those which re-export their fish by sea to foreign markets.

A fishery in an advanced area is a great, complex and inter-related assemblage of vessels, fishing equipment, harbour works, and machinery for fish handling, preservation, and processing. There are market and storage buildings, railway sidings, plants producing fertilizer, meal and oil, factories providing nets, ropes and ice, specialized shipbuilding yards, and finally the houses and other social capital of the communities needed to operate all these aspects of the fishery. To obtain a satisfactory geographical conception of such a fishery, none of these aspects must be neglected, for they react upon one another. All these activities blend into the organic whole that is the fishing industry.

All tonnages given in this book are metric (1 long ton of 2,240 lb. = 1·016 metric ton). National totals given as 'catch' or 'production' represent full weight at time of catch, before any heading or other treatment.

*Section I*

# THE PHYSICAL ENVIRONMENT

# CHAPTER I

# THE PLANKTON PASTURAGE

Two main groups of elements determine whether an area of sea will develop an important fishery. First are the physical conditions, which determine the quantity of fish available and the suitability of the area for the operation of commercial fishing methods. These conditions determine the potentialities of the area, and set the upper limit to its long-term rate of production. The second group, which may broadly be termed 'human', includes such matters as the density of the populations in the lands around the sea, their food habits, their purchasing power, and their degree of maritime skill. This group determines the proportion of the potential resources that is exploited. This section of the book will deal with the main bases of the first group: the physical environment of the fishing industry. This in turn can be divided into two main aspects: that which affects the life within the sea, and that which affects the fishing operations. The first aspect will be dealt with now.

The quantity of fish in a given area of sea, and the rate at which it can be 'cropped', obviously depends on their supply of nourishment. The food relationships of the sea are mainly of a predatory nature; the more powerful fish feed on the less powerful, and the least powerful in turn feed on the plankton. This, however, is an over-simplified statement. Some very large fish, such as the whale-shark, by-pass most of the chain and feed directly on the very small fish and larger plankton, while some fish, which may be compared to land herbivores, feed only on plankton. Yet, however the food relationship operates for any one species, it is clear that the total weight of fish which can be supported must depend on the rate of production of their basic food, whether they eat it directly, or indirectly in the form of other fish.

This basic food is the plankton, the mass of small or microscopic living organisms, frequently of simple structure, which inhabits the sea. Plankton can be divided into two groups: zooplankton, or drifting animals (including the eggs and larvae of larger creatures), and phytoplankton, which are drifting plants. As the zooplankton themselves live on the phytoplankton, it is the

3

phytoplankton stock which is the final pasture on which all sea creatures ultimately depend. In shallow waters this pasture is augmented by the plants which grow on the sea-bed. The possible production rate of all other sea life is therefore dependent on the production rate of these two forms of plants.

On what, in turn, does the plant production rate depend? Now the border between the organic and inorganic fields has to be crossed. The sea-bed plants, which are less important than the phytoplankton as a basic source of fish food, have requirements in some respects similar to land plants. Their first need is sunshine, and the limit of their outward extension from the shore is chiefly determined by the depth of water which the sunlight can penetrate. This varies with the latitude and the clarity of the water. Other determinants of production are the chemical composition, structure, stability, and other attributes of the surface layer of the sea floor. Sea-bed plants are normally most abundant in areas well replenished with nutrient salts by rivers, though in some places this may be more than offset by muddiness of the water reducing the penetration of the sun's rays. Their maximum depth may, however, be taken as about 100 metres in the tropics, while in latitude 60° N. it is rarely much above 20 metres.

Growing phytoplankton also are only found in the upper sunlit layer of the sea, to a maximum depth of about 80 to 100 metres, though zooplankton may exist at considerable depths below this, feeding on sinking dead plankton. The bulk of zooplankton are, however, also obliged to live in or near this sunlight-penetrated or 'euphotic' zone, where lies their main food supply.

Apart from the factor of the Sun, the phytoplankton production and type is mainly determined by the amount, type, and relative proportion of the nutrient substances and gases dissolved in the sea, and by the temperature of the water. These in turn are affected by such factors as nearness to land, the amount of river discharge from there, and the ocean currents in both horizontal and vertical planes. There are marked seasonal variations in the phytoplankton stock, especially in areas well away from the Equator.

The biological processes in the sea are in continuous operation, though varying seasonally in intensity. The materials for the manufacture and maintenance of phytoplankton include the nitrates, phosphates, and carbon dioxide dissolved in the water.

The water itself is a raw material, indeed, making important contribution to the weight of active protoplasm. The other main constituents of the organic content of phytoplankton are carbon, nitrogen, and phosphorus. The carbon is obtained from the carbon dioxide dissolved in the water by photosynthesis under the influence of sunlight into carbohydrate, as shown by the formula:

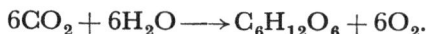

$$6CO_2 + 6H_2O \longrightarrow C_6H_{12}O_6 + 6O_2.$$

It has been found that carbon, nitrogen, and phosphorus bear a fairly constant ratio to each other in averages of plankton. The average ratio in a number of hauls of mixed plankton has been found to be respectively $41 : 7 \cdot 2 : 1$, by weight. N : P ratio is significantly close to the normal relative amounts of these elements in sea water, showing that plankton are adapted to make optimum use of these resources in the sea.

The density of phytoplankton has been found, when other factors are favourable, to be related to changes in the phosphate supply of the water, and annual variations of this in certain areas, due to vagaries of currents, have been found to be broadly correlated with variations of plankton production. The proportion of phosphorus in normal sea water is, nevertheless, very small, reaching a maximum of about one-tenth gramme per ton.

The cycle of transformation which organic and inorganic matter in the sea is continuously undergoing (which is not to be confused with the seasonal cycle in the intensity of this organic cycle) is, broadly, that indicated in Fig. 1.

Dead animals and plants are attacked by bacteria, which, by various complex processes, turn them back into the basic substances, the plant nutrients, which begin the food chain. Whereas the initial portion of this cycle, the forming of the phytoplankton, must take place in the euphotic zone, the action of the bacteria takes place at all depths. The sinking dead matter is attacked by the bacteria right down to the deepest sea-bed. It is also eaten by the creatures, both fish and zooplankton, which live below the zone of sunlight. Animals of various types can live even down to the greatest depths. The density of animal life, however, decreases rapidly below relatively shallow depths, because the supply of dead and sinking food naturally diminishes with depth as it is eaten or decomposed. The fish living in the middle and lower depths of the ocean are sparsely distributed, and specially adapted to their conditions of darkness and high pressure. Some carnivores possess various devices, such as illuminated appendages, to lure their scanty prey. These deep-water fish have no interest from the point of view of commercial fishing.

Because of the constant sinking of a proportion of dead matter and excreta below the surface layers before it can be fully transformed into inorganic nutrients, the concentration of these

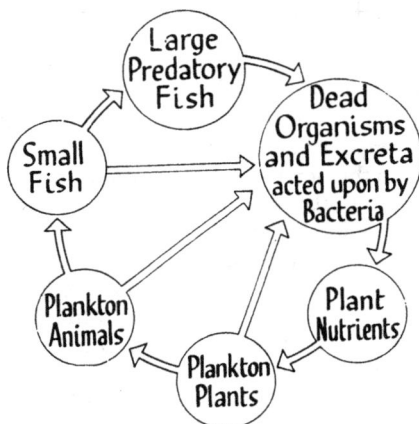

*Fig. 1.* Simplified diagram of some of the food relationships

nutrients normally increases with depth. At 1,000 metres depth at points in the western Atlantic, the phosphate concentration is some ten times what it is at 100 metres, while below 1,000 metres the concentration usually increases steadily but relatively slowly.

There is thus a large permanent reservoir of nutrients in the lower layers of the sea, though local variations in concentration may be considerable. In most areas of the sea there is little opportunity for this deep reservoir to be tapped and put to use by the local euphotic zone, but a good deal of these nutrients ultimately reach the surface by vertical movements after a long slow journey in deep water, to benefit certain regions greatly. In regard to carbon dioxide there is never any lack in such cases, as deep water is rich in this gas, which is also a product of organic decomposition. The loss of nutrients from the surface layers by the sinking of decaying material is ultimately made good by nutrients brought up from lower depths by vertical water movements, or fed into the sea by rivers.

Vertical mixing of waters from any cause commonly leads to vigorous organic activity. A degree of such mixing takes place in the upper layers of the sea in most regions because of wind-made and other turbulence, but there are also greater vertical movements.

Regions where upwelling takes place along the coast to replace water moving away from the shore because of the drive of

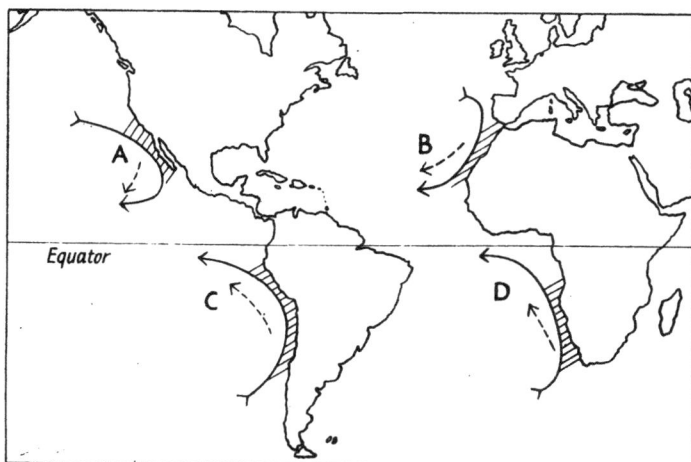

*Fig. 2.* Important Trade Wind coastal upwelling areas (shaded)
- - - - ➤ Direction of Trade Wind
➤——➤ Currents projecting nutrient-rich belts away from coasts
A. California.   B. Canaries.   C. Peru.   D. Benguela.

prevailing offshore or alongshore Trade Winds, coupled with deflection due to the earth's rotation, are more fertile in plankton and fish than they would otherwise be (see Fig. 2). The seas off California, Peru, and North-west and South-west Africa with this upwelling have proved in practice to be rich in fish. Upwelling also takes place along the Equator in the Pacific, because the westward-moving water tends to be deflected by the rotation of the Earth to the right in the northern hemisphere, and to the left in the southern. The part of this upwelling area near the Galapagos is much used by American tuna fishermen.

A high productivity of phytoplankton is to be found in a world-circling belt at about 50°–60° S., varying with longitude, where deep water, relatively very rich in phosphates and nitrates after its long creep southwards in the depths of the great ocean basins, wells to the surface. It does this to replace water which is leaving the surface layer about Antarctica in two ways. Water which is cooled by loss of heat to the cold air sinks to the very bottom of the ocean, where it begins to creep northwards, while the extreme surface layer, despite its cooling, does not sink because it is lightened by a lower salinity due to rain, snow, and melting ice. It moves away from the continent for some distance on the surface. The upwelling water essential to replace these movements has come great distances southward as deep, though not bottom, water. During this journey it has collected large quantities of nutrients from the sinking and decomposition of dead matter and excreta from the layers above it. When this great conveyor-belt of life-giving materials reaches the sunlit zone near the surface it bursts into life in the form of phytoplankton, particularly diatoms, and indirectly supports the abundant whale production of this circumpolar belt.

In similar latitudes in the northern oceans there is not so definite a large-scale circulation, partly due to interference by the land masses, but there is nevertheless a strong 'overturn' of the water during the winter, due to cooling and sinking of the surface layers and their replacement by deeper nutrient-rich water. Thus, although the tropical waters have the advantages of higher temperature and more sunlight, they are generally prevented, save in the areas of Trade Wind and equatorial upwelling, from using these to the full because of their poverty of nutrients. Tropical water tends to be vertically stable, because the surface water, warmed and therefore lightened by the hot sun, stays on the surface (although in some areas really high evaporation, with consequent high salinity and density, may lead to sinking).

Life production goes on throughout the year in the warm latitude waters, without great seasonal fluctuation. In higher latitudes the life production is small in the low sunlight and temperature of winter, but nutrient salts are building up richly in the euphotic layer, by local overturn and by larger-scale movements, ready to feed the great burst of life with the spring sunlight, which makes the annual production greater than in most tropic waters.

For the purpose of estimating the potentialities of a region, it is important to distinguish between the stock of phytoplankton and the daily increase, which is the true determinant of the possible daily fish weight increase. The daily increase of phytoplankton is surprisingly high. It was estimated by Hans Lohmann in the Kiel area to be about 30 per cent by weight of the standing crop, taking an average of seasonal variations. The rate of consumption of phytoplankton is also very high. The simpler plankton creatures may at times daily consume roughly half their weight in phytoplankton, though higher forms consume less in proportion to weight. The relative rate of depletion of phytoplankton must, however, be very high. Nevertheless, in spring the phytoplankton increase rate succeeds in passing the depletion rate, leading to a cumulative burst of growth—the 'bloom'— which in many areas markedly deepens the green colour of the sea. In winter depletion rate exceeds production rate, and stock falls.

The seasonal march of events in the English Channel, for example, is broadly as follows. In February the nutrient content of the water is high, but phytoplankton concentration is low. Increasing sunshine in early spring then leads to the phytoplankton outburst, while the using up of the nutrients reduces their concentration. In later spring the phytoplankton content falls greatly because it is now being heavily grazed by the spring outburst of larvae. During the summer there are a number of fluctuations, but by August nutrient concentration has normally fallen very low. A month or so later, however, nutrient concentration has risen markedly with the death and decay of the summer plankton, and it can now support the autumn outburst of phytoplankton, less intense than the spring one but nevertheless substantial. Finally, the winter fall in sunshine reduces photosynthesis and the phytoplankton content of the water falls sharply at the year's end, while the nutrient content builds up ready for its use in the spring.

Can estimates be made of the maximum productive capacity of any area of sea? At present, such estimates cannot be made with great accuracy. In theory there should be no reason why, given all the relevant data concerning nutrients, temperature, water composition, currents, sunshine, and so on, the productive capacity in plankton, and thence in commercial fish, should not be calculated.

The relative importance of the different controlling factors in plankton production varies, and this complicates the problem of productivity estimation. If all the factors varied in the same proportion between regions, and at any given point maintained the same relative importance, it would be fairly simple to isolate one index factor and use this as an indicator of the plankton productivity in any area. However, no such single index appears to give more than a rough estimate.

Productivity of plankton or a species of fish is in practice generally governed by a limiting factor, which is the measure of the least favourable of the group of controlling factors in the area. This limiting factor differs between regions, and in some cases between seasons.

We have not yet discussed the influence of gases on the geographical distribution of sea life. Carbon dioxide, necessary to the photosynthetic activities of plants, appears to be ample everywhere, either as dissolved gas, or as a constituent of bicarbonates. The carbon dioxide in the sea is replenished by respiration, decay of dead organic matter, and solution from the air. Withdrawal of the carbon dioxide from the water to become a constituent of phytoplankton, which ultimately feeds fish whose death once again releases the gas to the water, forms one of the typical cycles of sea life. As for the supply of oxygen, essential to nearly all organisms save anaerobic bacteria, this also does not normally appear to be a factor limiting the abundance of commercial fish. It is in good supply in the upper layer, because of the general turbulence of the surface water, due to wind, waves, and tidal currents, as well as larger movements, which bring it into intimate contact with the atmosphere. Photosynthesis itself also produces oxygen at the same time as it consumes carbon dioxide. Oxygen in the upper water thus normally appears sufficient for the needs of the life found there, and this includes all the creatures with whom we are concerned in commercial fisheries. At greater depths, of course, shortage of oxygen may prove to be the factor limiting life before others take effect. Even in relatively shallow bodies of water, if they are closed or nearly closed, as are some fiords, sea life may be possible only within a short distance of the surface. Stagnation of the water means that below a thin upper layer the oxygen used up in the decomposition of dead sinking organic matter cannot be replaced, until ultimately only bacteria can live, and the water becomes charged with hydrogen sulphide from putrescent matter. Such areas, however, are not relatively very important in the world's water.

It may be noted that, in any case, the oxygen capacity of temperate zone surface water is higher than that of the warmer latitudes, for the solubility of gases rises markedly as the temperature decreases. The maximum capacity for oxygen solution of sea water of average salinity is about 8 c.cm. per litre at 0° C., and only 4·5 c.cm. at 30° C.

While we have seen that the lower temperature of higher latitudes does not generally reduce their organic production as compared with warmer seas, this does not mean that temperature is unimportant as a factor. If in high latitudes temperature could be increased while other conditions were maintained roughly as they are, there would presumably be an increase in life productivity there. Again, as one progresses polewards, lower temperature may exert a greater and greater effect until it becomes a true limiting factor. There has been little occasion to study this effect. Fishing vessels have obtained good catches right up to the ice in the Spitsbergen and other northern Atlantic areas. What happens to the rate of life-productivity farther northwards under the ice is difficult to estimate precisely, but other factors, such as sunlight penetration, will clearly then change more than temperature. Sea water rarely falls below − 1·5° C. anywhere at any depth or any season, whatever the air temperature, as the ocean is a vast circulating fluid body of high specific heat.

Another limiting factor, then, which operates generally in the same direction as temperature, is the amount of sunlight. Though sunlight is the ultimate cause determining changes in temperature, the two elements must for our purpose be considered as separate factors. Changes in amount of sunlight in a given place are only loosely correlated with changes in water temperature, for the matter is complicated by currents, winds, and the conservative nature of water. Again, the photosynthetic properties of sunlight are in a different category from its effects on temperature.

The amount of sunlight is a general limiting factor of life in the sea in that it directly determines the total volume of water in which the essential photosynthesis can take place. Total yearly insolation, of course, decreases towards the Poles, though not by any means as rapidly as might be imagined. The low or absent insolation of winter is partly balanced by the high insolation accompanying the long days of summer. Therefore, while amount of sunlight is generally the limiting factor in the far north and south, it does not operate at all drastically in any of the areas at present fished commercially. There are, of course, local movements of fish farther from the Poles in winter and nearer to them in summer, in response to variations in temperature and plankton supply, both primarily due to insolation variation. But plankton and fish densities are normally fairly high quite near to the pack-ice. In the regions of permanent ice there is presumably a rapid falling-off in plankton density because of the weak or absent photosynthesis, though in certain localities currents under the ice may bring in considerable quantities of plankton and oxygen and so support a fair number of fish.

Growing diatoms have, however, been found under Arctic ice in March. Freezing naturally means a further interference with the already low mean illumination of the Arctic and Antarctic areas. Certain types of diatom and other algae, however, are adjusted to thrive best in poor light. Photosynthesis must have light in order to take place, but the rate of photosynthesis does not fall proportionately with the rate of illumination. Indeed, really high rates of illumination, such as the intensity reached at or near the surface in clear oceanic water in the tropics when the sun is at its zenith, are far above the optimum requirements of most phytoplankton, many species of which react by grouping their scattered chromatophores to reduce the effect of the intense light.

In the above discussion the concept of limiting factors, those present in the least amounts, has been stressed rather than that of the total of factors. While this is considered the most useful approach in determining geographical boundaries of regions of fishery potential, it is not intended to imply that such limits operate inflexibly, irrespective of the degree of abundance of the other factors. There are complex interactions between the factors which, under certain circumstances, may enable a deficiency of one to be made good—up to a point—by a more than proportionately greater value of another. Different types of plankton and other creatures have differing relative demands on the various factors, and evolve to meet the special circumstances of a given area.

Present research is revealing the importance of 'trace' substances as an influence on productivity. Although required by organisms in far smaller quantities than nitrates or phosphates, they may nevertheless be the limiting factor in productivity in several areas.

The basic study of the oceanic distribution of sunlight, temperature, the various plant nutrients dissolved in the sea or found in the eulittoral sea-bed, and the dissolved gases, is a concern of the geographer of the food resources of the seas, in the same way as sunlight, temperature, rainfall, plant nutrients in the soil, and their limiting values, occupy the geographer of land food resources. The only major difference is that due to the nature of the medium. In the sea the water is so abundant that it can be taken for granted and ignored as a factor, while on land the same can be said for the atmosphere. As regards a comparison between land and water productivity, it has been estimated that the whole area of the world seas has roughly the same total basic plant production as that of the smaller area of land. However, of this basic production a good deal more is available to man from the land, because he eats more of it directly, or through only one link in the food chain; whereas he nearly always eats the basic sea production indirectly in the form of animals, often after many links in the food chain, each representing a large wastage. The feasibility of the large-scale consumption by man or domesticated animals of food prepared from plankton directly collected is a question which must await more research.

CHAPTER II

# THE FISHERY PRODUCTION AND POTENTIAL OF THE WORLD

THE relative fish productivity of the world's regions may now be considered. While we have concluded that the geographer of the food resources of the seas should concern himself with a study of the distribution of the basic conditions, we find that little material for any detailed study is available for many regions, and even where reliable data have been produced, the intensity of coverage of the area concerned is often low. Sunlight conditions are of course well known over most areas. Even where detailed observations are lacking, simple calculations can be made of the daily duration of sunshine, and its various angles of incidence, at different seasons for different places. From these, by application of the approximately known degree of cloudiness prevalent, the actual sunlight conditions can be estimated.

Surface and near-surface temperatures are fairly well plotted for many areas frequented by vessels. In regard to the distribution of density of dissolved nutrients, data are less plentiful. Collection of such material involves the use of a well-equipped research vessel, expensive to maintain. There have been several important cruises in recent years, such as those of the *Dana, Discovery, Meteor, Carnegie, Atlantis*, and *Galathea*. Such cruises, however, naturally produce information only along the line of track, which might cross an ocean roughly along a meridian or parallel and provide, for instance, knowledge of the characteristic change of a given property of sea water with changing latitude along the track followed. Such information can only be applied with reserve to areas other than those actually crossed. At present there are not enough data available for the production of detailed maps of the world distribution of such features as phosphate supply or the essential result of this and other factors, the plankton concentration and rate of production. The plankton concentration is, of course, found experimentally by towing plankton nets or by centrifuging samples of sea water, although it might be possible ultimately to calculate the maximum possible concentration from the other basic data. It is, however, simpler to find the concentration experimentally. Even this apparently straightforward operation may yet give only approximate results. Estimates for the same area by different workers often differ considerably.

The *Meteor* expedition made hauls of plankton in the upper 50 metres of water at various stations in the South Atlantic, away from the continental shelves. At 55° S., for example, they obtained about 100,000 plankton organisms per litre of water. At 45° S., there were about 40,000, at 35° S. only about 10,000, and within the tropics mainly around 5,000, save in the belt fed by the upwelling off South-west Africa. Such counts do not, however, reveal the full conditions. For one thing, the euphotic zone is deeper in the tropics.

The rate of plankton production is, of course, more significant than the total plankton stock, from the point of view of fish support. As production in the tropics continues fairly steadily, without strong seasonal contrasts, the difference in yearly production between the tropics and the temperate zones may be far less than the maximum difference in stock.

Several authorities have made estimates of plankton productivity, measured in terms of grammes of carbon per square metre of sea surface per year. The experimental methods differ, and results are by no means in close agreement. Annual production in tropical seas away from upwelling zones would appear to be generally below 100 grammes of organic carbon per square metre, while in the more productive parts of the Trade Wind upwelling zones and on the cool temperate shelves it may rise to well over ten times this figure.

Attempts have been made to relate quantitatively the production of plankton in a given area to the production of fish, which is the matter of ultimate economic importance. There is naturally a relation, but the ratio varies from place to place according to the type of fish concerned. Again, commercially desirable fish may form only a small proportion of the total end product. The number of stages involved is important. Some useful fish, such as herring, mainly feed directly on plankton. Hence the ratio of valuable sea production to plankton production will be relatively large in a herring area. It will be relatively smaller in an area where the chief commercial species is a predator, living on animals which feed on the plankton. There is a land analogy. A lower density of human population can be supported as, in effect, predators, where meat is an important staple food, obtained from herbivorous animals, than can be supported by land where the human population depends directly on vegetable produce.

The greater the number of stages from the original photo-synthesis, the greater the wastage in commercially useless production. At certain times, for example, the prevalent food chain of the cod off Newfoundland involves three stages from the plankton, chiefly via shrimps and then lance and other fish.

While precise ratios cannot be computed on present-day knowledge, it is established that, away from littoral waters, where sea-bed plants offer another basic source of food, the long-term productivity of fish varies broadly in proportion to plankton productivity, other things being equal. This applies to all species of fish, whether or not they are themselves plankton-feeders.

In shallow waters close to shores, where the sea-bed is within the euphotic zone, the basic food supply from plankton is augmented and indeed sometimes overshadowed in importance by marine life anchored (not necessarily rooted in the biological sense) to the sea-bed. This is one of the reasons for the greater density of fish in these waters, though plankton density is also normally higher because of the greater proportions of nutrient salts in the sea water, replenished by land rivers. Approximate estimates of the fish-supporting power of sea-bed plants were made by C. G. J. Petersen in an area of inshore Danish waters where the chief basic food is eel-grass (*Zostera*). He estimated that the consumption of 24 million tons of *Zostera* produces 5 million tons of various animals of no value to man in themselves or as food for commercial fish. In addition, about a million tons of small animals forming fish food are produced. These in turn produce when eaten, either directly or through further stages in the food chain, about 10,000 tons of commercial fish, chiefly plaice and cod, in addition to larger quantities of useless creatures such as starfish. The ultimate ratio of plant crop to commercial fish crop is therefore over 2,000 : 1 in this example. Whether this can be taken as typical of such ratios where sea-bed plants form the main basic food there is not enough evidence to state, but there is no doubt that the economic 'wastage' in the food chain is very high. For areas away from the shore, where the basic food is phytoplankton, the ratio is lower than where sea-bed plants are concerned, for these tend to harbour a large quantity of useless creatures. Work at the Plymouth Marine Biological Laboratory has led to estimates that about 0·06 per cent of the wet weight of the yearly production of phytoplankton in the English Channel is harvested as fish.

Knowledge of ratios of production, coupled with knowledge of the rate of basic organic formation under given conditions of sunshine, temperature, nutrient, and gas supply, might ultimately enable reasonably accurate estimates of potential commercial productivity of undeveloped areas of the world to be made without the need for large-scale testing by actual fishing. At present, however, the best test of the fishery possibilities of an area is the direct one of actual catching on a commercial scale.

For many fishing grounds in the Pacific, Indian Ocean, and South Atlantic there are insufficient data for a satisfactory estimate to be made of the possible optimum production. In judging the possibilities of a new area, the first step normally taken is to carry out a series of trial fishing voyages with standard craft and equipment, and to note if the rate of catch per unit of effort makes the grounds commercially profitable. Such was the procedure recently adopted, for example, under Colonial Office sponsorship, to test the under-developed areas of Nigeria, Sierra Leone, Gambia, Aden, Mauritius, Seychelles, Sarawak, and Borneo. Such empirical methods of estimating stocks are the only really feasible ones. Whereas the cropping or grazing possibilities of an area of land can be estimated fairly accurately in advance from the relevant conditions of climate and soil, an analogous estimate of the cropping potential of the sea is not possible. As we have seen, sea conditions are not revealed as clearly as those on land; much of importance in the composition and characteristics of the sea water at different levels in a given area, and in the nature of the sea-bed, can only be discovered by painstaking and expensive research.

Again, when estimating the possibilities of land, it is possible to specify what crop or livestock is to be employed. In the sea, on the other hand, man has no such close control over the method of utilization. The species composition of the fish stock of an area is a given fact. Many of the creatures in some areas may be of no direct or indirect use to him, but it may not be economically possible in the open sea greatly to reduce their numbers and to replace them by more fish of useful species. A course sometimes adopted is to hatch out fry of the desired species in protected waters, so that they survive the first extremely dangerous phase of their lives in much larger numbers than otherwise, and then to release them into the sea. This is done by several governments, and may be of value in certain conditions in semi-enclosed waters, but cannot appreciably increase the adult stocks in the vast areas of the open sea.

Thus it will be seen that adequate estimation of the potential of under-developed fishing areas of the world is not possible until practical tests are made. Even the results of these must be viewed with caution. Trial trawls on ground previously little used will give a rate of catch higher than that to be expected when the grounds are fully used: for the stock will be higher than that which would result from the optimum rate of fishing. As large-scale fishing develops over a period of years, the proportion of older and heavier fish in the catch will go down, and with it the total weight of catch per unit of effort. Hence the only satisfactory way of finding out the possibilities of an area is to work it on a commercial scale from the start. The degree to which the fishery should safely be expanded without danger of over-fishing may then be found by study of developments in practice. Sometimes, of course, lack of co-operation between the firms and nationalities using the ground may prevent effective restrictive action being taken.

The problems involved in the study of over-fishing and its prevention are complex. It is important to bear in mind, however, that the normal aim of commercial fishing, and any regulation of it, is to get the maximum sustained output. This is not the same thing as keeping stocks at their highest. Obviously, fishing depletes stocks below their natural maximum, but this reduces the competition for food, and so allows more food and a faster rate of growth to the remaining individuals. Fish have considerable elasticity of growth rate. A well but not excessively fished stock has a low proportion of old, slowly growing fish, wasteful of food, and a high proportion of quickly growing younger fish turning a bigger amount of their food into flesh. The total yearly production of fish will therefore be greater than in an old, dense stock, and able, up to a point, to support the increased rate of fishing. If excessive fishing occurs, however, among other effects stocks will become so thin that catches per unit of effort or cost will be too low for fishing to pay. The aim of regulation is generally to use the optimum fishing effort, in which the industry pays its way and the yearly catch, replenished by fresh growth, is sustained at or near its highest possible level.

A very rough estimate of the probable yield of a given area can be made by analogy with other areas of similar type already being fished. For example, the Patagonian shelf, and particularly its extreme southern portion, appears to be a region worthy of more commercial attention. In water of less than 100 fathoms depth and a mean yearly surface temperature of below 55° F. it has an area of about double that of the shelves of the north-east of North America.

For a given sea area, of course, the continental shelves are generally much greater producers than the open ocean. Organic remains from the euphotic zone are only partly decomposed in their short fall to the bottom, so there is much food for small sea-bed creatures which finally feed fish. The shelf sea-floor thus forms a rich producing horizon, and one within convenient reach of vessels.

The 100 fathoms depth contour has long been generally accepted as the approximate edge of the continental shelf, but is, of course, an arbitrary figure. In some areas the edge of the continental shelf may be in shallower water, beyond which the sea-floor then plunges relatively steeply downwards; in others this change of slope may not occur until much farther from shore and at a depth of, say, 150 fathoms. For our purpose the matter is further complicated by the fact that, particularly in European waters, trawling on the continental slope at depths down to 180 fathoms is now common and profitable, and in some areas exceeds 300 fathoms at times. Nevertheless, the 100-fathom contour is normally a satisfactory general indication of the limit of the intensive shelf type of fishing. Beyond this the water usually deepens fairly rapidly. Fig. 3 shows the main world areas shallower than 100 fathoms.

The width of the continental shelf is, then, an extremely important factor in the general intensity of fishing activity in an area. It is not our function to discuss here the causes of the varying width of the continental shelf about the continents, as from the point of view of the fisherman the extent of the shelf is easily ascertainable and, in terms of human history, remains more or less fixed. The charting of the depths of all shelf areas in the world is now virtually complete, save in areas covered by ice, and much more detailed work has lately been rendered feasible by the development of echo-sounding. Most of the larger British vessels now have such equipment fitted, and with its aid the identification of fishing banks, as well as of schools of pelagic fish (those that normally spend their time swimming at some distance above the sea-bed), is made easy.

3

In the present relative disposition of shallow and deep areas about the continents, the influences of continental drift, deposition of material eroded from the land, isostatic adjustment of continents to their large-scale erosion or glaciation, vulcanism and faulting have all played parts, though it is beyond our scope here to attempt any detailed assessment of their relative importance. Some broad generalizations may be made, however. The supposed westward drift of the Americas and their longitudinal coastal folding has resulted in a consistently narrow shelf, save in the Bering Sea, which is not on the oceanic side of the main axis of Tertiary folding which runs down the Alaska peninsula.

The narrowness of the shelf has an adverse effect on the supply of demersal fish (those which spend much of their time on or near the sea-bed), but, fortunately for the countries concerned, other factors are particularly favourable to the development of pelagic fish. The upwelling waters off California and Peru have a dense plankton production which is dispersed over large areas by the California, Peru, and North and South Equatorial currents. The ocean to the west of the Americas in warm latitudes is thus rich in pelagic fish, tuna being particularly valuable. Washington, Oregon, British Columbia, and Alaska are outside this influence, but here the sea temperatures, coupled with the high relief and rainfall of the coast which have caused many clear streams, have combined to make them the world's greatest producing area of the salmon, which uses freshwater streams for breeding.

The east coast of North America has a much wider area of shelf, particularly off New England, the Maritime Provinces, and Newfoundland, and here is the greatest density of fishing activity. Hudson Bay has a large area of shallow water, but has so far attracted little attention because of its ice-closed season and distance from east coast ports. In South America, the east coast again, especially off Argentina, has a much wider area of shelf than the west coast.

Africa is the worst served of the continents in regard to its shelf area. On both east and west sides its mass of ancient hard crystalline rocks approaches closely to the coast in most areas, and the land falls away in a relatively steep gradient beneath the sea. In the Mediterranean it has a wider shelf in places, but the sinking of the sea-floor has left only a narrow shelf off Algeria. The tendency to poverty of fishing grounds is

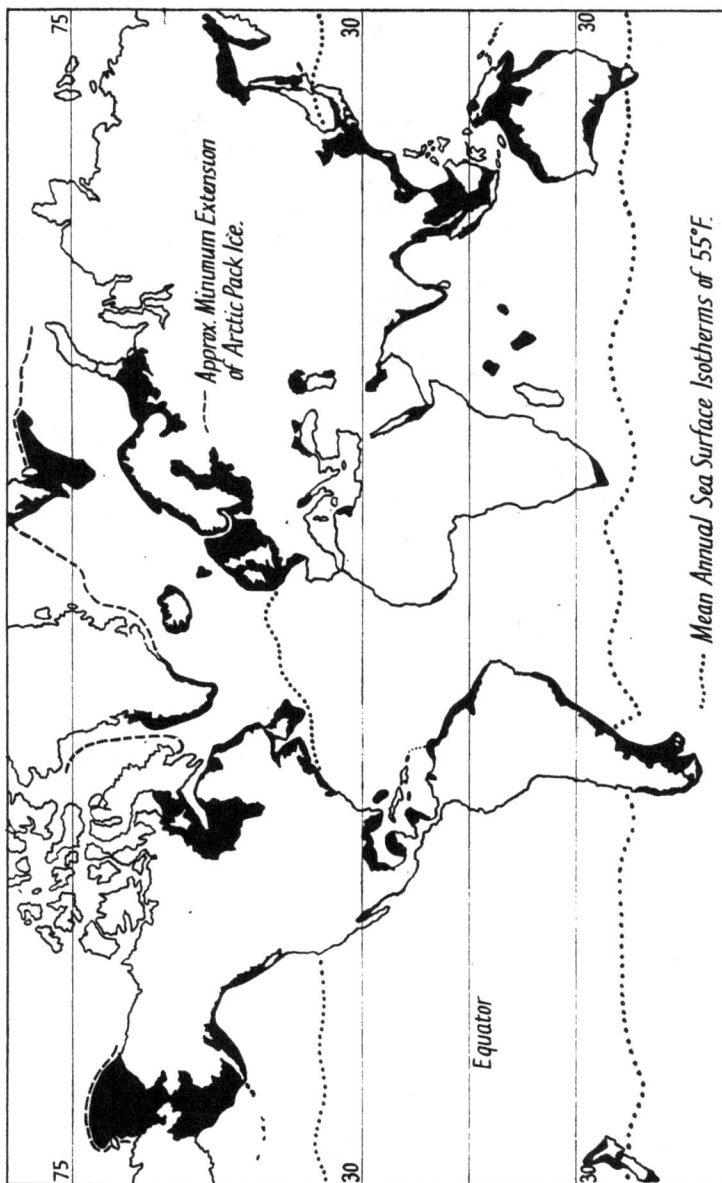

*Fig. 3.* Main areas of water shallower than 100 fathoms, and free of pack-ice for part or all the year. (While Mercator's projection markedly exaggerates poleward areas, it is used here to preserve shapes and directions.)

Labels within the figure:

- - - Approx. Minimum Extension of Arctic Pack Ice.

......... Mean Annual Sea Surface Isotherms of 55°F.

Equator

counterbalanced on the west coast, as with the Americas, by up-welling off Morocco and S.W. Africa, and currents moving away from these areas are rich in pelagic fish. They are the areas of greatest fishery production in Africa in relation to their coast length. Improvement on Africa's low total production is likely to come with better methods, but it seems bound to remain a minor fishing continent for physical reasons.

The Eurasian continent is well provided with shelf area on its eastern, western, and northern sides, though the value of the latter is limited by ice. The Indian Ocean has a narrower, though by no means negligible, shelf. The Persian Gulf is quite important as a fishing area when the fairly sparse populations about its shores are considered. The Caspian is important, particularly as a source of sturgeon. The Black Sea has a much smaller area of shallow water, and the Mediterranean a relatively small amount in proportion to its area, because of its foundered eastern and western basins. The Mediterranean fisheries nevertheless have a substantial, though not high, production, because their resources are fully exploited by the large population bordering the sea. The most important fishes, however, are pelagic: the sardine and tunny.

Finally, Australia has a good area of shelf, but most of this is off the north coast in tropical waters outside the zone of upwelling on the west. Again, the bulk of the shelf area, with the exception of Bass Strait, is remote from the main centres of population. Australia is thus a low fish-producer, particularly as she has large supplies of home-killed meat. There is, however, a signifi-cant and expanding fishing industry off the south-eastern coasts and Tasmania. New Zealand, with a much smaller area of shelf, has about the same total output as Australia. All its shelf is within the temperate zone of good organic production, and within easy reach of well-populated coasts.

Fig. 4 shows the relative production by continents and leading countries, while the table at the end of the book shows the production of all countries with an annual production of over 5,000 tons. Fig. 5 shows the dominant belts of fish production in the world.

The majority of the important demersal grounds lie polewards of the 55°F. (12·8°C.) mean annual surface isotherms, and are dominated by a few characteristic cool-water types of fish. Japanese waters lie across the isotherm, while the large demersal output of the Gulf coast of the U.S.A. in warmer waters is mainly accounted for by shellfish. The annual range of temperature in the sea is low, because of the high specific heat of water and the very large masses involved. Seasonal variations of surface temperature are greatest in the temperate zones, though even

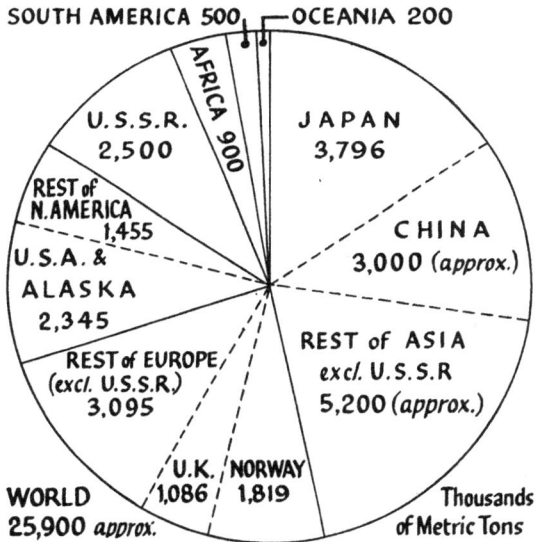

Fig. 4. Annual catch of fish, shellfish, and other non-mammalian sea and freshwater products, by continents and countries producing over 1 million tons. Figures are for 1951 (China, 1949), from F.A.O. sources. Some estimates have subsequently been somewhat altered; for details see regional chapters

here the total yearly range is in few areas much above 10°C. In the intertropical regions, and polewards of 60°N. or 60°S., it is rarely more than 5°C. At depths greater than 100 fathoms the seasonal variations are very small practically anywhere in the world.

The degree to which fish migrations are affected by seasonal variations in temperature is not fully known for many species, but some detailed studies have been made. Cod, for example, have been found to react critically to temperature changes, and thus to occasional variations from normal of the currents in the Grand Banks area. There is also a regular seasonal migration of Banks cod northwards to the shelf off Labrador in summer, the fish returning in late autumn. Not all cod migrate geographically; others move relatively short distances, to deeper water on the continental slope, for summer and early autumn.

As we have already mentioned, not enough is known to estimate the extent of organic production in the Arctic Ocean. In any case, the question has little significance for a study of commercial fisheries. The actual situation is that at present in the associated waters of the North Atlantic: the Barents Sea, the shelves off Spitsbergen and off East Greenland, and the Davis Strait, commercial fishing is at times pursued profitably to within a fairly short distance of the ice edge. The Bering Sea area is not so heavily fished, but expansion of fisheries will doubtless occur there. Much development may also well take place in Antarctic and adjacent waters, which at present are unimportant for fisheries despite their importance for whaling, although they appear to have substantial stocks of fish, such as nototheniids.

The limiting factor in some areas will for some time be economic rather than physical. The distance of some grounds from the main world areas of dense population renders the cost of transport to the chief potential markets high. Yet there is no doubt that pressure of world demand for food will ultimately, and perhaps fairly soon, compel a larger use of these areas. The densely populated Indian sub-continent, for example, is a likely market for the fishery production, at present negligible, of the banks of the Kerguelen-Gaussberg ridge, the Crozet Swell, and about Amsterdam and St Paul islands. The development of profitable fisheries in such areas is dependent on the setting up of suitable bases there, either on land or in the form of large mother ships and factory ships. The function of transport to markets may then be performed by specialized vessels instead of by the fishing vessels themselves, as is done in the Arctic fisheries of the North Atlantic region.

World pelagic production will also undoubtedly increase, though not generally to reach the same average intensity as in demersal areas. At present, some of the chief world pelagic fisheries, such as those for the European herring, are mainly in shallow seas which are even more important for demersal fishing. In addition, there are extensive pelagic fisheries for such fish as sardines in areas of deeper water, but fairly near to coasts. Further development of these, particularly in areas of upwelling, or down-current of upwelling, is likely. The widest ranging pelagic fisheries are those for tuna and related types, and these

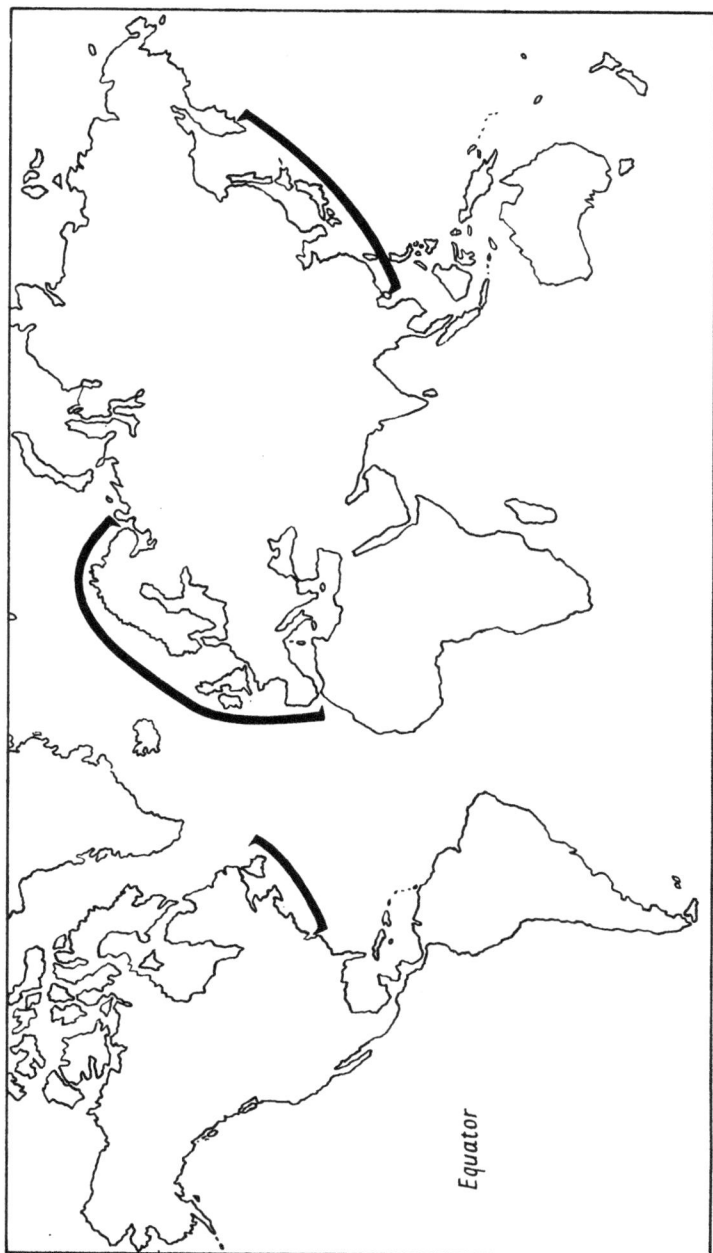

*Fig. 5.* Approximate extent of the fishing belts of the world landing more than 1 million tons per annum per thousand miles of continental front

Equator

will doubtless continue to increase production as improved range, speed, and fish-preserving equipment of craft bring more areas of ocean within economic reach. Long-range diesel-engined tuna 'clippers' from California range as far south as the latitude of Peru, and great distances into the Pacific. Japanese tuna vessels similarly cover great areas of the western Pacific, while mid-ocean waters are increasingly fished by modern long-range craft based on Hawaii and other islands.

There is scope for further pelagic development in the North Pacific, and a considerable increase over present production should be possible in the South Pacific, Indian, and South Atlantic oceans. Such development will, however, depend on whether the consumer can pay sufficient to support the necessary large investments in craft and gear. Low-priced markets such as South Asia can better support intensive demersal and pelagic fisheries fairly near coasts, where there are usually greater concentrations of fish and larger catches per unit of time and effort. The development of these up to their optimum output is likely to take precedence over that of long-range oceanic pelagic fisheries, save where these supply high-priced markets such as the U.S.A.

The exact limits of oceanic pelagic fisheries cannot be de-marcated clearly. They cover large areas in which, as one proceeds farther from the land bases, frequency of visits by fishing vessels gradually diminishes. Due both to the widely roving nature of the tuna and other quarry, and to the fluctuations in fish prices and costs of operating, which vary the effective range of the vessels, no clear and permanent outer limit can be set to such fisheries. As we have seen, such boundaries are in any case generally extending farther and farther from the land. For example, in Japan the north limit of commercial tuna fishing can be placed at about mid-latitude Hokkaido, because it is determined by water temperature, but in other directions no clear limits can be set. The Japanese tuna craft range great distances in normal times. The post-war occupation restrictions on Japanese fishing vessels have been largely released, and they are now operating in waters off East Australia.

# CHAPTER III

# ECONOMICALLY IMPORTANT TYPES OF SEA-FISH

THE zoological classification is extremely detailed and made with regard to several criteria besides those which chiefly interest a study of commercial fisheries. Closely allied species may have differences of concern to the zoologist but unimportant to the commercial fisherman, who often has but one name for several species. Creatures may be divided first into phyla, then classes, sub-classes, orders, sub-orders, families, genera, species, and varieties. Zoological authorities, however, differ in their classification systems, which are liable to change.

In the list below, sea, estuarine, or anadromous (freshwater spawning) fishes are placed according to a classification used by the British Museum of Natural History. Several orders of extinct, economically unimportant or freshwater fish are omitted. The list is by no means exhaustive, but the fish included account for the bulk of the world's catch. Under the orders are given the chief families of commercial value, with the British common names of some of the chief genera or species. Common names used by other English-speaking countries are sometimes given, when they differ.

CLASSIFICATION OF COMMERCIAL SEA-FISH

Class Selachii (fish with cartilaginous skeletons. Also known as Chondrichthyes).
  Sub-Class Euselachii (also commonly known as Elasmobranchii).
    Order Pleurotremata (Sharks and Dogfish).
    Order Hypotremata (Rays, including Skates).
Class Pisces (fish with essentially bony skeletons. Also known as Osteichthyes).
  Sub-Class Palaeopterygii.
    Order Chondrostei (in which the skeleton has partly changed to cartilage).
      Acipenseridae (Sturgeons).

Sub-Class Neopterygii.

   Order Isospondyli.

      Clupeidae (Herring, Sprat, Pilchard, Anchovy, Shad, Menhaden), Salmonidae (Salmon, Trout), Osmeridae (Smelt).

   Order Apodes (Eels).

      Congridae (Conger Eel).

      Muraenidae (Moray Eel).

   Order Synentognathi.

      Scomberesocidae (Saury), Belonidae (Gar-fish), Exocoetidae (Flying fish).

   Order Anacanthini.

      Gadidae (Cod, Haddock, Whiting, Coalfish, Pollack, Poutassou, Ling, Torsk or Cusk), Merluccidae (Hake).

   Order Zeomorphi.

      Zeidae (John Dory).

   Order Percomorphi.

      Serranidae (Grouper, Bass), Carangidae (Horse Mackerel), . Lutjanidae (Snappers), Pomadasidae (Grunts), Bramidae (Black Sea Bream), Sciaenidae (Meagre, Drum, Croaker), Mullidae (Red Mullet), Sparidae (Common Sea Bream, Spanish Bream, Bogue), Labridae (Wrasses), Gempylidae (Snoek or Barracouta), Scombridae (Mackerel, Spanish Mackerel, Kingfishes, Tunas, Albacore, Bonito), Xiphiidae (Swordfish), Anarrhichadidae (Wolf-fish), Mugilidae (Grey Mullets), Sphyraenidae (Barracudas).

   Order Scleroparei.

      Scorpaenidae (Norway Haddock or Rosefish), Triglidae (Gurnards), Platycephalidae (Flatheads).

   Order Heterosomata (Flatfish).

      Bothidae (Turbot, Brill, Megrim, Scaldfish), Pleuronectidae (Halibut, Dab, Plaice, Lemon Sole, Witch, Fluke), Soleidae (Soles), Cynoglossidae (Tongue Soles).

   Order Pediculati.

      Lophiidae (Angler).

Species of several of the above families will be referred to frequently in the regional chapters, when the scientific name of the individual species concerned will also be given when needed to aid precise identification.

We may here briefly consider some of the chief commercial groups, together with molluscs and crustaceans. Certain orders are far more commercially important than others; indeed, certain families are much more abundant than several orders. The attention devoted here to a group therefore depends on its economic importance, not on its rank in the zoological classification.

The first division of fishes for our purpose must be into demersal and pelagic types. It is one of great practical importance in its influence on the fishing method required, though from the point of view of a zoologist the distinction may be less important than others made between types of fish. Some fish, of course, do not fall very clearly into either division. However, we may define demersal fish as those which spend sufficient of their time on or near the sea-bed to be caught predominantly by gear operating there, such as trawl nets or long lines. The relative importance of this group varies greatly as between regions. In England and Wales, demersal fish form over 80 per cent by weight of the total landings, but in the U.S.A. they form a minority of the catch. Such fish live mainly on the continental shelves, where the sea-floor is within or near the euphotic zone, so that food is abundant for them. They feed, according to species, on other fish, on worms, shellfish, and other sea-floor dwellers, on the larger plankton and on sea-bed plants, where these exist. They include powerful and mobile fish like the cod, as well as the flatfish, which spend much of their time lying on the floor, and usually swim only short distances at a time.

Pelagic fish are found in greatest density on the shelves, but some pelagic species are also found far out in the open ocean. They are generally less tied to specific localities than demersal fish. They may be defined broadly as those fish which spend a good deal of their time swimming at or near the surface, some species feeding on plankton, others being carnivorous. They are caught chiefly by drift net, purse seine net, trolled lines, and other such gear adapted to work at or near the surface, although at certain seasons some essentially pelagic types may be caught by demersal methods. Pelagic fish are in general more mobile than demersal fish, and set the fishermen a more complicated problem in estimating their movements. They include very strong swimmers such as the tunny or tuna group, whose red flesh shows the richness of the blood needed to sustain their powerful muscles.

A summary of some salient features and the world distribution for commercial purposes of some of the main types of sea fish and shellfish is given below. The scientific names are given of the regional forms most important commercially. Fig. 6 shows the relative importance of the main groups of fish and shellfish in world landings.

A. DEMERSAL FISH

1. The Cod Group (Order Anacanthini)

*Cod.* (*Gadus callarias*, North Atlantic; *G. macrocephalus*, North Pacific.) The most important. This is pre-eminently the fish of the cooler waters of the North Atlantic shelves, although a form of it is also found in temperate waters of the North Pacific. It is abundant on the North-west European shelf from the North Sea up the Norwegian coast to the Barents Sea, and on the North-east American shelves from New England through the Maritime Provinces and Newfoundland areas up to South-west and South-east Greenland. It is also abundant on mid-oceanic shelves such as those about Iceland, Spitsbergen, Bear Island, and The Faeroes, and is the staple fish of the great long-distance trawling industry. In 1951 cod formed nearly half, both by weight and by value, of the total fish landings of England and Wales, and the bulk of this cod came from the far northern grounds. Cod is also important in the catches of Canada, U.S.A., Norway, Iceland, Germany, France, Russia, Portugal (from the Grand Banks), Sweden, and Denmark. In Japan the landings are appreciable, although small in relation to the immense total of all fish landed there.

Codfish are found chiefly on rocky, pebbly, or sandy ground. Muddy ground does not attract them. They feed on other fish and sea creatures, both pelagic and demersal, such as herring, the smaller flatfish, squid, shellfish, and starfish. They migrate to a number of definite breeding grounds, in fairly shallow water, and the height of the spawning season is in many areas the early spring. A water temperature of 41°–47° F. is the most favourable for spawning. The eggs, and the male milt to fertilize them, are released into the water near the bottom, but not on it. For this purpose the fish gather in dense schools. The eggs, only some of which are fertilized, rise and float in the upper layer of water, though turbulence may disperse them through a certain depth. They become temporarily part of the plankton. The incubation period may vary from ten to forty days, depending on temperature.

Mortality of the eggs is, of course, very high, because fish feed on them with the rest of the plankton. Of the several million eggs produced by the female cod, very few finally become adult fish. At the end of the incubation period the young fish are hatched. They still have the yolk sac attached as a swelling of

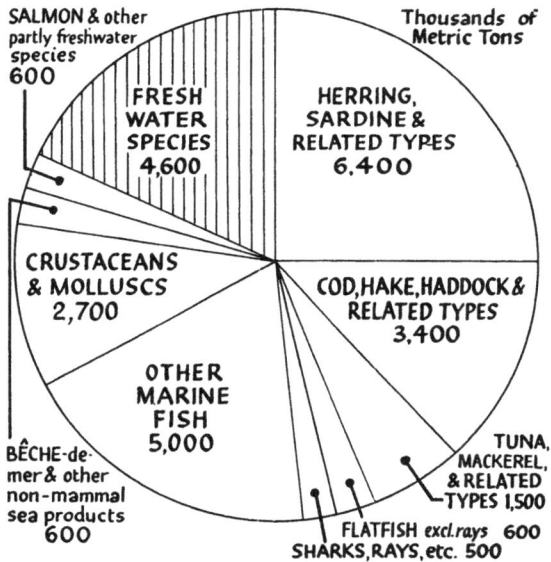

*Fig. 6.* Relative importance in world catch of main groups of fish and shellfish, 1951

the stomach, to serve as a source of food. This is used up in between six and twelve days, when the feeding organs of the fish, which is now about $\frac{3}{16}$ in. long, are fully developed, and it can start to eat plankton. It is still pelagic, and normally does not reach the sea-bed until at least two months have passed, even in shallow water. It is then about 1 in. long, and can commence eating sea-bed food, such as small worms.

Cod are voracious feeders, save at spawning time, and grow to be large fish. In its third year, an average Grand Banks cod reaches about 10 in. in length. By its seventh year it is over 2 ft.

long, and by its twelfth, if it has survived so far, it will be about 40 in. long. Cod over eleven years old, however, are not an important proportion of the catch.

*Haddock.* (*Gadus aeglefinus* or *Melanogrammus aeglefinus.*) This fish is related to the cod, and is found in the cool temperate waters of the North Atlantic. It prefers rather warmer water than the cod, although its area coincides fairly closely with that of the cod. Its optimum temperature is about 8°F. higher than that of cod. On the North American grounds, for example, it is never found north of the Straits of Belle Isle. Nevertheless, on most of the important cod grounds on both sides of the Atlantic, haddock are also an important trawler catch. British trawlers operating in the Barents Sea catch about a third as much haddock as cod, by weight. In the North Sea the haddock ratio is roughly similar, while in New England, haddock landings have in recent years been about double those of cod. Haddock are important in the catches of Britain, U.S.A., Canada, Norway, Sweden, Germany, Iceland, Denmark, and Holland.

These fish normally tend to move farther north within their zone with advancing age, though each winter they retreat some distance southwards. Unlike cod, they are rarely found close inshore in bays or fiords, though in other respects they frequent the same type of ground. They are more markedly bottom feeders than are cod, particularly liking worms and shellfish. Their early stages of development are similar to those of cod, but they mature earlier, at about four or five years of age, and rarely exceed 2 ft. 6 in. in length.

*Hake.* (*Merluccius merluccius*, East North Atlantic; *M. bilinearis* (West North Atlantic: whiting); *M. productus*, East North Pacific; *M. capensis*, South Africa; *M. gayi*, East South Pacific.) Another fish related to cod, hake is nevertheless a decidedly warmer water fish. In North America it is not important north of the Gulf of Maine, nor in Europe north or east of Cape Wrath. While most important in the warm temperate waters of the North Atlantic, hake are found in warm temperate seas elsewhere in the world, substantial landings being reported by South Africa (of 'Cape hake' or stockfish) and Chile. In the North Atlantic, hake landings are important in Spain, France, Britain, U.S.A., and Portugal. At present the world's most important grounds are in the European shelf south or west of the British Isles. The hake is also found in deeper water than cod or haddock.

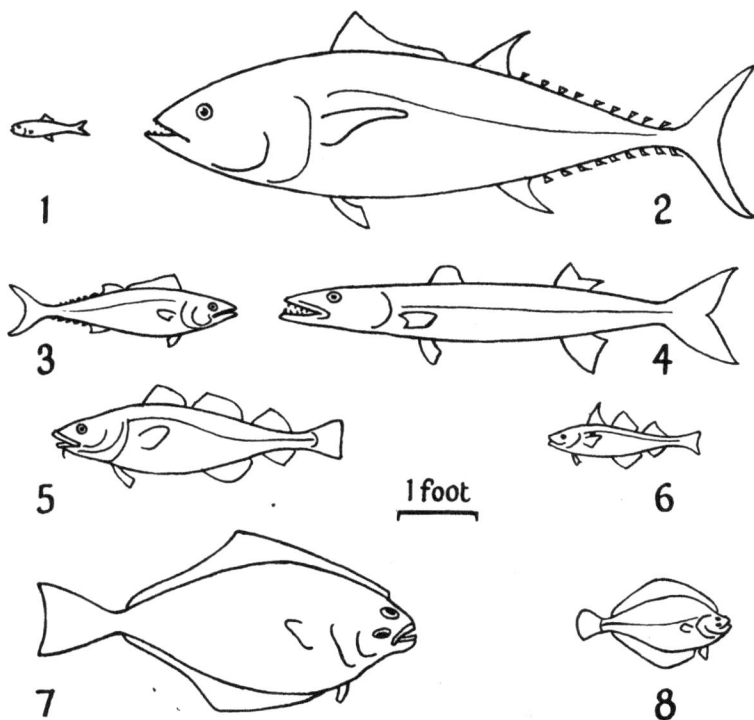

*Fig. 7.* Some commercial fishes. Specimens are medium sized or large, depending on varied local standards
1. Herring. 2. Bluefin tuna. 3. Bonito (*Sarda sarda*). 4. Barracuda (tropical W. Atlantic species: *Sphyraena barracuda*). 5. Cod (E. Atlantic). 6. Haddock (W. Atlantic). 7. Halibut. 8. Plaice (*Pleuronectes platessa*)

Adults may be found on the continental slopes as well as the shelves, at any depth down to 300 fathoms. Hake also differs in that it prefers soft, muddy ground, avoided by cod and haddock.

Its early life history, however, is broadly similar to the cod's, although it does not take to the sea-floor until it is at least 2 in. long. Its food is chiefly small crustaceans such as shrimps, together with squid and small fish. It feeds mainly at night.

*Other Cod Relatives.* Several of the other demersal species caught in appreciable quantities are again related to the cod, and are found on the shelves in temperate seas. The most significant in amounts landed are whiting (*Gadus merlangus*), pollack (pollock), coalfish (saithe), ling, and cusk, species caught wholly or chiefly in the North Atlantic.

CATCH IN TONS IN 1951 OF COD, HADDOCK, HAKE, and ALLIED
SPECIES BY CERTAIN COUNTRIES

| | |
|---|---|
| U.K. | 733,800 |
| Norway | 485,800 |
| Iceland | 224,900 |
| Japan | 211,000 |
| Newfoundland | 196,200 |
| U.S.A. | 195,100 |
| W. Germany | 187,700 |
| Spain | 183,600 |
| Canada (excluding Newfoundland | 158,200 |
| France | 97,400 |
| Denmark | 50,600 |
| Sweden | 48,200 |
| Chile | 42,800 |
| Belgium | 22,200 |
| Holland | 20,700 |

2. Flatfish (Order Heterosomata)

These differ markedly from the group considered above. While varying widely in size, they have certain features in common. Presumably as an adaptation to their mode of life, mainly on the sea-floor and feeding on the creatures there, they are flattened and wide. Their eyes and mouth are in the front of the body, but are not symmetrically disposed. These fish have apparently evolved from fish with the more normal bodily orientation of greater depth than width, and with eyes and other external features symmetrically placed. After hatching, the infant flatfish swims with its greater width in the vertical plane, with an eye on each side of the head. In a short time, about seven weeks for the plaice, the fish has changed its habit to swimming or lying on its side, and one eye has gradually migrated round to what is now the upper side. Another interesting feature is that the skin of the upper side has the power of changing considerably in its colour and textural appearance, so that the creature resembles its background of sand, shingle, or mud. The skin alters when the fish moves from one area to another.

The eggs of flatfish float after fertilization by milt at the time of extrusion. After some weeks young flatfish take to the bottom, where their food consists mainly of crustaceans, molluscs, and echinoderms.

The flesh of these fish is generally a more delicate food than that of most other groups, and in many countries flatfish fetch higher than average prices per unit of weight. In most countries they do not form a large proportion of the catch, however. They are important to inshore fishermen, but longer range vessels on most grounds catch flatfish incidentally to other demersal fish, in which cod and related fish are the chief haul. One important exception is Denmark, where flatfish represent about a third of the value of the catch. There are other parts of the world where flatfish are the object of specialized industries, as in the halibut fisheries of the north-west of North America. Flatfish are dominantly cool temperate fish, but some, such as a number of species of sole, also frequent warm temperate or tropical waters.

The largest flatfish is the halibut (*Hippoglossus*), growing occasionally to over 7 ft. and 300 pounds. It frequents the cool temperate shelves of the North Atlantic and North Pacific, and is important in the catches of U.S.A. and Canada, especially on the Pacific coast (including Alaska), while it is also of moderate importance to Norway and Britain, who obtain it chiefly from grounds about Iceland, The Faeroes, West and East Greenland, and Norway.

The common names of many other flatfish are somewhat confusing when applied to a world survey; for there is much ambiguity. For example, whereas in British waters the term 'flounder' is used for a single species (*Pleuronectes flesus*) with a maximum length of about 18 in., in North America it is used generally to cover several species. Terms such as 'plaice' and 'sole' are also often used loosely in translating names for flatfish in other languages. In Europe the plaice (*P. platessa*) achieves a maximum length of about 2 ft., and the common sole (*Solea vulgaris*) rather less.

The plaice, flounder, dab, soles, and some other flatfish have small mouths, and are not very active. They feed mainly on shellfish, sea urchins, worms, and such small creatures. On the other hand, the halibut and turbot (*Rhombus maximus*) have large mouths, good teeth, and active habits, and feed chiefly on other fish.

4

CATCH IN TONS IN 1951 OF FLATFISH BY CERTAIN COUNTRIES

| | |
|---|---|
| Japan | 99,400 |
| U.S.A. | 77,100 |
| U.K. | 64,500 |
| Denmark | 49,000 |
| Canada (excluding Newfoundland) | 35,800 |
| Holland | 23,900 |
| Belgium | 14,100 |
| Norway | 9,700 |
| Newfoundland | 8,500 |
| W. Germany | 7,400 |
| Iceland | 6,000 |
| Spain | 5,200 |
| Sweden | 4,800 |
| Chile | 500 |
| Portugal | 400 |

The relatively small quantity landed by Norway, West Germany, Newfoundland, and some other important fishing countries is significant. It is explained in some countries by the tastes of the population or the problems of handling for export; in others, such as Chile, partly by sparser flatfish resources in most of the warmer seas.

### 3. Other Demeral Fish of Bony Skeleton

Among a wide variety of other fish we may mention particularly others of the order Percomorphi. Several families, mainly demersal, are of substantial importance commercially in warm temperate or tropical waters; they include the Serranidae, such as the groupers (*Epinephelus* spp.), Sciaenidae, such as the croaker, Sparidae (sea breams), Labridae (wrasses), and Lutjanidae (snappers). In the order Scleroparei there are also important food fish, particularly the rosefish or redfish (*Sebastes marinus*), now caught in large quantities on both sides of the cool northern Atlantic, and the Triglidae (gurnards). The conger eel is also of significance in some temperate areas.

### 4. Cartilaginous Fish

Another commercially important group is composed of the sharks and rays. Having cartilaginous skeletons, gill clefts usually opening directly to the exterior, and other important structural features distinguishing them from the majority of fish, they form a separate class of creature. Although their total world catch is far less than that of the bony fish, it has been growing in importance recently.

The rays (Order Hypotremata) are shark-like creatures closely adapted to a life on the sea-bed by their flattened shape. There are many species, of which the common skate (*Raja batis*) is caught in substantial amounts in European waters, where it may achieve a 'wing-spread' of about 7 ft. The diet of rays is chiefly of molluscs and other fairly small sea-bed creatures, the mouth being well back on the underside of the head to facilitate easy scooping of these from the floor. Rays are symmetrical, in contrast to the flatfish. They are common in many warm or temperate areas, though never to the extent of dominating the catch. Landings are substantial in Britain, Spain, Japan, Korea, and some other countries.

Several forms of shark (Order Pleurotremata), mostly those of demersal habit, are used as food in various parts of the world. In Britain, for example, piked dogfish (*Squalus acanthias*) and spotted dogfish (*Scyliorhinus*) are landed in considerable quantities for use in fish-and-chip shops. The liver of certain sharks has also found an important market as a source of vitamin-rich oil.

APPROXIMATE TONNAGE CATCH OF SHARKS AND RAYS IN 1951 BY
CERTAIN COUNTRIES

| | |
|---|---|
| Japan | 85,000 |
| Norway | 66,000 |
| U.K. | 35,700 |
| Spain | 11,600 |
| Belgium | 4,700 |
| U.S.A. | 3,400 |
| Denmark | 2,900 |
| Eire | 2,400 |
| W. Germany | 1,500 |
| Iceland | 300 |
| Canada | 200 |

## B. PELAGIC FISH

The fishing grounds for pelagic species are not limited to the shelves and adjoining slopes, as are those for the commercial demersal species. Nevertheless, the bulk of pelagic catches are in the same areas as those of demersal catches, because it is on the shelves that food is most abundant. Yet a fairly clear distinction can be made between the demersal and pelagic fisheries of an area. Their methods differ, and the pelagic industry often tends to be seasonal, because pelagic fish are more migratory in habits than demersal fish, many of whose species are to be found continuously in a given area.

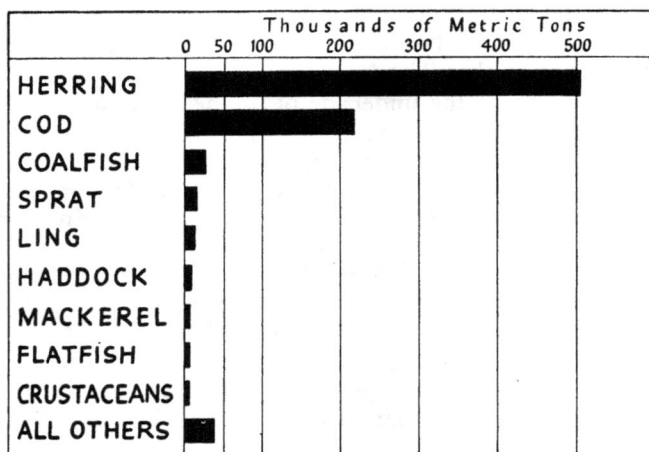

*Fig. 8.* Norway: landings by species, 1946

1. The Herring Group (Order Isospondyli, Sub-order Clupeoidea)

These are mainly small, plankton-feeding fish given to dense schooling.

*Herring.* (*Clupea harengus*, Atlantic; *C. pallasii*, Pacific.) The most important of cool temperate fish in terms of weight caught. A small fish, reaching in Europe a maximum length of about 14 in., it gathers in enormous schools near the surface at certain seasons, which vary according to place. In Britain, the main schooling first occurs off North-west Scotland in May, and occurs progressively later in the year down the east coast of Scotland and England, ending off East Anglia in early December. These schools are not, of course, composed of the same body of fish travelling southwards.

Types of herring are very important in the catches of Norway, Japan, Canada, Britain, Iceland, U.S.A., Germany, Russia,

Holland, France, and Sweden, and substantial in several other countries such as Denmark. While they are low-priced fish, they are fatty and nutritious, and an excellent contribution to the diet of many countries, where they are eaten either fresh or preserved in various ways. Like the cod, they form an important article of trade.

*Sprat.* (*Clupea sprattus.*) This quite closely resembles a miniature herring, its maximum length being about 6 in. It is far less important than the herring, but enters in small quantities into the catches of a number of cool temperate countries, particularly Norway (the Norwegian sprat being known as brisling), France, and Belgium.

*Pilchard.* (*Sardina pilchardus,* East North Atlantic; *Sardinops caerulea,* East North Pacific; *S. ocellata,* South Africa.) An important fish, especially in its young form, the sardine, the European pilchard has substantial landings in Portugal, Spain, Italy, and Morocco, and is quite important also in other Mediterranean and warm temperate coasts. It ranges as far north as the southern North Sea. There is a regular catch in Cornish waters.

The pilchards or sardines of California, until recently landed in great quantities, and those of South Africa and the west coast of South America, are related types. The term 'sardine' is also used about the world for a variety of small herring allies, while

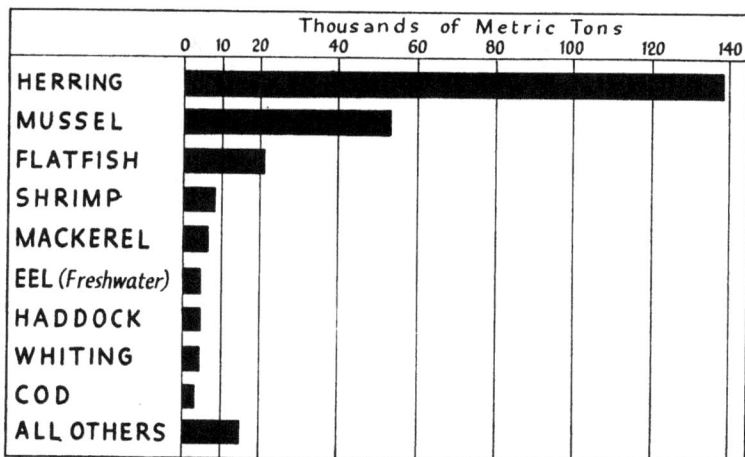

*Fig. 9.* Holland: landings by species, 1948

in north-eastern U.S.A. and eastern Canada the 'sardines' are young herring.

*Anchovy.* (*Engraulis encrasicholus*, East North Atlantic; *E. mordax*, East North Pacific; *E. japonicus*, West North Pacific.) A small and short-lived fish of mainly warm temperate habitat, it is landed in fair quantities by Portugal, Spain, France, U.S.A., and some other countries. The name is used for other small fishes.

*Menhaden.* (*Brevoortia tyrannus*.) This herring-like fish lives in eastern North and South American warm temperate waters, but is important only to the U.S.A., where, however, its landings reach vast proportions in the Middle Atlantic States. The U.S.A. lands by weight over seven times as much menhaden as herring, its menhaden landings being over twice the weight of the large British herring catch. Menhaden flesh does not apparently make good eating, and in the U.S.A. it fetches a low price, but is profitably used on a large scale for the manufacture of animal meal.

*Other Fish allied to Herring.* Species of significance include the alewife (fairly important in the U.S.A.) and a number of types of shad. The hilsa, or Indian shad, is a fish which ascends the Ganges, Indus, and other rivers to spawn during the south-west monsoon, and is then caught in large numbers.

CATCH IN TONS IN 1951 OF HERRING, PILCHARD, ANCHOVY, AND
ALLIED SPECIES BY CERTAIN COUNTRIES

| | |
|---|---:|
| Norway | 1,204,600 |
| Japan | 852,500 |
| U.S.A. | 740,200 |
| W. Germany | 316,800 |
| Canada (excluding Newfoundland) | 271,700 |
| U.K. | 179,600 |
| Holland | 150,000 |
| Spain | 130,900 |
| Sweden | 106,800 |
| France | 97,600 |
| Iceland | 84,600 |
| Portugal | 81,600 |
| Italy | 65,100 |
| Denmark | 31,000 |
| Finland | 30,000 |
| Newfoundland | 28,500 |
| Belgium | 9,900 |
| Chile | 8,600 |

2. The Mackerel Group (Order Percomorphi, Sub-order Scombroidea)

Whereas the herring and allies are mostly fairly slender, these are usually quite deep-bodied, but well streamlined. They are mainly warm temperate or tropical fish, and are all carnivorous.

*Tunny.* (*Tuna.*) A group of large and voracious species frequenting warm water, the largest of which (the bluefin tuna: *Thunnus thynnus*) reaches a length of 10 ft. and a weight of over half a ton. Others are the skipjack tuna, called 'striped bellied

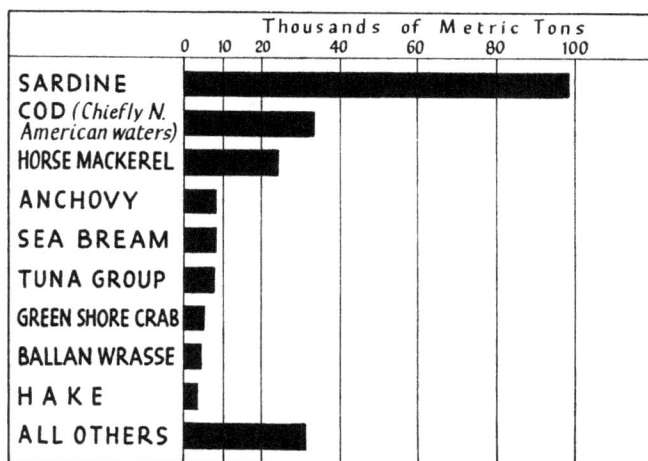

*Fig. 10.* Portugal: landings by species, 1947

bonito' in Europe (*Katsuwonus pelamys*), yellowfin tuna (*Neothunnus macropterus*), and little tuna (*Euthynnus alletteratus*). They hunt actively in schools, and have perhaps the best all-round swimming abilities of any fish. They possess not only high speed, but the ability to keep it up for long distances, and range widely over the oceans away from the shelves. Most tunny fisheries therefore use fairly long-range craft. Tunny are caught in large quantities by the U.S.A. and Japan, and fairly large amounts by France and Spain.

Albacores (*Germo*) are closely related fish also falling within this group of large mackerel-like fish, but statistically sometimes quoted separately. Their catches are important to the U.S.A., Japan, Portugal, and France. Bonitos (*Sarda*) are again fish within the tunny group, though much smaller than the 'great' tunny, rarely exceeding a yard in length. Their landings are large in Peru, and significant in the U.S.A., Spain, Morocco, and Chile.

*Mackerel.* (*Scomber scombrus*, North Atlantic; *S. japonicus*, West North Pacific.) Smaller than the tunny types, the mackerel nevertheless wreaks much destruction amongst fish smaller than itself. It ranges into cooler waters. The main catches are usually made closer to land than those of tunny, and they are caught mainly by nets rather than by the lines which in many countries are the most effective way of catching tunny. Mackerel catches are large in Japan, important in the U.S.A., France, Korea, and Norway, and significant in Canada, Denmark, Sweden, Holland, Spain, Portugal, and Britain.

There are several mackerel relatives, such as the Spanish mackerel, which are of fair importance, and will be mentioned where appropriate in the regional chapters.

CATCH IN TONS IN 1951 OF MACKEREL, TUNA, AND ALLIED SPECIES
BY CERTAIN COUNTRIES

| | |
|---|---|
| Japan | 338,400 |
| U.S.A. | 181,400 |
| France | 50,900 |
| Spain | 46,600 |
| Norway | 24,200 |
| Canada | 14,400 |
| Denmark | 12,400 |
| Sweden | 12,000 |
| Holland | 10,600 |
| Chile | 10,300 |
| Portugal | 9,100 |
| U.K. | 6,300 |

3. Other Pelagic Fish.

There is a wide variety of other pelagic fish, though relatively few of them approach first-rank commercial importance. An important exception is the salmon. This fish is, of course, anadromous, living mainly in the sea, but spawning in fresh water. When in the sea, it is caught by pelagic methods such as purse seining and trolling, although a large catch is made by stationary nets and traps at the mouths of the rivers. The salmon family (Salmonidae) is a member of the same order, the Isospondyli, as the herring family, having certain similar features, despite the difference in habits.

Salmon live chiefly in the temperate and arctic regions of the northern hemisphere. They spend their youth in fresh water, usually until the third year, when they proceed to the sea. Subsequently each salmon returns once or more to spawn in the river in which it was hatched. By far the greatest salmon fisheries in the world are those of the northern Pacific coast of North America.

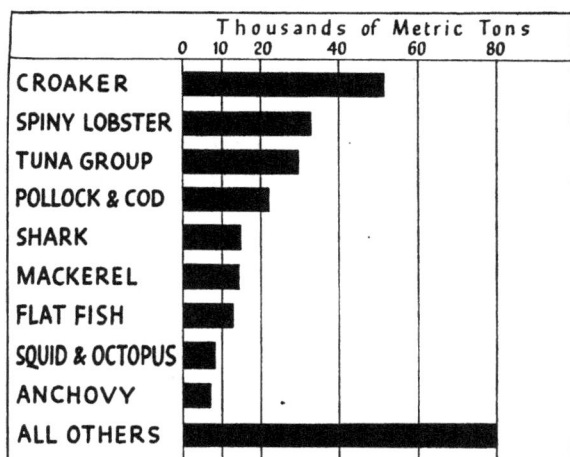

*Fig. 11.* South Korea: landings by species, 1948

### C. MOLLUSCS AND CRUSTACEANS

These are of decided importance, and in some localities dominate the fishing industry. The value-to-weight ratio of several types of shellfish is a good deal higher than that of most fish. These creatures are, of course, completely separate in zoological classification from the Bony Fishes and Selachians, both of which lie within the phylum Chordata, having a skeletal axis and gill slits. The phylum Mollusca is composed of creatures having in common the feature of the soft flat 'foot' used for creeping. In the class Cephalopoda, however, this 'foot' becomes divided into the 'arms' of the squid and octopus. The crustaceans belong to the phylum Arthropoda, animals having an external skeleton segmented to allow for movement.

Most shellfish are of demersal habit, and are normally obtained by dredges, trawls, or traps. They are mainly caught in shallow inshore waters, so that the industry based on them is usually one of small craft and small-scale financial units. There are, however, exceptions, as when oysters are 'farmed' by planting on prepared grounds. These operations sometimes lead to the growth of substantial enterprises.

### 1. Molluscs

There is a large number of species of mollusc, distributed widely about the world, though the chief commercial types are particularly important in fairly warm waters.

Pelecypoda. This class includes such creatures as clams, oysters, mussels, and cockles, which usually have the foot shaped for digging. They move but little, and often burrow. The body is enclosed by two shells hinged together, and the tiny particles of food enter with the current of water drawn through the part-opened shells. Oysters are, of course, renowned as a delicacy and fetch high prices in some countries. They may be dredged from the shallow inshore bottoms in which they grow naturally, or may be farmed on special grounds where suitable materials such as tiles are placed on the sea-bed to catch the 'spat'. This then grows into adult oysters under particularly favourable conditions, defended against natural enemies such as the starfish. Shallow estuarine shores are well placed for oyster production, and the Colchester and Whitstable oysters about the Colne and Swale on the outer Thames estuary are celebrated, though of small output in recent years. In France, oyster breeding has long been important. The large coastal lagoon of Arcachon has a high production. Here each tide renews the food supply of the oysters, but the sheltered, nearly enclosed water makes for ease of operation.

Many countries have some oyster production, but few have a really substantial output. The greatest is the U.S.A., whose chief grounds are in the estuarine waters about Chesapeake Bay. Japan, Canada, and New Zealand are also important, while Holland has a smaller but significant output. The U.S.A. and Japan lead in clam production, in which Canada, Spain, and Korea are other substantial producers. Holland appears to have the world's largest mussel landings, and uses over a third of these as poultry food. France and Chile also have considerable landings. The U.S.A. and France are the largest producers of scallops.

Cephalopoda. In contrast to the sedentary life of the usually small Pelecypoda, the creatures of this class are active and predatory, and can swim freely away from the sea-floor. They have several arms, and usually well-developed eyes, and their

shell is internal. Because of their habits, they are caught both
by pelagic and demersal methods. Various species are common
in most warm waters, and to a lesser extent in temperate waters,
but the chief factor determining the relative size of catches
appears to be the eating habits of the people. In many northern
countries the catch is negligible, but in Japan it is huge. In 1941
the Japanese landings of cuttlefish and squid were about 170,000
tons, and of octopus about 30,000 tons. Other Far Eastern
countries have substantial catches, while Spain and Portugal
also have sizeable landings.

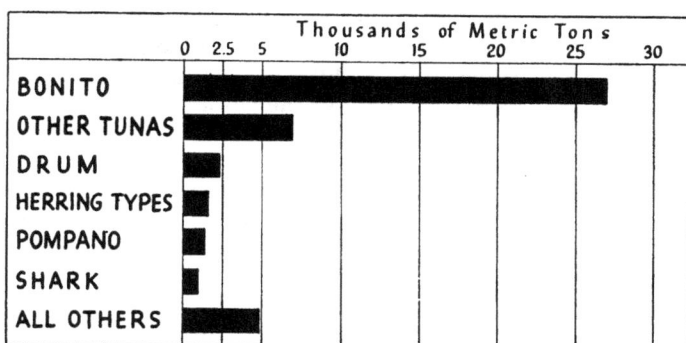

*Fig. 12.* Peru: landings by species, 1949

Gastropoda. This class includes the snail-type creatures with
spiral shells, such as the winkle and whelk. Although widespread,
they rarely attain major localized commercial importance.

CATCH IN TONS IN 1951 OF MOLLUSCS BY CERTAIN COUNTRIES

| | |
|---|---|
| Japan | 876,800 |
| U.S.A. | 434,100 |
| Holland | 43,000 |
| France | 39,400 |
| Italy | 22,500 |
| Canada | 20,800 |
| Spain | 20,200 |
| U.K. | 18,800 |
| Denmark | 18,100 |
| Chile | 16,100 |
| W. Germany | 7,600 |
| Portugal | 3,700 |
| Australia | (approx.) 3,000 |
| Norway | 200 |

2. Crustaceans

Of this class, the order Decapoda is of considerable commercial importance, as it includes the forms of crab, lobster, and shrimp. The crab and lobster live on the sea-bed, upon which they can move by strong legs. Their bodies are protected by hard external skeletons, and have powerful claws as offensive weapons. Prawns and shrimps similarly have external skeletons, but are, of course, much smaller. The bulk of crustaceans are taken in shallow water, usually fairly close to the shore. Baited cages or 'pots' lowered to the sea-floor are commonly used for lobster and crab, while towed nets of fairly fine mesh are generally used for shrimps. There are, however, many varieties and environments of each of them, with appropriately differing methods of catching. Easily the largest shrimp fishery in the world is that of the Gulf of Mexico and southern Atlantic States of the U.S.A. The wide area of shallow water of the continental shelf along this emergent coastline has a large shrimp population, which can be taken easily by motor boats towing trawls along the sea-floor. In 1947 the American shrimp catch was 87,000 metric tons. Many other countries have a small but significant production of shrimp, but Japan, Mexico, and Spain appear to be the only other countries with large catches. Holland, France, Britain, and Norway also have appreciable landings.

Many varieties of crab are widespread in the world. The U.S.A. again has a large output. Russia is an important producer, chiefly from her Far Eastern waters, and exports a considerable value of tinned crab. A good deal of this is prepared in floating cannery mother ships in the Sea of Okhotsk. Japan is also a large producer, while Britain, Norway, and France have substantial landings. Lobster, generally regarded as a greater delicacy than crab, is caught in smaller quantities, and fetches a higher price per unit of weight in most countries. The east coast of Canada is the world's leading producer. The U.S.A. also has a large production, while various other countries, such as France, Holland, and Scotland, have significant outputs. The spiny lobster, known in some countries as the crawfish, is a species which normally fetches a lower price. It is caught in many regions of warm or fairly warm water, and the biggest landings are reported from Korea.

CATCH IN TONS IN 1951 OF CRUSTACEANS BY CERTAIN COUNTRIES

| | |
|---|---|
| U.S.A. | 173,700 |
| Japan | 55,500 |
| W. Germany | 30,900 |
| Canada | 23,700 |
| Spain | 21,400 |
| Holland | 13,100 |
| Australia | (approx.) 8,000 |
| U.K. | 7,400 |
| Norway | 7,000 |
| Italy | 6,300 |
| Portugal | 2,000 |

The proportionate value of molluscs and crustaceans in the total sea fisheries catch during typical recent years was about 2½ per cent in England and Wales, 5 per cent in Norway, and 15 per cent in France. In North America the proportions were higher; about 18 per cent in Canada and 30 per cent in the U.S.A. This is presumably partly accounted for by the eating habits of the North Americans, with the importance there of canned foods, of which shellfish are an attractive and easily processed form.

Figs. 8 to 13 show the proportionate landings of the commercially important species of fish and shellfish in certain regionally representative countries. The chosen examples derive most of

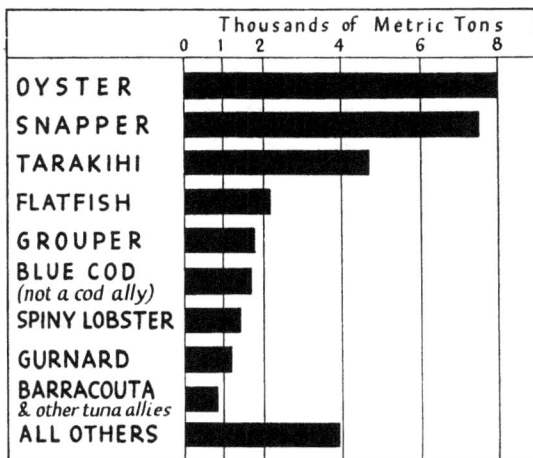

*Fig. 13.* New Zealand: landings by species, 1948

their catches from their nearby waters, and are located in different zones of temperature and shelf width upon or adjacent to the Atlantic and Pacific oceans.

Norway, with most of its waters having surface yearly means of between 40°F. and 45°F., has its catch dominated by the characteristic northern species of herring and cod. In Holland, where the yearly mean is about 50°F., cod are unimportant, though herring still dominate the catch. The large mussel production reflects the abundance of estuarine and inland waters. Farther south in Portugal, with means between 60° and 65°, there is a radical contrast with both the above countries. Sardines (pilchard) dominate the landings, while other warm-water species, such as horse mackerel, anchovy, and various species of tuna and sea bream, are also important. The cod is an exception, but is not obtained from home waters.

Turning to the Pacific, we find a broadly similar grouping in South Korea, with similar mean surface temperatures. The croaker is related to the sea bream, while tuna and anchovy are again caught in substantial quantities. The important landings of spiny lobster, shark, mackerel, squid, and octopus are also characteristic of fairly warm seas. The pollock and cod, on the other hand, are found only a short distance northwards in the cooler waters brought southwards by the east coast cold current.

In the warm Peruvian waters, of means between 65° and 70°, the tuna group is far the most important. Pelagic species form the great bulk of the catch, for the shelf here is generally very narrow. In New Zealand, with means between about 50° and 65°, there is a considerable range of type.

The summary given in this chapter will serve to indicate the enormous range of type of creature with which the world fishing industry is concerned. The great differences in size, methods of locomotion and feeding, and in habits of association, migration and breeding, pose many problems in the evolution of human techniques to catch, preserve and transport these sea resources.

# CHAPTER IV

# THE INFLUENCE OF THE TYPE OF COASTAL ZONE

THE coast itself is obviously one of the important factors in the moulding of a fishery. Variations in type of coast are reflected in variations in type of fishing activity, vessels, and settlement. If the first physical requirement of a fishery is the presence of a satisfactory fishing ground, the second is the presence of a satisfactory location for one or more ports. Where the coastline is everywhere suitable for port development, it is not a critical factor; the ports will grow at positions best in regard to the locations of the fishing grounds and of their markets, factors which are discussed in later chapters. But such a condition is uncommon. Marked variations occur in the suitability of the coast. Both the general positioning and the detailed siting of a fishing port normally owe a good deal to the form of the coast.

For the present purpose the term 'coast' will, to avoid any confusion, be enlarged to become the 'coastal zone', in view of the fact that some physical geographers prefer to reserve 'coast' for the precise margin of the land; the cliff line or its equivalent. We are concerned here with a zone of human use whose value depends not only on the nature of the coastline but on the nature of its immediate sea and land approaches. The 'coastal zone' is therefore defined for employment here as the area bounded on the seaward side by the outer edge of the abrasion platform (or offshore beach terrace, if this extends outside it), and on the landward side by a line slightly inland of the limit of penetration of navigable estuaries, rias, fiords, lagoons, and other inlets. If such inlets are absent or infrequent, then the limit must be fixed more arbitrarily along a line sufficiently inland to give adequate indication of the type of terrain immediately bordering the coast. On the seaward side, the limit is made flexible so that it can be extended outwards to include adjacent islands, rocks, or shoals, where these are significant in their influence on the human use of the coast.

Thus, whereas a coastline has no width, the coastal zone has a width which may vary considerably from place to place. This variation does not imply lack of precision in definition: it is a reflection of actual conditions. The coastal zone is the area in which human activities, directly in the establishment of commercial ports, fisheries, and holiday resorts, and indirectly in numerous other ways, is dominated or strongly influenced by the sea. Its width may be estimated, for example, at an arbitrary two miles on the middle Lincolnshire coast, lacking indentations, and where sea-controlled activities are unimportant, whereas in East Essex the coastal zone width has a mean of over fifteen miles, and in South-west Norway of over sixty miles.

The coastal zone may vary in its effects from being completely useless for maritime economic activity—an economic barrier coast—to being one which invites, virtually compels, such activity. The types of coast zones can be graded according to the degree in which they facilitate maritime economic development. Such grading must take into account their provision of sheltered and sufficiently deep harbours, the navigational obstructions in their seaward approaches, and ease of transport from the water's edge inland. We are here concerned only with transport in the immediate coastal zone. Easy communications farther inland *en route* to the hinterland, and within it, are obviously also of great importance, but these are more conveniently considered separately, and are dealt with later.

Conditions of climate, weather, and natural vegetation also clearly affect the suitability of a coast. However, as the basic coastal classifications are those of landforms, and as these cause marked local variations in coastal suitability within the same climatic region, they will be used as the basis for the grading which follows. The conclusions can then be modified in particular instances where climate, weather, and natural vegetation are seen to be significant factors. Severe weather conditions may render unsuitable an otherwise useful coast. In zones of frequent gales the relative advantage of coast types offering closely spaced sheltered anchorages is obviously increased. Climates in which the sea becomes ice-blocked for part of the year clearly render many types of coast useless for the ice period. Equatorial and tropical climates often make low-lying coastal zones too unhealthy and enervating for any appreciable human use. In some areas, also, dense forests and swamps may seriously impede the construction of land transport facilities in the coastal zone.

Whereas the suitability of coast zones for general maritime activity is broadly indicated in the grading discussed, it is the suitability for fishing activity with which it is essentially concerned. Certain types are therefore given a different importance from that which would be the case if their suitability for general cargo ports were being assessed. For example, a fiord coast zone may provide a good base for fishing, particularly when the products are being exported by sea, whereas it might prove a poor location for a general cargo port because of difficult communications with its hinterland.

Again, fishing craft are less critical in their demands than normal cargo or passenger ships. Fishing vessels are of small size; even a modern steam trawler rarely exceeds 200 ft. in length and 17 ft. in draught, and most other types are a good deal smaller. A modern motor drifter is about 70 ft. in length. The requirements of fishing also make these vessels highly manoeuvrable. Their needs in harbour space and depth are therefore less demanding than those of cargo or passenger ships. They are also robust craft; more robust in many ways than are large vessels. It is, of course, a popular mistake to assume that a large vessel is normally more robust than a small one. The large vessel has frames and skin often more fragile in proportion to the weight and momentum of itself and its cargo than those of a small craft, and its greater length gives greater leverage to disruptive forces. A large vessel may break its back on rocks when a small one would escape serious damage.

Fishing craft, therefore, are in less need of large, well-sheltered harbours than normal cargo vessels, and there are places, for example parts of the coasts of Holland and of north-eastern England, where fishing is carried on in the absence of such shelter. Such areas must, however, develop specialized craft. These must be capable of resting upright on the beach for unloading, and of taking considerable pounding against the beach when partly afloat. Hence the flat bottom and heavy construction of some Dutch craft. Alternatively, the boats must be capable of being hauled up the beach above high-water mark. Hence the light though strong construction of craft such as the Yorkshire coble. Such types are, however, becoming relatively unimportant today in advanced countries, and some form of shelter is generally provided as the base of operation of fishing craft. Such shelter is necessary if a modern standard of rapid and economical unloading is required. In a natural harbour the shelter is already there; the only artificial addition needed is the building up of quays in sufficient depth of water to permit the craft to come alongside to discharge. In the absence of a natural harbour, an artificial one must be made by the building of one or more breakwater arms. These may exist solely for sheltering the craft from waves and swell, or they may also serve the functions of unloading quays.

The main physical requirements of a base for fishing vessels are therefore adequate depth of water for vessels to come alongside at high tide, and preferably at all states of the tide, and adequate shelter from the sea to protect the craft from damage when alongside the quay, and to permit easy unloading. A third basic requirement relates to the land behind the shore-line: normally there must be satisfactory communications between the harbour and the area immediately inland. Locations otherwise suitable may be rendered useless if access to the land behind is barred by a continuous cliff-line. Satisfactory road or rail transport is essential to all but subsistence fishing communities, or those exporting the bulk of their produce by sea to other regions.

Many sites occur naturally which fulfil the above three basic conditions. If they are sufficiently near fishing grounds, if there is sufficient market available for them, and if labour and material supply are adequate, they almost inevitably become small fishing centres, if nothing more. In Britain, until the early years of this century, the fishing industry was mainly conducted from a great number of such small fishing ports, thickly distributed along many parts of the coast. In all areas, save those of sparse population, few potential sites were left unused as fishing centres. The industry was largely dispersed among many small but economically viable communities. More recently, for reasons to be discussed later, the bulk of the industry has become concentrated in a few important ports. In most of the other centres commercial fishing has dwindled to a minor though usefully picturesque adjunct to their now primary function as holiday resorts.

The degree of centralization of the fishing industry in Britain is, however, unique. Other countries, even of advanced fishery development, such as the U.S.A., Canada, and Norway, owe a large part of their production to many dispersed communities. It is likely that in most parts of the world, particularly in Asia and Africa, the industry will remain highly decentralized for some time, if not permanently. The study of the type of natural site suitable as a relatively small fishing base is therefore still important. As an industry becomes more centralized, the natural

conditions of course become less critical. A highly centralized—
and therefore usually highly capitalized—industry can afford
the construction of expensive harbour works which will transform
a poor site into a good one. It is prepared to sustain the expense
if the other factors, such as nearness to a large market, make this
worth while. It should be noted, however, that even large fishing
ports with much artificial construction have normally developed
from small ports whose location was originally determined by
natural conditions.

The class of zone which most facilitates the growth of fisheries
is the markedly submergent. The earth's crust is, of course,
liable to substantial movements with the passage of time.
Submergence may be due to subsidence of the land, or it may be
due to rise in sea-level. The latter process has been in operation
during the retreat of the ice sheets since the last Ice Age. Every
part of the world has been affected by this general, or eustatic,
change, so that many coastlines show some signs of fairly recent
submergence. The exceptions are where the land has been rising
faster than the sea, as, for example, where it has previously been
markedly depressed by the ice sheets. In many areas there have
successively been opposing movements of relative sea-level. We
are here concerned essentially with the resulting dominant
characteristic.

The dominantly submergent coast has many inlets, where
former valleys have been drowned by the sea. These provide
good navigational depth close inshore, closely spaced and well-
sheltered natural harbours, and normally adequate transport
routes inland along the valleys. They have a high ratio of total
coastline to coast frontage (that is, the span of coast, ignoring
indentations). They stimulate maritime activity, while fishing
is early encouraged by the well-stocked and sheltered fishing
grounds in the many inlets.

There are a number of types of essentially submergent coast
zone. The most conducive to fishing activities, other factors
being equal, is the ria type. Rias are drowned river valleys in
regions of previously fairly marked relief. They thus have good
depth of water. Many inlets lead on to good land routes up their
valleys to interior markets. Such areas of long-established fishery
importance as Brittany, Galicia, and South-west England are
examples of this type (see Figs. 14 and 15).

Where the interior is still very mountainous, easy inland
communications may be impeded. Such high lands in the cooler

latitudes are generally also associated with heavy past glaciation. The valleys have once been deeply eroded by glaciers to become fiords. These contrast with rias in their normally greater depth and steeper sides. While fiords make good natural harbours, they generally make poor locations for ports. They often lack sufficient area of flat land for extensive port works and town building. Communication inland from them by rail or road may be made difficult, sometimes impossible, by the steepness of the gradients involved.

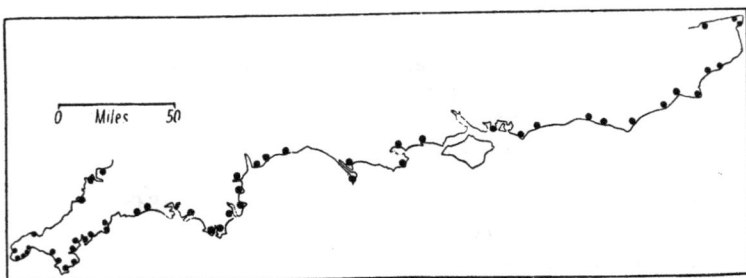

*Fig. 14.* South coast ports with significant fish landings. Closer distribution in markedly submergent south-west is evident

Yet, in spite of these difficulties, heavily glaciated coast zones of submergent type are among the most important fishery areas of the world. They occur in latitudes of prolific sea conditions. The fiords and inshore waters are rich fishing grounds, and offer numerous sheltered channels and anchorages as refuge from severe storms for vessels which operate farther out to sea. The lack of productivity of the rugged, thin-soiled land compels development of the fisheries, while the sparseness of inland settlement means that markets for the surplus fish must be found elsewhere. The large-scale development of fisheries in such areas is inevitably heavily dependent upon exports: this is the case particularly in Norway, Iceland, Newfoundland, Alaska, and British Columbia. Poverty of inland communications is then no handicap to coastal fishing settlement where the bulk of the production is shipped overseas or coastwise to entrepôts. A heavily glaciated highland coastal zone is thus a restrictive influence only where the fisheries depend primarily on a local inland market for fresh fish. The British fishing industry depends mainly on such a market. Fast rail communication to the inland areas of dense population is therefore essential here to a fishing

*Plate II.* BRETON TUNNYMAN. TANGONS (FISHING RODS) NOT IN USE:
STARBOARD ONE RAISED VERTICALLY, PORT ONE ACTING AS A BOOM

centre of importance. For this reason the fiord-type coastal zone of the Western Highlands of Scotland, with its poor communications from the coast inland, has developed no prominent fishing centres despite the good fishing grounds offshore. The main Scottish centres are all on the better transport routes of the east coast.

Another coast type is the estuarine. This is a relatively flat coastal zone, which may have been but recently (from the point of view of geological time) submerging, following upon a period of emergence. In many cases, indeed, the previous emergent movement may still dominate the character of the zone, having left it with a relatively level coastal plain which was once the bed of the sea. The recent rise in sea-level, however, will have encroached some distance upon the plain, deepening and widening the lower reaches of the rivers.

Such coast plains, penetrated by numerous estuaries and their branches, are normally important fishing areas. Indeed, the intensity of fishing production of, for example, the Chesapeake Bay area, is very high. This relatively shallow estuarine type is, however, graded as normally somewhat inferior to the markedly submergent coastal zone because it less frequently develops a dominant fishing industry; that is, one which dominates the human use of the coastal zone in question. A high value of fishery production in estuaries is often largely accounted for by inshore shellfish, which require skilled attention, though little in the way of vessels and fishing gear. The shores of estuaries are usually of shallow water, which in many cases gives place to extensive mud flats at low tide. This keeps the size of the vessels small and hence limits their range of operation. For the same reason fishing ports tend to remain small, situated at the heads of creeks which at low tide may be little more than ditches.

In days when most fishing vessels were small and of short range these ports had a higher relative importance than today. In advanced countries the main present centres are usually on other types of coast zone. Large estuaries are often the sites of important general cargo ports because they penetrate into populous lowlands with good land communications, and in earlier days found their shallow water no disadvantage. Where such large ports have been long established, their concentration of industrial and social capital has made it worth their while to stand the expense of extensive dredging and artificial dock works to keep the port open despite the increasing draught of vessels.

However, this has rarely helped the fishing activities of the estuaries. The large commercial ports are normally sited at the nodal point near the head of the estuary. Here also the freshwater current and the narrowed tidal currents scour a channel which may have fairly deep water close inshore. From this point the deep channel proceeds roughly along the middle of the estuary to the sea, but nowhere else does it approach the shore closely. Thus, at first sight paradoxically, ports nearer the sea have naturally shallower water than the port at the head.

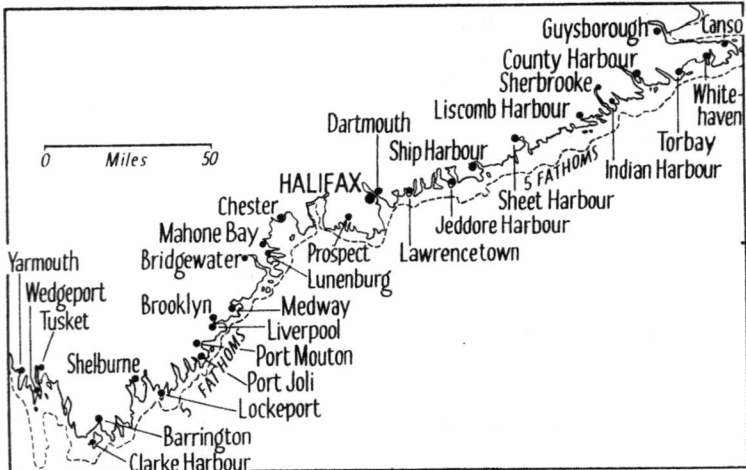

*Fig. 15.* Density of distribution of coastal settlements in a submergent zone of moderate relief: Nova Scotia, southern coast

Average frequency of distribution: 11 settlements per 100 miles of coast front, in a province of average population density of approximately 33 per square mile

Artificial deepening of the main channel only accentuates this discrepancy in depth. Any small ports along the estuary shores which continue to depend primarily on fishing can rarely afford to maintain deep-dredged harbours and channels to the main channel, so they rarely gain a new lease of life from the deepening of the main channel. Indeed, the fate of fishing ports in proximity to an expanding modern commercial port is sometimes extinction. As the large port expands downstream, with its new dock works and new tributary dredged channels where necessary, it engulfs the fishing port. Because of their different requirements in size and type of dock basins, and in specialized cargo-handling facilities, the work of general commercial ports and fishing ports cannot always be combined effectively in the same place. The fishing function is normally the less important from the local point of view, and so in cases of conflicting interest it has to give way. For example, the expansion of the Port of London down the Thames estuary has destroyed the once important fishing centre at Barking, and curtailed the fishing activities from other centres such as Gravesend. The advantages of estuaries for fisheries may therefore under modern conditions be neutralized by their still greater advantages as locations for large cargo ports.

Another factor sometimes limiting development of estuarine coast plains as fishing centres is the competing attraction of activities not connected with the sea, in these lowland areas of good agriculture and inland communications. This is sometimes the case in 'new' lands in early stages of settlement, but once a certain density of population is reached the resources of the sea can no longer be neglected.

To summarize, it can be said that estuarine coast plains are normally important areas of fishery development, while their large, easily accessible, sheltered areas of shallow water make them particularly suitable locations for extensive shell-fisheries. Their fishing settlements are usually small but closely spaced (see Fig. 16).

The submergent form of coast zone, therefore, is frequently important in fishery development. The exception is the submergent coast zone which, after the passage of considerable time without further submergent tendencies, has reached the stages of maturity or old age. There are few examples of old age, because before this stage has been reached new movements have initiated fresh cycles of development. There are a number of good examples of the mature stage, however, such as the eastern end of the south coast of England. In this stage, erosion by the sea has cut back the headlands and largely destroyed the indented nature of the coast, leaving it with a regular coastline of cliffs. Natural harbours are rare or absent. The small ports of Dover and Folkestone exist despite the adverse coast, chiefly because they command the shortest routes to France for passenger vessels, and because Dover has been of naval significance, but their harbours are formed artificially by breakwaters.

The remaining coastal zone types to be noted facilitate fishing activities to a markedly less degree than the immature submergent types. This is not to say that important fishing centres are not at times to be found on them; but such centres are sited there only because of the absence from the region of coastal zones of submergent type to provide better natural conditions. If a region is densely populated and provides an adequate market, it will, under modern conditions, tend to develop fishing centres even if the available coastal zone is naturally adverse. The economic power of the market will promote this. Under such conditions considerable capital outlay may be necessary to make

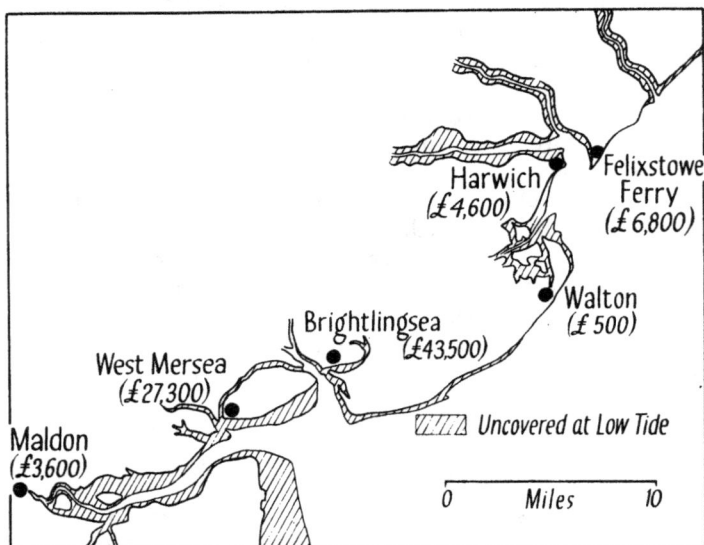

*Fig. 16.* Part of Essex and Suffolk. A typical estuarine coastal zone, showing close spacing of small ports with fishing industries. Figures show initial value of fish (mainly shellfish) landed in 1947

a serviceable artificial port on an unsuitable location. In building such dock works there are economies of size: a large dock site of a given capacity normally costs less than a number of smaller dock sites of the same total capacity. For this reason a region of unsuitable coast may paradoxically have larger fishing ports than an adjacent region with naturally superior coast. In such cases, however, the *total* fishing activity of the better coast will usually be the greater, other factors being equal.

In contrast to dominantly submergent coastal zones, there are the dominantly emergent types, in which the land has been rising and the coastline moving outwards. These present few or no good natural harbours in their little-indented shores.  Such harbours as there are occur at river mouths, and are usually shallow and impeded by shoals.  Approach to the coast from the sea may be prevented in places by the characteristic offshore bars parallel to the shore-line.  When they partly or wholly enclose lagoons, these rarely offer conditions of depth and shore terrain suitable for use as harbours.  The fringe of the shore, particularly in tropical and sub-tropical areas, is frequently a forested swamp seriously interrupting communications between the shore and the coast plain inland.

Emergent coastal zones thus normally lack satisfactory natural harbours, and do not encourage maritime activity by the inhabitants of the region.  This lack of maritime activity is enhanced, particularly in temperate climates, by the usually easy land communications along the coast plains, causing neglect of sea transport.  Again, the good agricultural possibilities of the plains reduce the need for exploitation of fishery resources, at least until the population becomes dense.

With most zones of emergence we may include for this purpose other types having somewhat similar results in rendering maritime development difficult and providing easier alternative activities. Forms of coast zone which may be built out seawards without any substantial relative change of sea-level fall into this category. Alluvial plains and deltas built of material carried down by rivers may normally be included here.  Such deltas may have numerous distributaries, but these may be too shallow and shoal-blocked to encourage seagoing activities, while the delta shore may in many climates be swampy and forested: a barrier shore.  Many deltas have important ports: but these arise because of their nodality in commanding a large inland waterway system or a populous inner delta agricultural area, not because of any advantage for port location on the delta coast.  In most cases, indeed, these ports are a considerable distance inland rather than on the coast.  The coastal zones of such deltas as the Mississippi, Niger, Po, Danube, and Ganges are notable for their absence of any large settlements.  Small fishing communities may be scattered about the zone; but these are more usually concerned with freshwater fisheries on the distributaries than with sea fisheries.  In any case, fishery resources of the sea off delta coasts are not necessarily good.  The advantage of the greater supply of nutrient salts brought down by the river may be more than offset by the reduction in the sun's photosynthetic effect by the muddiness of the water. Production of sea-bed plants and plankton is thus reduced in waters off mouths of rivers which bring down much suspended material. There are, of course, great variations in this degree of concentration.

Deltas influenced by submergence to a degree which makes their distributaries estuarine are better classified as the estuarine coast plains previous discussed. They are frequently important sea-fishing centres as, for example, the Rhine deltaic area in Holland, and the delta of the Si Kiang.

Other forms of coastal zone which normally may be grouped for our purpose with dominantly emergent types are glacial outwash plains, and coasts due to outbuilding of volcanic material into the sea. The latter, however, will vary considerably in form according to the nature of the volcanic material and, of course, their age. Other grading may, therefore, be allotted in individual cases.

The southern Atlantic and Gulf coasts of the U.S.A. offer an excellent example of the influence on fisheries of a coastal zone of emergent characteristics. Coastal settlements are much less closely spaced than in the northern Atlantic U.S.A. coast, and both general maritime and fishing activity is considerably less. There are a few large cargo ports existing to serve the hinterland: these are products of the hinterland, despite the coastal zone conditions. The main fishing activities in several areas are concerned with shellfish, for which the shallow waters provide good grounds. Even so, the average annual value of the fishery products of the roughly 2,200 miles of coastal front between Wilmington, North Carolina, and the Mexican frontier is somewhat less than that of the 550 miles of front of the New England submergent type coastal zone. This disparity cannot, of course, be accounted for solely by the contrast in coastal types, for the New England coasts have economical access to superior fishing grounds and larger markets. Nevertheless, the coastal types have an important bearing on the matter, by the difference in the natural facilities they provide for fishing bases, and in the different human outlooks they have bred. The New England states have exploited to the full their adjacent fishing grounds, and have extended their range of operation farther afield.

We may now consider the coast zones where there is strongly developed folding or faulting of the earth along lines more or less parallel to the coast. These are usually the least suitable type for fishing ports. The land rises steeply inland from the shore, high cliffs may be common, and the sea-bed slopes sharply downward. Lowland behind the coast will be a narrow strip, or completely absent, so that inland routes are difficult. The steep inland rise of the land prevents its penetration by inlets, so the coast is very poor in natural harbours. While the sea immediately offshore is deep and offers no impediment to navigation, the continental shelf is too narrow to support a large quantity of demersal fish. Fishing activity is therefore often unimportant from such coasts. Oceanic pelagic fish, such as tuna, may exist in economically worth-while quantities in the adjacent seas, but fishing for these may largely be by craft based on other areas. Peru and northern Chile offer good examples of this type of coast zone. Thanks to their good pelagic resources their local fisheries have grown rapidly in recent years, but they are still not of major importance by world standards. For a long time they remained neglected because of the unsuitability of the coast.

The review in this chapter deals, of course, with broad effects only. It is recognized that compound coast zones exist which defy easy classifications, and these must be judged on individual merits, though the above analysis offers appropriate criteria. Detailed effects, in matters such as the precise location of fishing centres, the forms of settlement developed, and the modifications in types of vessel and equipment in response to coastal conditions, will be discussed in later chapters.

## SOME BOOKS AND PAPERS ON SUBJECTS TREATED IN THIS SECTION

This list is not intended to be exhaustive. There are, for example, many research establishments in the world publishing frequent reports on various aspects of marine biology and fisheries problems. Lists of such reports may be found in the *Fisheries Bulletins*. of the United Nations Food and Agriculture Orgaization, Rome. (The abbreviation F.A.O. is used in subsequent references to this Organization.)

*The Oceans: Their Physics, Chemistry and General Biology*. H. U. Sverdrup, M. W. Johnson, and R. H. Fleming. (Prentice-Hall, New York, 1949.)

*The Seas*. F. S. Russell and C. M. Yonge. (Warne, London, 2nd. Edn., 1936.)

*This Great and Wide Sea*. R. E. Coker. (Univ. of North Carolina Press, 1948.)

*Zoogeography of the Sea*. Sven Ekman. (Sidgwick and Jackson, London, 1953.)

*Hydrography in Relation to Fisheries*. J. B. Tait. (Arnold, London, 1952.)

*The Journal of the Marine Biological Association of the U.K.* (Cambridge Univ. Press.) Several papers on plankton productivity have been published in this journal in recent years, for example:
'Phosphate in the English Channel 1933–1938, with a comparison with earlier years.' (L. H. N. Cooper, vol. XXIII, 1938.)
'On the production of living matter in the sea off Plymouth.' (H. W. Harvey, vol. XXIX, 1950.)

*The Overfishing Problem.* E. S. Russell. (Cambridge Univ. Press, 1942.)
*The Fish Gate.* Michael Graham. (Faber & Faber, London, 1943.)
*Rational Fishing of the Cod of the North Sea.* Michael Graham. (Arnold, London, 1947.)
*The Nations' Sea-Fish Supply.* E. Ford. (Arnold, London, 1937.)
*Conservation of the Pacific Halibut.* W. F. Thompson. (Annual Report, Smithsonian Institution, for year ending June 1935.)
Many studies on such matters as fish migrations and over-fishing problems have appeared in the *Reports* and the *Journal of the International Council for the Exploration of the Sea*, Copenhagen, for example:
'Some Observations on the Principles of Fishery Regulation.' (R. J. H. Beverton. *Journal*, May 1953.)
*An Illustrated Guide to the Fish Gallery of the British Museum of Natural History.* J. R. Norman. (British Museum Trustees, 1937.)
*A History of Fishes.* J. R. Norman. (Benn, London, 1947.)
*British Salt-Water Fishes.* F. G. Aflalo. (Hutchinson, London, 1904.)
*The Distinguishing Features of Fish.* (Fishmongers' Hall, London, 1949.)
*Herring and Allied Species.* (F.A.O., Rome, 1949.)
*The Natural History of the Herring in Scottish Waters.* H. Wood. (Fishing News, Aberdeen, 1932.)
*The Natural History of the Herring of the Southern North Sea.* William C. Hodgson. (Arnold, London, 1934.)
*The Cod Fisheries.* H. A. Innis. (New Haven, 1940.)
*The Plaice Fishery.* R. S. Wimpenny. (Arnold, London, 1953.)
*The Hake and the Hake Fishery.* C. F. Hickling. (Arnold, London, 1935.)
*Oyster Biology and Oyster Culture.* J. H. Orton. (Arnold, London, 1937.)
*Fishery Science.* George A. Rounsefell and W. Harry Everhart. (John Wiley & Son, New York, and Chapman & Hall, London, 1953.)
'Report on Trawling Surveys on the Patagonian Continental Shelf.' T. J. Hart. *Discovery Reports*, 1946.
*Yearbooks of Fishery Statistics.* (F.A.O., Rome published for 1947 and subsequent years).

*Section II*

# TECHNIQUES AND THEIR WORLD DISTRIBUTION

# CHAPTER V

# FISHING METHODS AND CRAFT AS RESPONSES TO ENVIRONMENT

THE fishing vessel, with its equipment, forms an instrument evolved to fulfil a function as efficiently as the knowledge of its builders permits. Though purely utilitarian, it often has beauty. This can perhaps be said of most devices of man constructed to deal directly with the forces of nature. They are obliged to achieve a harmony and balance of form reflecting that of nature herself.

Fishing methods are the basic control of the types of craft used. There is a great variety of such methods, but the most important can be classified functionally into a few major groups. They are determined by the habits of the types of fish caught, by the nature of the sea-bed, and related conditions. These limitations still leave a certain field of choice, and the methods most favoured by any particular community will partly depend on such matters as its ingenuity, available capital, size of market, and form of social organization. Local variations throughout the world are almost infinite, and include bizarre methods such as the use of harnessed cormorants in China. An exhaustive study of all of them would take a great deal of space. We will chiefly limit ourselves here to the main techniques used in commercial sea fisheries, as listed below.

A. FOR DEMERSAL FISH

    1. *Lines*   (i)    Hand lines.
             (ii)   Long lines.
    2. *Nets*   (i)    Gill or trammel nets or traps stationary on the sea-bed.
             (ii)   Beam trawls.
             (iii)   Otter trawls.
             (iv)   Pair-operated trawls.
             (v)    Danish seine nets.
             (vi)   Beach-hauled seines.

B. FOR PELAGIC FISH

  1. *Direct attack*—by harpoons, spears, etc.
  2. *Lines*  (i)    Hand lines.
              (ii)   Trolled lines.
  3. *Nets*   (i)    Drift and other gill nets.
              (ii)   Ring nets, purse seines, and lamparas.
              (iii)  Beach-hauled seines.
              (iv)   Vertically hauled nets.
              (v)    Bottom trawls (at certain seasons).
              (vi)   Floating or mid-water trawls.
              (vii)  Stationary traps.

These methods, and the vessels involved, will be described in turn in the following two chapters. Before such detailed consideration, however, it will be useful to discuss some of the general conditions influencing the development of fishing gear and vessels.

The method of direct attack by spears, harpoons, or other missiles, although doubtless the first method devised, and still of significance to the small-scale fisherman in parts of Asia, Africa, Oceania, and South America, has negligible importance in major commercial fisheries, with the important exception of whaling and sealing. These are not, biologically speaking, true fisheries, and will not be discussed in this section, though they will be considered under the appropriate regions in Section III. Direct attack is also used to a small extent in certain work such as the harpooning of sharks, but even in that fishery is, in several areas, less important than trammel nets or long lines.

The line accounts for a smaller proportion of the world's catch than does the net, and its relative importance is decreasing in many areas. For certain types of fishing, however, the line remains the most economically efficient method. Reasons for this are:

  (i)   Nets have to be heavy and costly to hold large and powerful fish, and even then need frequent repair.
  (ii)  Large pelagic fish are normally widely dispersed or in relatively open schools: this must be so because they depend for their sustenance on smaller fish, which can support only a limited number of large predators in a given area. Hence the net, which in pelagic fisheries

is essentially for the capture of dense homogeneous schools, is unsuitable for many types of large fish.

(iii) Some grounds have many outcropping rocks or other obstacles on which trawl nets can catch and be lost. Some areas off South Greenland, for example, have many large boulders dropped by melting icebergs. Many tropical grounds are littered with coral formations. In such cases line fishing has obvious advantages for demersal fish.

(iv) Where other factors influencing the choice of methods are inconclusive, the line gains the decision by virtue of its simplicity of maintenance and operation and low initial cost.

Most of the methods discussed are operated from vessels, ranging from small wooden canoes in many parts of Asia and Africa to the large steam trawlers on Arctic grounds and the imposing Portuguese four-masted schooners working the Grand Banks and Davis Strait. Some techniques, such as the use of beach-hauled nets, or stationary traps between high- and low-water levels, can be operated entirely from the shore without the use of vessels. These are usually important only in less advanced areas, such as the tropical coasts and islands of Asia. Even in these areas, however, fishing from craft, or with the co-operation of craft, is generally more important. Shore-operated methods can only exploit a very narrow fringe of the sea resources of their areas.

A very important exception is the group of shore-operated fisheries which are concerned with fish having partly sea and partly freshwater habitat, particularly the salmon fisheries of the northern Pacific coast of North America. The value of pound nets and fish weirs in Canada in 1945 was $620,000, or about 17 per cent of the total value of net or line equipment in use in the country.

The basic aim of the fisherman is to use the method giving the greatest catch per unit of effort. This simple principle, however, is frequently modified by other considerations. The adoption of a more efficient and, in the long run, cheaper technique may be delayed by the capital cost of the equipment and the necessary modifications to the craft. Further, fishermen are often of a conservative disposition, and reluctant to try new methods save under strong economic spur, such as a large fall in fish prices

6

making larger catches per man essential if the standard of living of those remaining in work is to be maintained. Such economic conditions are, however, precisely the time when the fishing vessel owner's resources are least able to stand the expenditure.

The situation is further complicated by the fact that fishing can become, in one sense, over-efficient, because wholesale destruction of fish may so deplete fishing grounds that finally a lower rate of catch is obtained despite the improved technique. This has seemed to be the final result of the development of power-trawling in the North Sea. Few large areas are, however, at present in imminent danger of such a fate. What does happen is that the introduction of more efficient methods in a limited locality may ultimately so reduce the fish density there that boats are obliged to make longer voyages to obtain reasonable catches. The spur of competition thus opens up new fishing areas, and in most parts of the world is still succeeding in increasing the total catch. Any increase in the prices of fish, or any new technique lowering the cost of catching, has the effect of enlarging the area intensively fished up to the point at which the non-paying part of the voyage—the journey to and from the place of actual fishing—is so long that the costs in the outer marginal areas once more equal the prices.

Major revolutions in technique in the fishing industry are not frequent. It has been practised so long that the basic methods by which fish can be caught have been pioneered many centuries ago. The greatest single change was the development of the steam-drawn otter trawl technique by Britain in the latter part of the last century. This method could exploit the steam engine fully by drawing a much larger trawl net over the sea-floor, keeping its mouth open by means of two opposing boards inclined at an angle to the water flow. It is a significant commentary on the conditions of the fishing industry that, in the advanced areas of New England and the Canadian Maritimes, the otter trawl has since then only gradually been displacing their older long-line dory-fishing methods.

The adoption of the otter trawl generally leads to a lower requirement for fishermen. Labour costs are the bulk of the total cost for long-line fishing, whereas fuel and depreciation costs of equipment are more important in trawling. Widespread displacement of long-lining by trawling may therefore increase owners' profits by a relatively small amount, and this perhaps only temporarily until fish prices tend to fall (relatively to other prices) in response to greater output. On the other hand, unemployment and social dislocation may be caused in the fishing community.

Revolutionary changes of technique apart, there is in progress a gradual improvement of old techniques, together with the adoption of new ancillary techniques connected with the handling and preserving of fish. Of increasing significance is the fitting of full refrigeration to long-range craft, instead of the mere carriage of ice or salt.

Few fishing craft are 100 per cent specialized, in that they cannot be adapted at all to other methods. Nevertheless, most vessels are equipped primarily to deal with one type of fishing, or with two which have different seasons and for which the boat can be prepared without much adjustment. In Britain, for example, the trawler is exclusively concerned with demersal fish, chiefly the cod, allied species, and flatfish, whose habits are similar in their effects on fishing method. The majority of drifters, similarly, concern themselves with their own special method, evolved for pelagic fish. These are the two most important groups in the country. However, the medium-sized, motor-powered drifter-trawler is now becoming an important class of vessel where certain local conditions encourage it.

The great bulk of the British long-distance catch is by large steam trawlers, which have evolved in response to the particular requirements of the fishery: high power to drag a large trawl, and considerable range and hold capacity. Britain has developed the use of the large trawler to a greater extent than any other country. Specialization is carried furthest in craft dealing with fish that are within range throughout the year; examples are the British steam trawler and the American diesel tuna clipper. Boats which have not the range to follow their quarry outside local waters are naturally obliged to be less specialized in type and equipment, so that they are ready to take advantage of whatever marketable species may arrive for a period in their waters. Such is the case with a large number of small craft in North American inshore waters. The degree of stability of relative prices for various types of fish also influences the amount of specialization. Fairly rapid changes in the United States, for example, may have contributed to the generally lesser degree of specialization there than in the United Kingdom.

In size, shape, and equipment, fishing craft must be a compromise between conflicting requirements. The well-designed vessel is the optimum case. Draught requirements for load-carrying, net-towing, and stability conflict with the needs of shallow harbours. Powerful engines for higher speeds, to reach grounds and markets quickly, conflict with the demands of long-range operation and low fuel consumption. Complex equipment, leading to higher rates of catch, conflicts with the requirement for rugged, dependable gear unlikely to break down out of reach of the technical resources of the land.

Once certain environmental factors are understood, it is possible, from a drawing of a craft (including her underwater portion), to make a good estimate of the type of coast from which she works, the type of fish she is primarily concerned in catching, and in some cases to state her most likely home port.

The main factors influencing the design of fishing vessels and their equipment can be listed as follows:

1. Features of the types of fish caught in the area, such as their size, and habits of feeding, schooling, migration, and so on.
2. The distance from the base at which the main grounds lie.
3. The abundance of the fish.
4. The nature of the sea-bed on the grounds (in demersal fishing).
5. The type of coastline.
6. Climate and weather conditions.
7. Natural materials locally available for construction.
8. Type of fuel most economically available.
9. Conditions influencing the outlook, maritime skill, and organization of the fishermen.
10. The size and type of market for fish.

The dictates of these conditions are sometimes conflicting, sometimes complementary, and they vary greatly in relative importance in different cases. For clarity of presentation the physical and human factors may at times be treated separately, though this does not, of course, imply that they are completely independent of each other. Some societies are more skilful than others in adapting themselves to the limitations imposed by physical factors, while the societies themselves owe their special skills in part to the demands of their physical environment.

Oceanic conditions affecting the fish supply are, of course, of primary importance everywhere, and will be discussed in detail subsequently. The type of coast, with the harbours it offers, is also a factor still of importance everywhere, though in advanced regions its degree of control may be modified by dredging, by large harbour works, and so on. Climatic and weather conditions have less influence than in the past in advanced countries, but are still significant. They are more important, of course, in the areas relying on sail power.

The nature of the material locally available for construction is a factor now of less importance than formerly, because of the fairly free international movement of steel and timber. Generally, however, where there is a cheap and plentiful local supply of suitable timber, it takes precedence over steel as the basic material for fishing-vessel construction. Such is mainly the case in North America, Russia, Japan, and Scandinavia, among the more advanced fishing areas. In backward areas, using traditional types of craft, there is obviously no question of any material save wood or other vegetable materials being used. The material in turn affects the design of hull because of its particular limitations in shaping, and influences the cost and the economically optimum size of craft.

The group of human factors is in some ways tending to decrease in importance. Modern ease of interchange of information means that regions less advanced in design and fishing techniques can draw on the knowledge of the more advanced. Yet large differences in the level of skill and knowledge still remain. The size of market is a limiting factor in many less advanced regions where fish-preserving and transport methods are primitive, and where local demand for fish is low. In such conditions the introduction of larger, longer-range craft with improved gear would merely lead to a useless glut. In passing, however, it may be noted that often enough the small local demand—in terms of money—for fish may occur where the need for more fish, to supplement a meagre protein food supply, is great. Such is the case in India and many other countries. The problem of increasing the effective demand for fish in such areas is naturally part of the wider one of their general economic improvement.

Broadly speaking, the greater the effective market in a fishing port's economic hinterland, which may include foreign countries, the larger the craft it employs, and the more advanced its techniques. Though there are notable exceptions, this is the paramount tendency. The larger the effective market, the larger tends to be the financial size of the unit of fishing organization, and its capital resources. The large effective market in Britain has led, in this century, to increasing centralization of fishing in the hands of large owners concentrated in a few large ports. These can afford to finance harbour improvement, either directly or indirectly by paying port dues, and develop their vessels in size, range, speed, and equipment up to the optimum for the conditions of the market. Such vessels are beyond the capital resources commanded by smaller fishermen. Larger catches from the larger sea area tapped by the longer-range craft tend to depress fish prices, not necessarily in absolute terms, but relatively to the general price-level prevalent in the country at a given time. Small fishermen thus find it increasingly hard to survive independently.

In areas having a less concentrated market than Britain, the best size of vessels for any particular type of fishing is usually smaller. There is less economic pressure towards increase of range, and therefore of size of craft. For short-range work the large vessel has normally few, if any, advantages over the small one. In seas fringed by advanced maritime nations there is, however, always a tendency towards increased range of fishing craft. The nearer fisheries are becoming steadily less productive in terms of return for effort because of the intensity of fishing practised. Higher catches can be obtained by going farther afield, and this may prove economically worth while because the loss due to a lower proportion of actual fishing time may be more than compensated for by increased catch. North Sea countries regularly send numerous vessels to operate out of the area.

We may briefly analyse here why longer operating range requires a larger vessel. To make the trip profitable a considerable time must be spent on the distant banks, to cover the non-paying journeys out and home. The catch therefore requires a large hold. Further, as long-distance vessels are now solely engine driven, with few exceptions such as the Grand Banks schooners, a large bunker or tank capacity is required. British long-distance craft are mainly steam driven, and many are still coal-fired, though oil-firing has grown rapidly in importance. Most countries, however, have predominantly internal combustion-engined fleets, such as the large Californian tuna clipper fleet.

Another factor tending to increase the size of the craft is the need for more generous accommodation facilities for the crew when voyages last for several weeks. Increasing distance and duration of fishing journeys may lead in the near future to further development of the 'mother-ship' system, in which a large vessel, equipped for storage, preserving, and even processing of large quantities of fish caught by smaller vessels, remains in the fishing area for a protracted period. She also affords recreational and medical services to the crews of the small craft. This system has already reached a high stage of development in the whaling industry, and has been considerably used by the Japanese and Russians in normal fisheries.

If the fish are of a migratory character, or alternatively are most abundant at different periods in different areas, this is another factor tending to increase the size of vessels, even though the distance from port of each fishing trip may not alter greatly. As craft need to operate for long periods from ports other than their own, more accommodation must be provided. The more predictable the seasonal variations, the less important is this factor. The timing of the British herring seasons along the coast is well established, so that each of the ports in turn provides from long experience the facilities in stores and ancillary services required. Herring drifters are thus relatively small craft.

As a general rule, it can also be said that the size of vessel increases with a greater abundance of fish, other factors being equal. Abundance of a given species in an area means easy and high catches; therefore, a tendency to low prices per unit of catch. To pay its way each crew therefore needs to bring large catches to market, and a craft with a substantial hold capacity is necessary. It should be noted that as the size of craft increases the crew does not increase in proportion, so that each member's share of the proceeds, or the wage he can be paid, will rise.

Local variations in the sizes of fishing craft can often be related to the relative abundance of fish in their waters, but broad comparative generalizations about regions some distance apart are not always possible because of other factors which must be considered.

Another significant factor affecting the design of fishing vessel is the type of coastal zone. It is particularly noticeable in the control of the form of the hull of the craft. Coast type is reflected particularly in the draught, and hence in the proportionate beam and length necessary for a given load capacity, and in the structural strength it is necessary to impart to the hull.

Craft operating from shore-lines of dominant submergence, faulting, or heavy glaciation, are usually in marked contrast to those of shore-lines of dominant emergence, with which, for this purpose, one may include deltas and other outward-building forms. The former offer deep water close inshore, and frequently provide ready-made harbours. The vessels are not seriously limited by considerations of depth of water, and therefore tend to be deep and relatively narrow-beamed. In days when sails provided the sole motive power, the rig also reflected the deep draught, as a generous spread of canvas could be carried without fear of capsize. While all fishing craft must be reasonably sturdy, these vessels need not be reinforced in extreme manner to withstand pounding on beaches, as they operate from shore waters deep enough to allow them to come alongside the jetty without the possibility of touching bottom. Further, as they are normally unloaded when afloat alongside the jetty, their midships section need not be flat-bottomed, and they may have a deep keel. Such deep-hulled types, able by virtue of their depth and consequent stability to operate in severe seas, reach their most characteristic development in such areas of submergence as the west of England and Brittany. The Brixham trawler and the Douarnenez lugger are representative types.

They are very different from similar-sized vessels of a deltaic coastline such as the Dutch. These are of shallow draught, and hence, to maintain their load capacity, broad-beamed and slow. Those that carry sail are limited in the height of their masts by the danger of capsize. The sparse distribution of harbours with deep water alongside the jetty, save where expensive long piers or continuous dredging of channels can be afforded, means that the craft of small fishing centres have often been designed to be unloaded from the beaches at low tide. They are therefore flat-bottomed. Further, because of the stresses set up in the hull when all its weight, including its cargo, is taken by the bottom, and especially when on slightly uneven ground, the hull must be built very stoutly. It is particularly liable to damage when the tide is coming in or out and it is just on the point of floating, and thus pounding up and down upon the beach. The flat-bottomed, broad-beamed, heavily built, and low-masted botter and hoogars are representative types. However, the general process of centralization of the fishing industry in a few major modern ports has affected Holland, and its fishing is rapidly becoming less distinctive.

These contrasts of type are more marked in small craft than in the larger, and are becoming less clear in such areas as western Europe, the U.S.A., and Canada. Where the fishing industry has become centred in large ports that can provide artificial deep-water facilities, standard large deep draught modern types of craft have evolved irrespective of the type of coastline. But, over the greater part of the world's coastlines, fishing is still done from small dispersed ports, and the craft are closely related to the natural conditions of the coast.

Climatic and meteorological conditions are another important group of factors. These are more important in areas the bulk of whose craft still rely wholly or partly on sail. Such areas are still surprisingly extensive, apart from North-west Europe, the U.S.A., and the British Dominions outside Asia. Even important fishing countries such as Japan, Spain, and Portugal still have a substantial proportion of their fishing craft without engines. Fig. 17 shows the approximate proportions of different forms of motive power found in various important countries. All registered sea-fishing craft, including those engaged in collecting shellfish, are included.

Meteorological conditions affect the type of the boat in these main ways:

(*a*)   Intensity and frequency of storms affect the necessary strength of build, and the freeboard and amount of decking.

(*b*)   Normal strength of wind affects the size of the working sails, and thus of the masts and standing rigging.

(*c*)   The prevalent direction of wind in relation to the coast, and its variability, may affect the type of rig, and also, in extreme cases, the power of the motor used.

(*d*)   Temperature conditions sometimes affect the degree of protection needed by the crew of small craft in the way of decking and superstructure.

The demands made on the vessel by stormy weather have an obvious effect on its design. Vessels built to operate in open waters of the stormy westerly belts are noticeably more strongly built, though not necessarily heavier, for their size than those operating elsewhere. In France, for example, there is a contrast between the strongly constructed craft of the Atlantic seaboard and the less sturdy, often half-decked, ones in the Mediterranean. Vessels built for stormy seas are also usually somewhat larger, other things being equal, than those used in calmer areas, but the difference is not as marked as might be imagined. As we have seen, it is fallacious to consider that a larger craft can necessarily withstand storms better than the smaller one.

In areas such as the West Indies or South-east Asia, normally calm, but subject on relatively infrequent occasions to very severe storms, the design of fishing craft is not greatly affected by the existence of these storms. The boats normally operate at a short range from the shore, and their best protection is to return to port at the first signs of any severe storm. The attempt to design a boat capable of withstanding a typhoon or hurricane as a matter of routine would be uneconomical in terms of local resources.

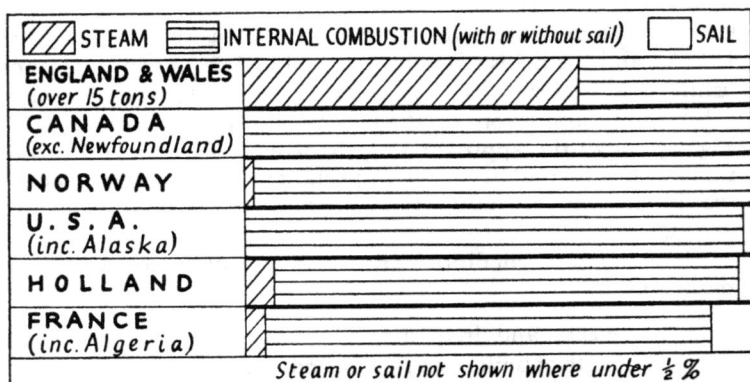

| | STEAM | INTERNAL COMBUSTION (*with or without sail*) | SAIL |
|---|---|---|---|
| **ENGLAND & WALES** (*over 15 tons*) | | | |
| **CANADA** (*exc. Newfoundland*) | | | |
| **NORWAY** | | | |
| **U.S.A.** (*inc. Alaska*) | | | |
| **HOLLAND** | | | |
| **FRANCE** (*inc. Algeria*) | | | |
| | | *Steam or sail not shown where under ½ %* | |

Fig. 17. Approximate proportions of total number of sea fishing craft, excluding small boats, powered by various means, 1950

Normal strength of wind determines the sail area, where sail power is used. The higher the mean wind strength, obviously the smaller the sails that need to be, or can be, carried. Sailing fishing craft of the eastern Mediterranean, for example, have a higher normal sail area/tonnage ratio than those of the western Mediterranean, and these in turn have a higher ratio than those of Portugal. It is again the normal conditions which are determinant of the type. Abnormally high winds are handled by reefing, and light winds by lightweight sails carried on extra spars not in true harmony with the basic rig.

The direction of the wind in relation to the coast is particularly important in primitive areas where boats are small and the art of sailing 'close to the wind' imperfectly mastered. Thus, in many tropical coasts where the condition of regular alternating land and sea breezes is well developed, the normal procedure is for the fleet to go out on the land breeze in the early morning, and return in the afternoon on the sea breeze. Simple sailing with the wind is thus all that is required. Where such regularity and predictability of the wind is not found, however, so must the rigs used become more complex and subtle so that the boat can travel easily in any ultimate direction irrespective of that of the wind. There is a noticeable correlation between the degree of maritime skill of a region and the degree of variability of its winds. The native craft, both fishing and trading, of the Indian ocean, where winds are notable for their regularity in timing and direction, are behind the standard of design and performance reached by the sailing craft of the North Atlantic, Mediterranean, and China.

The variability in direction and strength of the wind is further an important factor in determining the desirability of fitting a motor, and the power of the motor if fitted. Where winds are normally low or unpredictable there is clearly a greater incentive to fit a motor. However, a clear correlation between wind suitability and percentage of craft motorized cannot be drawn for various regions, for the issue is obscured by the variation in financial resources.

Finally, conditions of general weather, especially of temperature, affect the design of the upper structure of the boat. In the Mediterranean and tropics quite large craft may be only partially decked, and little provision made for the shelter of the crew. In the North Sea, on the other hand, practically all craft above about 30 ft. long are fully decked, or fully decked save for a small protected cockpit. Boats above about 40 ft., if modern, have a fully enclosed wheelhouse. The same generally applies to the world areas in and polewards of the westerly belts; new craft even in backward areas approach these standards of crew shelter.

The descriptions in the following chapters of various types of fishing craft are mainly concerned with mechanized boats of fairly modern evolution. However, a by no means negligible total catch is made in various areas of the world by small unpowered craft of traditional designs which have changed little for a long period. Such craft are important in many parts of Asia, Africa, South America, and the Pacific islands. There is no point here in an account of the innumerable detailed local variations in such craft. This is an interesting study, but perhaps one chiefly concerning the anthropologist. We may note, however, that despite much superficial difference, the basic geographical factors of type of coast, climate, and natural vegetation impose an essential similarity on all those which have evolved under comparable conditions.

In areas where tropical hardwood forests are found near the sea, the small boat is usually of dug-out canoe type, where a single large log is hollowed by adzes, sometimes with the help of fire. A sturdy craft is so made, but its beam will be limited by the width of the log, and most dug-out canoes are too narrow for reasonable lateral stability. Thus in many areas one or two outrigger floats are added. The device appears to have first been used in the Pacific islands where stability and seaworthiness were essential for the long voyages undertaken by the canoes. The system has spread widely along the coasts of South Asia, and is common, for example, in East Africa. Fig. 18 shows a gharawa, or outrigger fishing canoe, of Zanzibar.

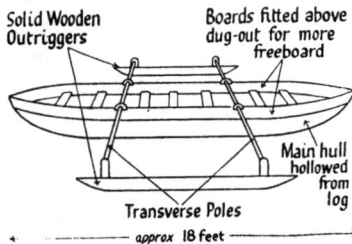

Fig. *18*. Outrigger dug-out canoe of East Africa

Where boats are required larger than the thickness of the available trees, composite building has to be used. This does not make so sturdy a product as the dug-out method, until the community has advanced sufficiently to have evolved precision tools and methods of fastening planks. In primitive areas, therefore, the dug-out remains important. Even in these, however, the increasing availability of tools, nails, and screws from traders has led to the recent development of non-traditional types which are usually inferior imitations of Western-type small boats.

Where tree vegetation is scanty, and the region is not sufficiently developed to import suitable wood, the normal method of construction is to use a framework, perhaps of saplings bound with cord or leather thongs, with skin stretched over it. The Eskimo kayak is a good example of this form of construction. In skilled hands it is perfectly seaworthy, and has the important advantage of portability over the land and ice.

The rate at which simple traditional types of boat will evolve into more typically modern types will vary considerably in different areas, depending on the capital available, the degree of government encouragement, advances in technical education, and the changing conditions of the market. The Colonial Office has recently been sponsoring energetic programmes of research and education in several colonies to evolve types of inexpensive craft superior to those at present in use, and to persuade the fishermen to adopt them. In the Gold Coast, for example, work with a small motor surf-boat, using mainly types of local gear, has shown its ability to catch far more fish than local canoes. In trials with a crew of six men it caught five times as much as two canoes, each with seven men. In Malaya a school for fishermen has been developed, with tuition in the use of power craft.

In other parts of the Colonial Empire similar vigorous action is being taken. It also includes experiments with large European-type vessels, usually with British crews, but the aim here is to open up new offshore fishing grounds rather than to compete with native fishermen in their own grounds. The diet situation in most colonies is such that there is room for expansion of both native and modern type fisheries. The paramount aim, however, is to enable the native fisheries to expand and develop technically by gradual stages. There is no intention to cause sudden revolutions in technique with consequent social upheaval and distress among fishermen.

In the Philippines similar developments are occurring under the stimulus of technical advice from the U.S.A. India, Pakistan, Ceylon, and other Asian countries are receiving technical aid from Western countries individually and through such agencies as the Indo-Pacific Fisheries' Council of the Food and Agriculture Organization of the United Nations. Nevertheless, progress in modernizing equipment, and modifying or replacing traditional craft, can only take place slowly because of lack of capital, both by governments and by individual fishermen. A few publicized new craft are of negligible importance compared with the many thousands required in South Asia.

In Japan, with her greater technical and material capital resources, modernization of the great numbers of small craft still of traditional type is proceeding again after the set-back of the war. In China progress has been slow: whether the new régime will succeed in forcing the pace by totalitarian measures remains to be seen. Until an adequate industrial base to produce motors and other equipment is available, no decrees can succeed.

In South America development is patchy. Credit for develop-ment is difficult to obtain in several countries where demand for fish is still low, but during and since the late war, when import of fish from Norway, Iceland, Newfoundland, and other northern areas was severely restricted, many governments have awakened to the importance of modernizing their fisheries. Venezuela, with its large oil revenues, has been able to provide many of its fishermen with marine engines on hire purchase or other credit systems. The Fisheries Development Corporation conducts this motorization programme. From 100 motorized fishing vessels in 1941, the number increased to 800 in 1948, out of a total of some 4,300. In 1938 production was 21,700 metric tons; by 1948 it had reached 92,300. Such figures are eloquent of the gains to be expected from technical improvement in many other under-exploited areas of the world.

# CHAPTER VI

# DEMERSAL FISHING METHODS AND CRAFT

THESE usually differ markedly from pelagic methods. Modern specialization of fishing gear generally, though not invariably, has led to more differentiation between types of vessel. Whereas in primitive communities methods of catching pelagic and demersal fish may not differ greatly, this is not so in advanced areas.

In demersal fishing the problem is simplified by the fact that the bulk of fish sought are to be found in one plane—the sea-bed. On the other hand it is complicated by the fact that the sea-bed being fished may nowadays be well over 150 fathoms below the vessel. Demersal fishing in deep waters may therefore call for strong, bulky, and expensive equipment, which needs a large and expensive vessel to handle it.

Demersal fish may be found in fairly dense association at times, but not to the extent of many pelagic species. Cod may be found in large numbers in a given area, while at another time they will all have moved elsewhere. They all naturally respond to the same stimuli of temperature, spawning needs, food supply, and so on. They are predators, and may follow the movements of a school of herring in the course of the hunt. The average degree of concentration of cod, however, is under normal circumstances much less than that of most pelagic fish, and each cod operates as an individual. Unlike the wholesale catching of pelagic fish that takes place when a herring school is caught up in a drift net, or surrounded by a ring net or purse seine, the capture of each demersal fish is rather more an individual event, and methods have to be adapted to these circumstances.

The majority of demersal fish are predators, and so one important group of methods involves their snaring by baited hooks. These can be divided into two main types:

*Hand Lines.* These are not of major world importance today, and are mainly confined to small craft working inshore (see Fig. 19). They are, however, still of local importance in the large cod fishery of the Lofoten Islands of Norway. They are lines carrying one or a small number of hooks, baited or with lures.

They may be allowed to rest touching the sea-bottom with their lower ends, or they may be trailed from a slowly moving vessel. Each line is usually the responsibility of one man. Quite large vessels using this method are the Icelandic schooners, which find it a good method for some of the grounds, particularly those less suited for trawling. It also requires only a small capital outlay, and each man, when paid on a basis proportionate to his catch, has an incentive to work hard. The technique most

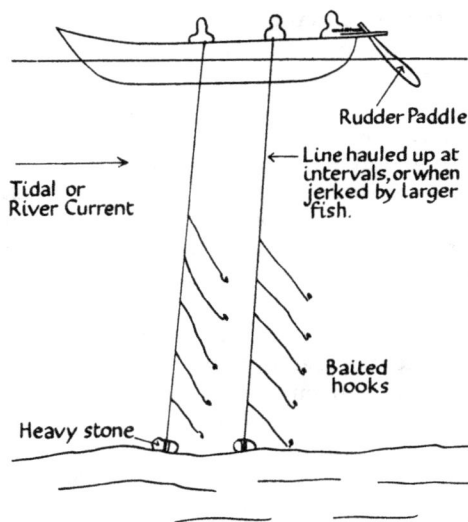

*Fig. 19.* Hand lining from a small boat in shallow water and weak current as practised in south-east Asia

frequently used here is 'jigging', where the line carries a barbed metal 'fish' which is pulled through the water just above the bed in a series of smart jerks. Jigging is also used occasionally from long-lining vessels to catch cod when live bait is short.

*Long Lines.* Long-lining is still a very important method of fishing, though diminishing under the impact of the trawler. It is used in the Grand Banks cod fisheries, the halibut fisheries of the Pacific coast of North America, and is fairly important in some European waters.

Long lines are made up by joining lengths of cod line, each of about 50 fathoms, and are laid out upon the sea-bed in a straight line. At intervals of about 1 to 3 fathoms, depending on the type of fish to be caught, is attached a short line or 'snood' to which is fixed the baited hook. Each long line may stretch for a mile or much more, and its ends are anchored and marked by buoys. In the mother-ship and dory system, in the form practised by the Portuguese, each fishing member of the crew has a small boat, a 'dory', stocked with the line and bait. He sails or rows to his selected position some distance from the mother ship, and lays out his long line. Thereafter through the day he works along it at intervals, hauling it in and removing the catch, then relaying it with the hooks rebaited where necessary (see Fig. 20). The dories are so constructed that they can be 'nested' into each other and thus carried on the ship's deck in the minimum of space. The mother ship remains on the Banks until her hold is filled, which may take four or five months.

Canada, U.S.A., Portugal, and France still send dory-carrying sailing vessels to the Grand Banks, although these are invariably also powered by auxiliary oil engines. In the propulsion of the Portuguese and French vessels, sail is as important as power, and indeed vital to their system of working. Even though they are capable of travelling under auxiliary power alone, sail is needed, as they could not cruise about for this period under power without carrying great quantities of fuel, or refuelling at intervals. Such methods would in any case be expensive. Sail is therefore used whenever possible. Portugal does now employ some purely motorship dory-carriers, but the construction of new schooners recently tends to show that the use of sail has been found to be the most economical method.

The French vessels may be dealt with briefly. Until the First World War a large number of sizeable three-masted, square-rigged 'terre-neuvats' operated from St Malo, Fécamp, and other Breton and Norman ports. Their number has now dwindled until there appears to be but one such vessel recently in regular operation, the steel *Lieutenant Réné Guillon*. This ship now has cut-down masts and sails, and the mizzen-mast is hollow and acts also as the engine exhaust. The square-rigged banker is clearly almost a thing of the past. The French Grand Banks fleet is now dominated by large trawlers.

From ports in New England, the Maritimes, and Newfoundland, dory fishing is declining, though still fairly substantial. From these coasts the voyages to the fishing grounds are much shorter than for the Europeans, while the dories are usually manned by two men. Even so, there appears to be difficulty in

7

recruitment. Those who still work on dories are mainly from traditionally-minded communities, which include the appreciable Portuguese-descended population found in the New England fishing settlements.

The schooners from eastern Canada and New England are normally about 100 to 140 ft. long, with two masts, and are usually more dependent on their large engines than on their sails. Their rig has often been severely cut down, with short masts and no bowsprits. They carry about a dozen dories, often motor-

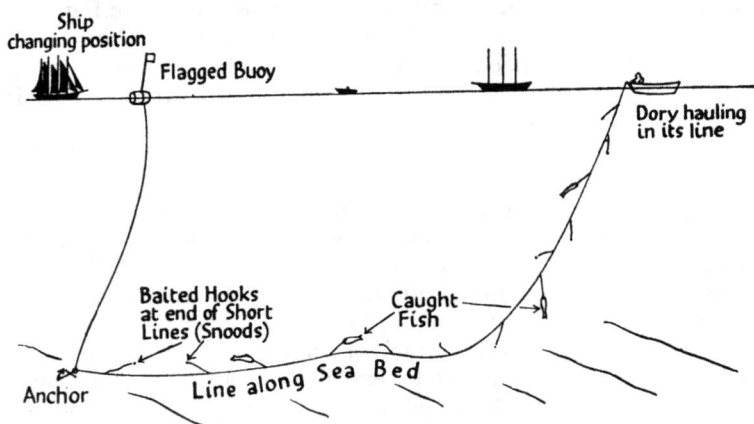

Fig. 20. Grand Banks long-line fishing

equipped, and each crewed by two men. Unlike the Portuguese system, this one does not require the line to be hauled right in before rebaiting. As the dory works along the line, one man removes the catch and the other rebaits the line as it is pulled in ahead and paid out astern.

The Portuguese have developed a type of sailing ship and dory-carrier whose continuing satisfactory performance is proved by new construction. The major part of their Banks sailing fleet consists of good-looking three- and four-masted schooners. The *Argus*, for example, is a steel four-masted schooner of about 700 tons. Her length is 209 ft., beam 32 ft., and her diesel engine is of 400 h.p. She carries some fifty dories and a crew of about sixty. No power is needed for refrigeration of the catch, though a fairly small apparatus is needed to preserve the bait. These sailing vessels preserve the fish with salt, as Portugal is still a large market for salt cod.

These large schooners are by no means anachronisms persisting because of human inertia. They are an efficient response to certain conditions. These are basically:

1. The assured Portuguese market for cheap cod, which requires vessels which can
2. Make long voyages on low fuel consumption, and
3. Catch fish cheaply, which is best done (by the Portuguese) by dory-fishing methods, because they possess
4. A substantial labour force of hardy and hard-working fishermen needing relatively low wages.

Hence the evolution of the modern Portuguese Grand Banks and Davis Strait schooner. Though scientifically designed, she is nevertheless a traditional type because she carries a full or nearly full area of sail, and she fishes by an old-established method which requires much labour and virtually no mechanism. Certain power-driven devices are used to assist the handling of gear on board, but these are not essential. The dories themselves carry only sail and oars, and their long lines are worked solely by hand. To permit nesting, they must be of very simple design, lacking decks or any form of protection for the dorymen from the harsh weather conditions.

The schooners themselves are stoutly built of wood or steel, with lines that combine reasonable speed with ability to ride the steep seas often raised by high winds on the shallow waters of the fishing grounds. Their rig is simple; much simpler than that of the square-rigged ships. The sails on all four masts are practically identical, and the running rigging has been reduced to the minimum, so that its demands on labour are small. Only a small proportion of a vessel's complement is concerned primarily with running the ship.

It would seem that these ships have still many years' economic service before them. One can speculate, indeed, whether the development of long-range fisheries in the southern oceans, to supply such areas as India, southern Africa, and South America, does not offer scope for the further development of such craft. They are eminently suitable for use by countries of low purchasing power, small capital resources, and lacking much technical skill of the modern variety, but having resources of seamen willing to work hard for fairly low pay. Use of dory fishing is perhaps often a more logical development for such countries than the use of steam or diesel trawlers, which have normally to be purchased abroad at high cost, and often need foreign crews to man them.

The crux of the matter, of course, is in the supply of suitable seamen. Dory fishing by Europeans and North Americans, as we have mentioned, has declined greatly. This is partly because most European nations, and the U.S.A. and Canada, can build and operate steam or diesel trawlers more economically, having regard to their own conditions. In addition, it seems likely that, even if these countries had wished to continue large-scale dory fishing, they would have found it impossible because of the absence of enough men willing to undergo the hardships, monotony, and hazards of the doryman's work.

To fish alone on a stormy sea in a tiny boat with no flotation gear or other safety apparatus, liable to be swamped or driven away from the ship by a high wind, or cut off from it by fog, demands a calm, almost fatalist mentality that is increasingly rare. Of the social factors conditioning dory fishing, an important one is perhaps that of religion. The Portuguese fisherman is, beneath the seaman's rough manner, usually a devout man. The service to bless the fleet before it sails from Portugal, the religious devices painted on the dories, and the 'Praise be to God' with which the ship's helmsman takes over the wheel at the beginning of his watch, are still of real import to him, not archaic survivals.

Were this form of dory fishing to be taken up on such Indian Ocean grounds as the Mascarene plateau and Chagos Ridge it might provide an important source of cheap fish, particularly for the Indian sub-continent. The most suitable type for training as fishermen in such ventures would seem to be the Moslem seamen of Pakistan, Java, and, particularly, the Arab seamen manning the ocean-trading dhows ranging from Zanzibar to Muscat and along into India. These have a background and outlook which, though different from the Portuguese, is nevertheless generally one of fortifying belief which can support them through hardship and loneliness.

Long lines are used also in other ways than from dories, and for a wide variety of fish other than cod, such as haddock, hake, pollock, and all forms of flatfish. In the halibut fishery of the North American Pacific coast, the line is worked directly from the fishing vessel, a medium-sized oil-driven craft with a large power-driven winch at the stern, which pays out the line to a length of up to 8 miles as the vessel moves ahead. After the line has been down about an hour, the boat moves back along it, hauling in the line by power while the men remove the catch from the hooks.

Long-line methods in European waters are now much less practised by modern craft than is trawling. The longer-range British 'long-liners' are often trawler-type steam vessels. Instead of the gallows and heavy winches characteristic of trawlers, however, there is a steam-driven line hauler to wind in the line, which may be some 15 miles long, with over 5,000 hooks. Long-lining of this type is carried out in parts of the North Sea, Irish Sea, and in waters about The Faeroes, Rockall Bank, Iceland, and even Greenland. For short-range work there is a substantial number of medium-sized motor craft in Norway (particularly the Lofotens), Britain, and other West European countries. Japan also has a considerable number of lining craft. They include, however, many fairly old sailing craft fitted with auxiliary engines. This method of fishing does not so strongly dominate the design of fishing vessels as do some others. The craft do not, therefore, form a particularly distinctive type.

It seems likely that line fishing will persist in the future in two main spheres. Firstly, there is the fishing close inshore by independent fishermen with small boats, for prime quality fresh fish. Here the circumstances favour the small unit, and large amounts of capital for investment in trawling gear are neither necessary nor available. Further, in Britain and many other countries, these inshore fishermen, operating from small ports and seaside resorts, are protected by law from competition by large trawlers, which are not allowed to use inshore waters. Local fishermen thus maintain a supply of very fresh, unbruised fish to their immediate neighbourhoods. The second main sphere where line fishing is likely to remain important is, as previously mentioned, over extensive areas of rocky bottom, where trawl nets can be severely damaged or even lost.

The net methods may now be discussed. These are, of course, normally more complicated and expensive equipment than lines. They pay for their cost by their increased effectiveness. The line is a more or less immobile snare, which must wait for the fish to come to it, and its range of operation is therefore limited to its immediate vicinity, as most species of fish cannot sense their prey from very far off. The trawl, pair, and Danish seine nets, however, are weapons for actively hunting the fish. These demersal nets contrast also with pelagic nets in that they are hauled speculatively through large stretches of water, whereas pelagic nets are in general either passively drifting or, like purse seines or ring nets, only moved through water when an actual 'set' is being made at a school of fish. There is, however, one demersal exception to this statement:

*Stationary Bottom-set Gill Nets, Trammel Nets, and Traps.* Such nets take a very wide variety of forms and sizes, but are alike in that they are a type of wall whose lower end is attached to, or near to, the sea-bed, and whose upper end is raised above the bottom by floats (see Fig. 21). In action the bottom-set gill net is similar to the drift gill net. Bottom nets, however, frequently

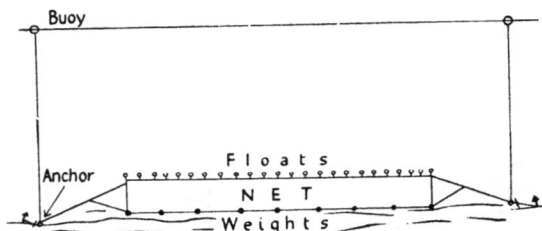

Fig. 21.
Set gill net

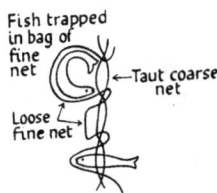

Fig. 22.
Trammel net principle

employ the trammel principle, which normally takes the form of a loose net of fine mesh placed alongside a taut one of coarse mesh, or between two coarse-meshed nets, so that fish coming against the fine net push part of it through the coarse one to form a bag which holds them (see Fig. 22). This is a more expensive gear, but one which is very effective against species which, because of their shape or power, cannot be caught easily by the gills.

Both gill and trammel bottom nets are confined to fairly shallow water, and are most used in rivers, estuaries, or other partly enclosed waters. They are most effective when placed so that tidal or river currents tend to lead or drive the fish to them. World distribution of the bottom-set net is very general, nearly all areas having examples in regular use. The trammel net, being more complicated in conception, is less general than the gill net.

Stationary traps are also quite important for demersal fish. This class embraces an almost infinite variety of devices, linked only by the fact that they consist essentially of a method whereby the fish can get into, but not out of, a chamber formed of net, posts, or basket work. Frequently the entrance is by an initially wide but progressively narrowing channel leading the fish into the chamber. Once inside, there is little chance of a fish finding the small exit. Nets are often very large, and maintained permanently in place attached to stakes driven into the sea-bed. The distinction between demersal and pelagic fish loses much of its point, of course, where this class of devices, operated in shallow water, is concerned.

Traps are important in many parts of Asia and Africa. They lend themselves well to construction by less advanced areas, needing only wood and some type of fibre in their construction, which is often very ingenious. Estuarine waters are especially suitable for their location, river and tidal currents being used to direct the fish into the traps, while the waters are relatively sheltered from large waves which might damage the structures.

Some of the simpler forms of large traps do not have any form of non-return entrance, but are situated between tide levels, so that fish can swim over the top into them at high tide and are trapped when the tide goes out. Such a type is the moka of Fiji.

Smaller portable traps, which can be placed in position and removed by boats, are often made of basket work. They are sometimes baited, and may be lowered to the bottom, or suspended from anchored floats. Basket-work traps are common on the Palk Strait and Gulf of Mannar coasts of India, and in Brazil, where they appear to have been introduced by Portuguese who had seen similar forms used in India. Such traps are also relatively important in the Pacific islands and in the Mediterranean.

Many types of trap are operated without boats, or with small and simple canoes, but quite large craft are sometimes used. As an example we may mention the Rua Chalom of Siam (see Fig. 23). This is used particularly to tend elaborate fishing traps installed fairly close to the shore. These consist of converging lines, about half a mile long, of stakes driven into the sea-bed, forming funnels along which the fish swim into the final enclosure.

The boat may be as much as 50 ft. long, though of small

draught to negotiate the shallow inshore water of the Gulf of Siam. It is mostly undecked. The crew of seven stand up to work the long oars when there is no wind. The sail is a single lug of simple nearly square cut, with a boom along its foot. Steering is not by rudder but by twin oars slung over the quarters, similar to those of the Roman and other ancient ships. Indeed, in her rudders, sail, and high stem and stern posts, the Rua Chalom has much in common with some types of vessels of the ancient civilizations of the central and eastern Mediterranean. However, it would be difficult to assess the extent to which the Siamese may have

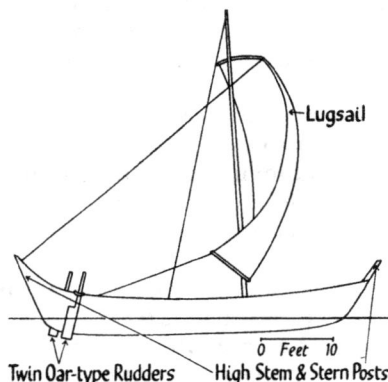

*Fig. 23.* Rua Chalom

been influenced by ideas slowly spreading from the Mediterranean or other sources, and to what extent the similarities are due to parallel but independent lines of evolution.

*Beam Trawls.* These are the simplest type of trawl. They consist of a large bag of net, roughly conical in shape, which is towed over the sea-bed, the mouth being held open by a long horizontal beam. At each end of the beam are skids to raise it a little off the sea-floor, and prevent the net ploughing into the bottom. These trawls were used a good deal from sailing craft in western Europe in the last century, but, in Britain, were steadily superseded in the latter quarter of the century by the otter trawl, which exploited the full possibilities of the steam engine. Beam trawls are now used in British waters only by small inshore fishing craft, though they are still used to a certain extent in West European and Mediterranean coastal waters from medium-sized motorized sailing vessels, and also in East Asian waters from fairly small sailing craft. Their total contribution to world catch, however, is far below that of the otter trawl, which has long been the standard method of trawling in the advanced areas.

The beam trawl retains the advantage, for small scale or primitive use, of simplicity of principle, and ease of handling when in small sizes. In large sizes, however, the long and heavy beam makes it much less wieldy than the otter trawl.

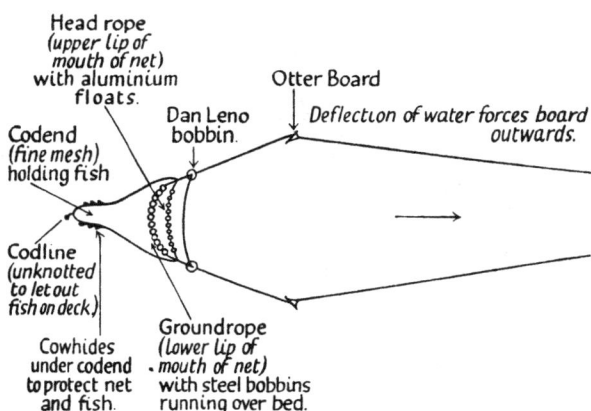

*Fig. 24.* Plan view of otter trawl in action

*Otter Trawls.* The introduction of steam power to fishing vessels in the latter part of the nineteenth century had numerous advantages in increasing speed, range, and particularly in making fish landings more dependable; less controlled by wind and weather. It also opened up the possibility of the use of power in the fishing operation itself. The limit to the maximum size of beam trawl was imposed by the difficulty of handling such a heavy beam during the process of emptying the net. Steam power, with its ability to provide a more powerful and steady pull than was obtainable from sails, enabled the beam to be dispensed with. In the otter trawl the net is held open by the otter boards at each side of the mouth, which are towed at a suitable angle and thus forced sideways by the flow of water in a manner analogous to the operation of the airflow over an aircraft wing (see Fig. 24). During trawling a steady speed of about two knots is maintained.

On modern, large, long-distance trawlers the headline of the mouth of the net is up to 130 ft. in length, and the net is about

120 ft. long. The size, shape, and the strength of rope vary with
the type of sea-bed of the area; a rocky bed requires a heavier and
stronger trawl than a sandy one. The otter trawl has perhaps
controlled the form of vessel more than has any other major
type of fishing gear. A large and powerful vessel is required for
trawling, save in shallow water. The majority of British trawlers
are steam-engined, because steam is a flexible form of power.

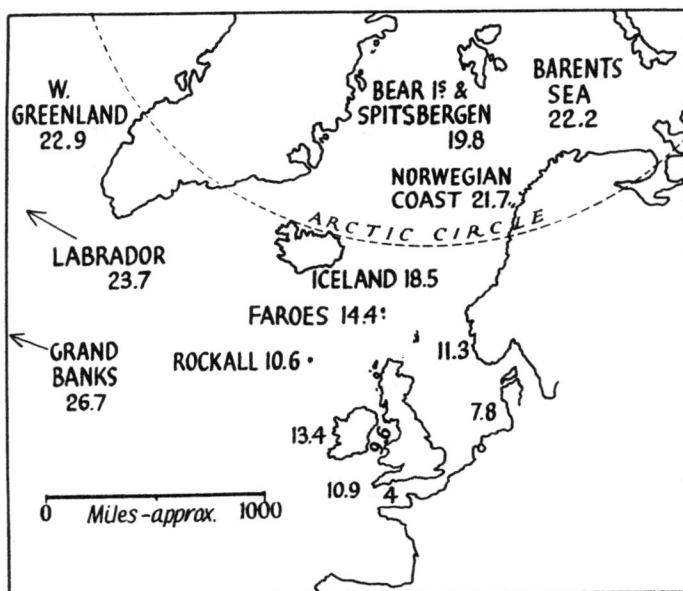

*Fig. 25.* Average duration of voyages, in days, of steam trawlers from
ports in England and Wales to the principal grounds (1953). Greater
distances do not in all cases mean greater duration, because of higher
rates of catch

The boiler can supply steam to the heavy winches required to
haul in the trawl for emptying, a process performed once every
two to four hours throughout the day and night. North American
trawlers (or 'draggers') are mainly diesel-driven, but these have
the disadvantage of requiring a completely separate winch engine
or electric motor, or complex gearing between the main engine
and the winch.

Trawling by large steam vessels of 140 to 200 ft. in length
dominates the British long-distance fishery to the Barents Sea,
Bear Island, Iceland, and, recently, Greenland areas. Quite apart

from the power required, only large vessels could have the necessary range, and the hold capacity to make round trips lasting three weeks and more worth while (see Fig. 25). Medium-sized steam trawlers are important in the North Sea and other waters nearer home.

In no other country is the otter trawler so dominant in fishing. It is important, however, in Germany, France, Iceland, the United States, Canada, and Japan. In the fishing grounds of Newfoundland, the Maritimes, and New England, it is steadily gaining ground, as we have seen, on the older method of long-lining from dories, which, however, still remains a common method of the area. In North America the bulk of the trawlers are oil-driven and, as they normally operate closer to home, smaller than the European. In Japan the majority of the newer trawlers are also oil-driven, presumably because of the poor Japanese resources in coal, and its greater scarcity than oil in world markets.

Power trawling is naturally limited to advanced countries because of the capital involved. Since the war, however, several countries hitherto using less advanced methods have been investigating its possibilities, spurred on by their general protein shortage. India has been testing the use of trawlers in its waters, and the British Colonial Office Fisheries Department has been using large steam trawlers experimentally in the West African and Seychelles areas. Good catches have been reported from all these places, and expansion of steam or motor trawling may therefore be expected in them in the near future. Other areas where trawling is developing on a moderate but significant scale are in the southern temperate waters off South Africa, South-east Australia, and Argentina. These, particularly the last, have sizeable areas of continental shelf in waters of temperature conditions well suited to large-scale fish production, and have considerable potentialities if the trawl is not over-used.

Power trawling, although expensive in initial capital outlay and in fuel and maintenance, is usually fairly cheap in proportion to the amount of fish caught. This assumes that the fishing grounds are reasonably prolific. Trawling, like all highly mechanized techniques in any field, requires a large turnover to make it worth while. In grounds carrying a low density of fish, trawling cannot pay its overhead costs. Again, we have already mentioned that in particularly rocky grounds trawling cannot displace the line methods. An otter trawl is an expensive piece of equipment whose components have risen very sharply in price in recent years. A large trawl now costs over £400. Risks of its severe damage or total loss on some types of uneven rocky ground occur at sufficiently frequent intervals to make trawling unprofitable on them. This is the case in some banks off Newfoundland and Greenland.

Other factors in the assessment of trawling must be considered. Firstly, the trawl is, if uncontrolled, at times too effective an instrument. It enables very large catches to be made initially in prolific areas, yet ultimately the density of fish may fall so low that fishing becomes unprofitable. Over-fishing has certainly occurred in the North Sea, and may well be occurring in a number of other areas. Conclusive evidence is sometimes difficult to produce because increased efficiency of catching methods maintains the level of total catch and so masks for a while the drop in biological production.

Nevertheless, the trawl has certain economic advantages, and is now very well established. The sensible course is to limit its use in inshore waters, as is done by several countries, and to enforce other suitable regulations, such as a minimum mesh size to enable small fish to escape and grow to economic size, as in the recent European International Fisheries Convention.

At present, however, the trawling grounds are gradually being extended. With development of the gear, trawling is now normal to depths of 200 fathoms and frequently well below this, so that the outer portions of the continental shelves and the inner portions of the continental slopes are being exploited.

In Europe the most characteristic type is the large steam trawler used pre-eminently by Britain, but also important in Germany and France, and to a lesser extent in Spain, Belgium, and other countries. The type is of very small relative importance in the U.S.A. and Canada, and of comparatively small importance in Japan, while there is a relatively small number distributed elsewhere about the world, as in South Africa. The first reason for the concentration in the western European countries is to be found in their especial use in long-range fisheries: the Barents Sea, Bear Island, Iceland, Greenland, and Newfoundland areas. The second main reason is the availability of enough coal to these countries, which established steam firmly as the long-range motive power, although the more modern craft now use oil as boiler fuel. In various countries large trawlers driven by diesel engines are gradually replacing steam ones, but the proportion of large diesel trawlers in Britain remains small, despite their advantage of saving of engine room and bunker space, which can be devoted to larger holds. British owners have a traditional liking for steam. As previously mentioned, steam also has the big advantage of providing a flexible means of power for winches and other auxiliary machinery from the main boilers.

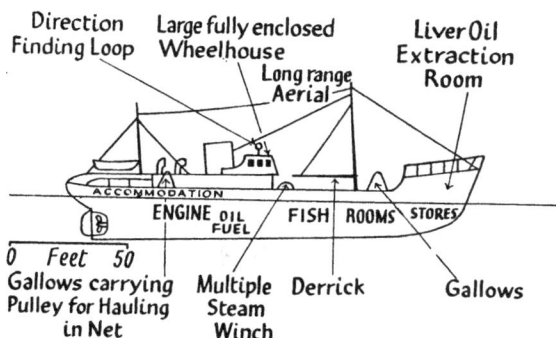

*Fig. 26.* Modern long-range steam trawler

In North America trawling is, as we have seen, of more recent general introduction than in western Europe, and is less important relative to other methods. Furthermore, trawling at long range is hardly practised from North America, which can supply its markets for demersal fish from fairly near waters. North American trawlers are therefore generally fairly small and motor-powered.

Pre-war Japan built a number of modern long-range diesel trawlers capable of staying at sea for a month when fishing the Sea of Okhotsk, or off the Aleutians, and elsewhere, but their total tonnage was small in proportion to that of the vast number of more traditional types. Japan was, of course, hampered by shortage of capital, steel, and fuel, rather than by any lack of enterprise or technical knowledge.

For a representative long-range trawler we may therefore take a British type. Fig. 26 illustrates such a vessel. (This drawing, like the others representing various craft, is intended to show only the salient features. Details of rigging, etc., are deliberately omitted for clarity.) The ship shown would be most likely to operate from Hull, Grimsby, or Fleetwood. The following dimensions are typical: length about 180 ft., beam 30 ft., and draught about 16 ft. She burns fuel oil in Scotch-type multi-tube boilers, supplying a triple expansion engine of about 850 to 900 b.h.p. capable of driving her at 12 knots maximum speed. The crew number about twenty. The cost of keeping such a vessel at sea is some £250 per day (in 1952). About two-thirds of this figure is accounted for by fuel oil and crew's pay.

Only a large and heavily capitalized organization can thus afford to use such a vessel; £5,000 worth of fish must be caught merely to cover the cost of an average trip, and a poor trip can therefore make very heavy losses. The complexity increases continually; since the war radar has become normal equipment. While a great aid to navigation and safety when fishing along remote coasts, it adds yet more to the amount of fish that must be caught to support the vessel. Post-war conditions of good fish prices may have encouraged the purchase of very well appointed but expensive craft. One result, however, may be to harden minimum fish prices because of the high cost of running the vessels. Nevertheless, the public should not grudge these expenses undertaken to increase the safety and comfort of fishermen, whose life is never soft at the best of times.

The long-range nature of the fishing requires a large engine to enable the distance to be covered in reasonable time, a large fuel capacity, and accommodation on a substantial scale for the crew. Another factor tending to increase size is that of the severe weather conditions experienced in winter in the northern fishing grounds which, although not necessarily dangerous to a small vessel, would render it an unsuitable base for continuous fishing operations. The considerable depth of hull is needed for fish and fuel capacity for the long voyage, for stability in rough seas, and particularly for efficiency in towing the trawl. This in turn prevents the vessel from using small ports without adequate depth alongside the quays, and is an important cause of the centralization of most British fishing in a few large ports.

Of the detailed equipment of the trawler, perhaps the most noticeable are the two frames or 'gallows' on each side which carry the pulleys involved in hauling in the trawl net.

The smaller steam trawlers we need not describe in detail, as in general features they resemble the ones already described. Their length is usually between 80 and 130 ft., and they are frequently 'flush-decked', that is, their upper deck is continuous, lacking a forecastle. Many are still coal-burning, though their numbers are falling steadily, and most possess the tall narrow funnel characteristic of the coal-burner. They operate chiefly in the North Sea and south and west of Britain from British, German, French, and Belgian ports. Medium-sized motor trawlers have, however, been increasing in relative importance in Europe.

The motor draggers of North America are usually modern types, chiefly because of the fairly recent spread of the technique there. Fig. 27 shows a representative Canadian dragger operating from Nova Scotia, chiefly on the Sable Bank. She is 100 ft. long,

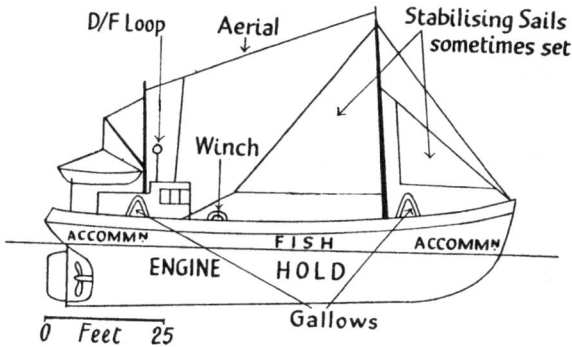

*Fig. 27.* Dragger

about the same as North Sea trawlers, but in other respects she is greatly different. The hull is of wood, because of the local abundance of timber and the relative expense of steel. Wooden fishing craft are still dominant in North America, and likely to remain so for some time. Propulsion is by diesel engine, again a characteristic of North American fishing craft save the very small ones. The foremast is rigged to carry a small sail area, chiefly to diminish rolling when fishing. This is a common practice amongst North American draggers, although it has practically ceased in modern European trawlers. Use of sail for this purpose, however, cannot be regarded as detracting from the modernity of the American craft.

Motor draggers are pre-eminently vessels of the east coast, particularly New England and the Canadian Maritimes, from where the main demersal fishing takes place.

*Pair-operated Trawls (Pareja Trawls).* Some of the criticisms advanced against uncontrolled otter trawling apply even more to this method. The arrival in post-war years on the Grand

Banks of pareja trawlers from Spain has provoked some ill-feeling. Power-drawn pareja nets have been common in waters off Spain for a long time, but reached Britain only shortly before the war. A number of pareja trawlers have recently been operating from Milford Haven, some of them with partly Spanish crews, and concerned chiefly in the hake fisheries in the south-western approaches to these islands. Pair-trawling involves the towing of a very large net over the sea-bed between two vessels steaming abreast. In essence the idea is simple. It is practised on a small scale in many primitive communities using canoes, and also by junks in Chinese waters. There, however, the net is relatively small. It is when the method is practised by sizeable power vessels that it becomes dangerous. Pareja vessels are usually smaller than otter trawlers, and of lower-powered steam or oil engines. Operating in pairs, however, they draw a net whose mouth has a headline of about 300 ft., or over double the normal otter trawl.

Its catching power is thus enormous. One pair of vessels can sweep one square mile or more of sea-floor per day. The net, however, has one advantage over the otter trawl. Because it is towed between two vessels, and therefore needs no otter boards and their associated heavy gear, it does not drag along the bottom, but only touches it lightly, thereby minimizing damage to the sea-bed and the small creatures there.

The vessels normally steam at about 1·7 knots, half to three-quarters of a mile apart, drawing closer together at the end of a tow when the resistance of the trawl is greatest. The ships come very close together when passing the tow-rope between them at the beginning of a tow, and also during the hauling at the end. They take it in turns to haul the net and stow the fish. Fishing is usually limited to daylight because of the need for the vessels to come close during these operations. In short winter days one long tow is made, in summer two or sometimes three shorter ones.

Pareja-caught fish are in better condition than those caught in otter trawls because they are subject to less buffeting. Nevertheless, except in extremely prolific grounds, and in newly opened grounds still under-fished, this powerful catching device must be used with caution. Uncontrolled pareja fishing in over-fished areas is efficient only in the sense that a large modern combine harvester would be efficient if used yearly on dry-farmed land that took two years to grow a satisfactory crop. It is important that the trawl should be operated with a frequency or intensity analogous to that of a harvester used only when the harvest is ready. Despite its immediate advantages, its use does not appear to be spreading very fast.

In the past a wide variety of small- and medium-sized vessels have been used for pair-trawling, often converted from other methods, but a characteristic type now appears to have evolved to meet the particular requirements. This is a vessel the size of a small normal trawler, about 100 ft. long, and broadly resembling

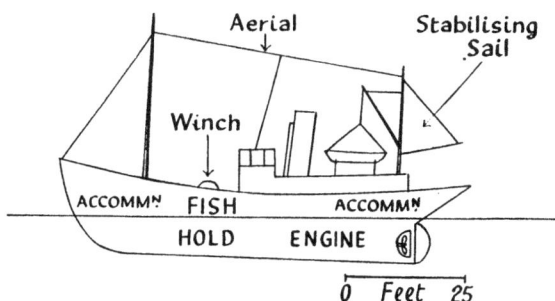

*Fig. 28.* Spanish pareja vessel

such a trawler in general lines. The gallows are missing, as the net lacks heavy otter boards and does not need complicated handling gear, though powerful winches are still required. Construction may be of wood or steel, and power by oil or steam, much of this choice apparently depending on where the ships are built. A number of steel pareja vessels, both steam- and oil-engined, have been built in Aberdeen for Spanish users.

The craft are usually for fairly short-range work in waters between Southern Ireland and Morocco. Although such vessels have crossed the Atlantic to the Grand Banks, they seem decidedly below the optimum size for economical use at such range. Presumably they refuel soon after arrival on the other side. Their method of fishing enables them to fill their holds quickly and return with the cargo in salt. The sturdy construction and seaworthy lines of these ships enables them to make the crossing satisfactorily. Fig. 28 shows a steam pareja type. The marked sheer, or curved profile of the top of the hull, is a Spanish characteristic.

Pair-trawling is an old-established and important method in China. Quite large vessels using it range substantial distances over the wide shelves of the Yellow Sea, East China and northern South China Seas. The ships are generally without auxiliary motor power, save in the case of Hong Kong, where under a recent government scheme auxiliary motorization of the fishing fleet has been started. Junks so motored have been found to average catches of about 70 per cent more than the purely sailing vessels.

The junk shown in Fig. 29 is of a common type in southern China, though considerable variations in size are found. Typical length is 50 to 60 ft., and beam 13 to 15 ft. Draught is rather shallow, but reasonable initial stability is attained by the broad, flattish bottom. A typical fishing feature is a rather lower poop than normal in trading or passenger craft, as less accommodation is needed. Windlasses are heavier than usual, for the hauling and hoisting inboard of the net, and the rigging is, for a junk, fairly simple. The trawlers are normally two-masted, whereas the average trading junk has three masts, sometimes four or five. The windlasses are of the traditional Chinese type: a horizontal beam running in bearings at each end, and round which the rope is wound. It is turned by a number of spokes which permit several men to work simultaneously on a windlass. Crews are large, as man-power is a plentiful resource.

Some observations may be made here on the junk type of craft. At first glance, to Western eyes, the junk appears an ungainly and inefficient vessel. Closer inspection reveals that she is, in fact, a good deal more efficient than appears to be the case. The southern Chinese vessel is also not without beauty, though this can hardly be said of northern Chinese junks. The southern junk has attractively-shaped sails with rounded leeches (trailing edges), whereas the northern type usually has sails cut in crudely rectangular form, like a window blind, both ugly and less effective.

Apart from the shape of the sails, both northern and southern types have many features in common. The sails have battens, which help to keep the airflow smooth in sails often roughly patched, and also permit sail to be shortened easily in high winds. The above-water lines of the hull are very bluff, but below the waterline they approach quite closely to a moderate streamline shape as found in Western craft, and some junks have a surprising speed. The rudder projects below the keel, and therefore has a slit in the counter above it through which it can be partially retracted in shallow water. It is also perforated, presumably in the belief that this increases its effectiveness. This would be the case only at very low speeds, above which the perforations must become an appreciable drag on the vessel. The most striking feature of the junk's hull is the high poop, as prominent a feature as the poops of late-medieval western European craft. This poop contains the crew's quarters, and also acts as a vantage point for the helmsman. Fierce eyes are still frequently painted on

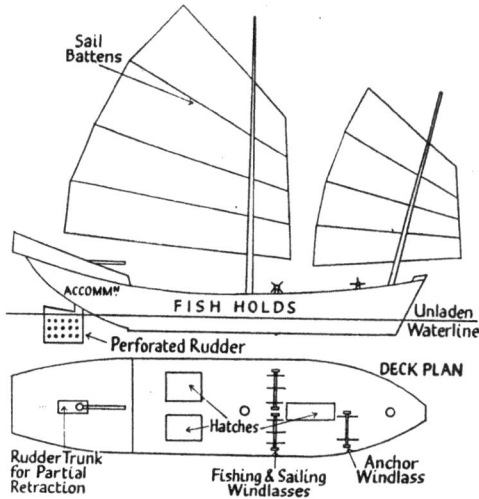

*Fig. 29.* Southern Chinese fishing junk. (Details of rigging omitted)

the bows of the junk. With them the vessel can see its way through danger and possibly overawe any evil forces contemplating harm. Such eyes are found in other parts of the world; for example, on Portuguese inshore fishing boats.

Working in virtual isolation, the Chinese have evolved a characteristic vessel which differs widely from both European and Indian Ocean craft. Yet the South China junk is almost equal in efficiency to the better types of commercial and fishing craft evolved in Europe up to the time of their eclipse in the nineteenth century. The Chinese battened sail is aerodynamically more efficient for sailing across and into wind than is the European sail, while the underwater lines allow reasonable speed with adequate stability despite the fairly shallow draught required to permit access to ports situated on the smaller rivers.

*Danish Seine Nets.* These use another 'wholesale' method of catching, but they are limited to smooth sandy ground in not very deep water. The net, because of its size, and the fact that it is operated by only one vessel's power, is necessarily of light construction, and is thus unsuitable for any but smooth, even ground. It is a large trawl with very extended wings, which is moved over the bed not by towing, but by the winch of an anchored or slowly moving vessel. By this method a relatively small and low-powered craft can operate a large net. The usual craft are oil-driven modern vessels of about 60 ft. length. The basic method is quite old, but the modern power version is comparatively recent, and in this country has developed mainly between the wars. It is not of great relative importance in British waters, however. The area of most use is off the east coast of Scotland. The system has been fairly widely adopted in Scandinavia, and is also used in Germany and some distant areas, such as New Zealand. The method is important in the waters of the Danes, its originators, where sea-bed conditions are well suited, and where particular stress is laid on obtaining the best quality prime fish fairly close to the shore. The light net does not damage the fish, particularly as the length of a haul is short.

European craft for Danish seining are rather smaller than American purse seiners, and frequently resemble the motor drifter. They are oil-driven, flush-decked, simple, and robust, with no superstructure save a wheelhouse aft. They normally carry sails for stabilizing, and for assisting propulsion. Typical dimensions of a Scottish seiner are: length 60 ft.; beam 17 ft.; draught 7 ft. 9 in.; power 75 b.h.p.; speed 9 knots. The relatively small size of the craft is due to the usually fairly short distance from base of suitable grounds, such as those in the Moray Firth fished by craft from Buckie, Lossiemouth, Nairn, and other local ports. The characteristic flush deck and small superstructure of the boats facilitates the handling of the net and gear. The essential feature of the gear is the large power capstan or winch for hauling the net along the sea-bed. (A capstan is a vertical drum, while a winch is horizontal.) Such equipment and general arrangement also fits the vessel for handling drift nets, and drifting is often carried out by these vessels during the herring season. Unlike the steam trawler, the most typical British craft, these British seine-netters are wood built, although in this case most of the wood has, of course, to be imported. In spite of this disadvantage, wood remains the chief material in Britain for fishing vessels of less than 100 ft. length, because it lends itself much more easily than steel to use by the small boatbuilding firms that cater for the demand for the smaller fishing craft.

We may note here that the powerful influence of the type of craft on the economic organization of the industry, and on the location and size of settlements, is well illustrated by these small Scottish motor seiners and drifters. They are sufficiently cheap to be within the range of ownership by a prosperous fisherman. Owner-skippers or part-owner-skippers are therefore widespread. For reasons both economic, in the relatively small capital required, and physical, in the small harbours required, the Scottish fishing industry is therefore still relatively decentralized, in contrast to the English. The conditions of the sea-bed impinge directly on the financial structure and settlement forms associated with the industry. It is true Scotland has one very large port for long-distance work, Aberdeen, where the industry is partly in the hands of large firms, and it has other sizeable fishing ports such as Leith and Peterhead, where centralization has progressed considerably. On the other hand, it has a string of medium importance fishing ports all the way down the east coast. At present, due to the good price of fish, these are fairly prosperous. They have, in general, avoided the final decay prophesied for them in pre-war days, and make a large contribution to the total Scottish catch. This state of affairs contrasts with most parts of the English and Welsh coasts. Here the proportion of owner-skippers, and the frequency of fishing ports of medium importance, is decidedly lower. A greater proportion of the industry is owned by companies, and the fishing ports are typically either very important or unimportant.

*Beach-hauled Seines.* As these are operated in shallow water, they obviously catch both demersal and pelagic fish. The bottom of the net is weighted and the top fitted with floats. These may be so adjusted that the net moves along the sea-bed or hangs from the surface, or if the net is sufficiently deep, it may stretch from surface to bed. The net is usually paid out from a small boat, which leaves one end of the net on shore, and moves roughly on a semicircular course to return to the shore with the other end. Hauling is then done by shore parties, or occasionally by winches. Beach seines of many forms and sizes are widely used in the world, but are now relatively unimportant in most of the advanced areas, save in the salmon fisheries of North America. In Japan, a country whose vast fishing industry, despite its many modern facets, also retains many traditional forms, beach seining is important. The method as normally practised needs plenty of man-power, and it is thus common in Asia and Africa. However, in heavily fished areas where the density of reasonably-sized fish in inshore waters is low, its use may become uneconomic.

*Shellfish-catching Methods.* The main methods of catching demersal fish have now been described. To complete the account, mention may be made of the methods of catching shellfish, which can conveniently be classified for this purpose with the demersal fish whose bottom-living habits most of them possess. The simplest group of methods involves the direct seizing of the creatures by tongs or rakes operated by hand from vessels in shallow water. These methods are used in fisheries for oysters, clams, scallops, and similar relatively immobile creatures, and the equipment may take a wide variety of detailed forms. Dredges towed by vessels are more elaborate equipment used in such fisheries. The dredge, in widespread use about the world's coasts, though mainly found in the more advanced areas, is normally a form of small trawl net or basket with its mouth maintained open by a rigid frame placed on skids, and sufficiently weighted for the lower edge of the mouth to dig a little way into the mud or sand and so remove the creatures living on it. For swimming creatures, such as prawns and shrimps, various types of trawl net are in general use, while push nets are used by waders close inshore.

Lastly, there is the group of devices to trap such creatures as the lobster, crawfish (spiny lobster), and larger crabs. These traps may take a variety of forms, depending on the type of sea-floor, the strength of currents liable to overturn them as they lie on the sea-bed, and the habits of the creatures they are designed to catch. Basically, the principle is usually that of a cage containing bait, with a tapering tunnel as the entrance, permitting easy entry but making exit difficult. These 'pots' are laid on the sea-bed from small boats, identified by buoys attached to them by ropes by which they can be hauled up after a suitable period. This technique is practised mainly on mud-free inshore grounds where currents are not too strong.

# CHAPTER VII

# PELAGIC FISHING METHODS AND CRAFT

PELAGIC fish offer markedly different problems to the fisherman from those of demersal catching. They are highly mobile in both the horizontal and vertical planes. The volume of water in which they have to be sought is thus much greater than for demersal fish, which spend the bulk of their lives on or close to the sea-bed. However, the habits of most pelagic species are such that at certain times they are normally near the surface. Catching them therefore involves, firstly, finding the area in which they are in sufficient quantity, and, secondly, using a device operating on or near the surface to capture them.

Finding the fish in the first place may not be at all easy. The habits of certain species in some areas are fairly well known, such as those of the herring in the North Sea. Yet even here their movements, the timing of their appearances, and their quantity, may fluctuate unpredictably and give rise to unexpectedly good or bad 'harvests'.

Searching techniques for pelagic fish, which range more freely than demersal fish, and are less limited to areas of certain depths, are therefore an important part of the fishing operation in many areas. In the North Sea the actual range of the search may be small, because the areas and times of appearance of the fish throughout the year are well known from long experience: the mass appearances start in May off the Shetlands and the Outer Hebrides; in the Orkneys and north-east of Scotland the season starts in June, and becomes progressively later (though with occasional exceptions) farther southward. The very important East Anglian season ends in December. These mass appearances are not, of course, the result of the *same* schools migrating steadily southwards.

Similar pelagic movements, well understood in their broader aspects, occur off the coasts of North America. The problem of precise location by individual fishing craft still remains, however. Off the middle Atlantic coast of the United States the craft catching menhaden are fitted with look-out positions on top of their masts. The herring craft of Britain and Norway are now generally fitted with the echo-sounding detector, an important post-war addition to their equipment. It is fortunate that most species of the smaller pelagic fish are given to dense schooling during the 'season', making detection fairly easy by echo sounder or by observation of bird activity and other signs. The schooling habits of a species play an important part in determining the technique of catching. The dense schooling of the smaller fish, such as herring, mackerel, pilchards, sprats, and menhaden, renders the use of nets feasible. On the other hand, the larger fish, such as tunny, are given to more open association, and this, together with their size and power, means that they are more generally caught by the totally different line technique.

In pelagic line fisheries, where the fish are near the surface, the lines are trailed from the boat to the optimum depth for the particular species required.

*Hand lines* are normally relatively short, with one or a few baited hooks along their length. Several lines are usually operated from one boat. They are not important in the more advanced areas, as they are often wasteful of man-power. They are normally operated from small craft of a wide variety of types and, indeed, have the least effect on boat design of any type of gear.

There is, however, one very important exception to the above statements. This is the pole-and-line technique of the large American Pacific coast tuna (tunny) fishery. It is paradoxical that this fishery, employing particularly large and modern craft, nevertheless uses such a basically primitive method of catching. The hand-line technique, however, has here reached a high degree of refinement, and is the most effective method for the tuna fishery in this particular region. Adult tuna here frequently weigh 1,000 lb. or more, and are particularly powerful and active. They tend to hunt in schools, but nets are plainly unsuitable. Their great weight and strength, however, often make quick landing by one man with a line impossible, and quick landing, when a school is encountered, is important if the opportunity is to be exploited fully. Therefore each hook is often operated by two, and sometimes three, men. Each 'rig' consists of a strong hook attached by short lines to two or three short stout poles. Live bait is carried in a tank on the vessel. When a school is sighted, bait fish are thrown overboard close to the vessel. These attract the tuna. The crew line the side and pull in the tuna on the hooks, flinging them over the rail into the deck compound behind them. No baiting of the hooks is necessary:

the voracious fish, once aroused by the live bait, strike at any object within sight (see Plate I).

The typical tuna clipper is mainly influenced in its size and design by the need for long-range operation. The tuna tends to a widely-dispersed, low-density distribution, rather than convenient concentration in a few grounds. The tuna clippers range widely over the ocean from the latitude of the Canadian frontier down to Peru, and to a distance from land of about 1,000 miles, though most of the fishing is done considerably closer to land. Fig. 30 shows such a vessel.

The method of fishing has strongly influenced its design. These craft are high at the bow and low at the stern, which carries the live-bait tanks and is the platform from whose edges the crew fish. Obviously, as the tuna are very heavy fish, the less distance they need to be pulled from the water the better. Seaworthiness, how-

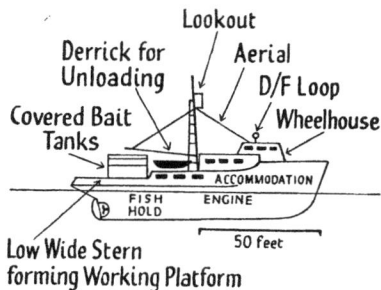

*Fig. 30.* Tuna clipper

ever, dictates the high bows, while the need for substantial accommodation for a crew of some twelve to fifteen men for a voyage of up to six weeks also leads to height in the forward part of the ship, both in the hull and the superstructure.

Despite their range, these ships are decidedly smaller than long-range European trawlers. They do not have heavy gear to drag, while their cargo has a higher value-to-bulk ratio than the usual trawled fish. As with all pelagic fishing, their work is more chancy than that of a trawler. They do not go to their chosen grounds and then fish more or less steadily. They must cruise about until a school of fish is sighted. The work is therefore often composed of periods of relative inactivity punctuated by short periods of feverish effort.

Typical of the tuna clipper is the crow's-nest on the mast. A feature of all oceanic pelagic fishing is the need for a constant look-out for the schools. Some modern tuna vessels even carry light seaplanes or helicopters. Tuna ships are diesel-engined; steam propulsion is almost completely alien to the west coast of North America, which had not developed any large marine engineering industry catering for small vessels before the advent of the internal combustion engine. Dimensions of a representative tuna clipper are: length about 100 to 120 ft.; beam 25 to 30 ft.; draught about 12 ft. The factor of availability of natural materials is significant. Although extremely advanced in design and equipment, the hulls of these ships are usually wood, abundant on the Pacific coast, in contrast to the relatively low production of steel there.

Engines are usually of about 500 h.p., capable of driving the

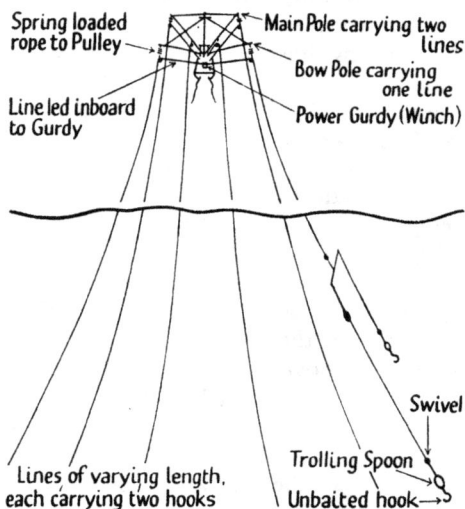

*Fig. 31.* Schematic diagram showing a method of trolling, as used for salmon on the U.S. Pacific coast

loaded vessel at 10 knots, though normally it will cruise when searching for fish at a lower speed more economical of fuel. The tuna vessel, it will be seen, contrasts with the long-range trawler in its smaller demands for power both for propulsion and other purposes. Like the trawler, however, it requires power for preserving its catch. Whereas normal trawler practice is still the carriage of crushed ice, demanding only enough refrigeration to keep it from thawing, the tuna clippers usually have the more advanced fully freezing method which keeps the fish hold below freezing-point by refrigeration without the aid of ice. More fish can therefore be carried in a given hold space. Full refrigeration, however, needs more power. In a diesel-driven craft power for this and other purposes is normally provided by auxiliary diesels which in some craft may need to supply a power of half that of the propulsion engine.

*Trolled Lines.* These lines are towed by a vessel moving at moderate speed. Often no bait is used, but the hook is attached to a lure or to a trolling 'spoon' agitated by the water flow, its movement and reflection of light attracting the fish. Trolling is used for large- or medium-sized fish. Up to sixteen lines are normally trolled simultaneously, being attached to the stern and quarters of the vessel, or to long poles which project outwards from each side (see Fig. 31).

The lines are often run through shock-absorbers, which serve the double purpose of lessening the strain on the line when the fish strikes, and by the subsequent jerk in reaction hooking the fish securely. From the shock-absorbers the lines are led inboard to a winch, power-driven in modern craft, which enables the fish to be brought aboard quickly. Major troll fisheries are the salmon and albacore

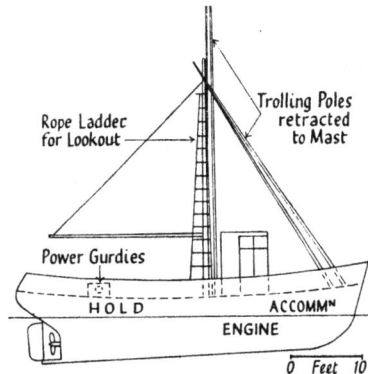

*Fig. 32.* Pacific coast salmon troller

sea fisheries of the west coast of the U.S.A. and Canada, and the tunny fishery in the East Atlantic, operated especially from Brittany.

Trolling does not greatly influence the basic design of the craft, though the long rods are a distinctive feature. In port they are raised vertically and project considerably above the masts. The North American vessels are characteristically flush-decked, with a wheelhouse situated just forward of amidships. Behind this is stepped the single mast which carries the rigging to operate the poles, which usually number two or three a side. A common feature of the mast is also a substantial rope ladder and look-out post to aid in the quick spotting of schools. An essential piece of equipment is one or more small power winches or gurdies, shaft-driven through clutches from the engine, for hauling in the fish once they have been hooked. The lines are led inboard over pulleys, mounted on the shock-absorbing springs on the poles, to the gurdies which are situated towards the stern. Average dimensions of a Pacific coast troller, which differ little from Alaska to Washington, are: length 40 to 50 ft.; beam 10 to 13 ft.; draught about 6 ft. Power is a diesel engine of 80 to 120 h.p. Fish hold capacity is usually between 8 and 12 tons. A typical vessel is shown in Fig. 32.

The noted Breton sailing trolling vessels, whose numbers have fallen rapidly in the past few years, are yawls or ketches, about 65 feet in hull length, 20 feet beam, and some 11 feet draught. They are designed to stand heavy seas in the Bay of Biscay, having straight stems, deep draught, and high freeboard. The long fishing poles or tangons, which project one on each side from the foot of the mainmast and carry up to eight lines each, are an easily distinguished feature. Few craft have wheelhouses, as these would necessitate shorter mainsail booms, and hence less sail area (see Plate II).

These traditional type vessels remained important until a little after the last war. Since then they have largely been replaced by oil-engined vessels, sometimes having auxiliary sails. The newer craft are usually designed to prosecute other fisheries out of the tunny season; the Breton trawler-tunnymen form a numerous type.

*Nets.* The net, bulkier and more complicated than the line, usually has a more pronounced effect on the design of the vessel using it. In pelagic fishing floating nets are generally used, depending for their result either upon the enmeshing or the containment of the fish. They are normally concerned with small, schooling fish.

*Drift Nets.* By far the most important form of pelagic net used by British vessels is the drift net, which is also important in Holland, France, and many other areas. It is a long floating 'wall' hung in the water (Fig. 33). Its upper edge is attached to floats, its lower to weights. Each net used in the British herring fishery is about 60 yds. long and 16 yds. deep, and a vessel normally 'shoots' up to 100 nets in a continuous line of a total length of over 3 miles. It then rides at the downwind end of the line. The mesh of the drift net is such that the particular species of fish required can swim partway only through the net, when it becomes caught by the gills and cannot extricate itself. Once laid, the net is a passive instrument and must await the passage of a school. There is both skill and luck in the successful placing of the net, though in the last few years the general adoption of echo sounding has enabled schools to be located much more easily than before.

The British steam drifter is a celebrated type using this method, but even in Britain the motor drifter is steadily replacing the steam vessel which has for many years been one of the most characteristic fishing craft of the east coast. By 1953 the catch landed by motor drifters in England and Wales exceeded that by steam drifters by over 10 per cent. The remaining steam craft are nearly all old, and still coal-burners. For reasons of fuel economy, and smaller engine space, the motor drifter is replacing them as they are withdrawn from service. The steam

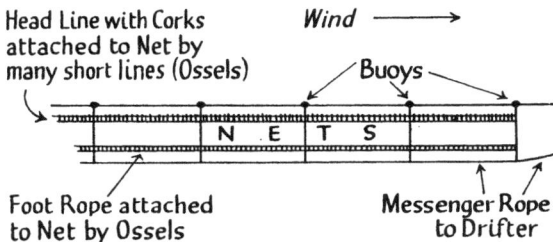

*Fig. 33.* Portion of a fleet of drift nets

drifter is pre-eminently a British type, little developed by other countries, in which the transition from sail to power was often late enough to permit immediate adoption of the internal combustion engine.

Because of the steam craft's still substantial tonnage in Britain, however, a brief description may be given (see Plate III). The typical vessel is of wood, though some are of steel, and in general appearance she resembles an old-type steam trawler, though she is smaller. She has a flush deck, with a small superstructure and wheelhouse aft, below which are the crew's quarters and engine. The funnel is usually tall and narrow. The forward and middle portions of the ship contain the stores and fish hold. An essential feature of the deck is the steam capstan for hauling the net. Other characteristics are the pivoted mainmast which can be lowered during drifting to reduce rolling, and the smaller mizzen (after) mast which carries a triangular sail which helps to keep the vessel stable and head to wind when drifting.

Length of the average steam drifter is about 85 ft.; beam 18 ft.; and draught aft 11 ft. Maximum speed is about 9 knots. Drifters must be sturdily built to stand severe weather, but do not have to remain at sea for long; about a day or so. Fishing grounds may be anything between 20 and 60 miles from port, depending on the locality and season. The ships may move from the north of Scotland down to East Anglia in the course of the year, but are always based on a port adjacent to the grounds being fished. Cramped accommodation for the crew of about six, and small space for stores, are therefore all that are strictly·necessary, and fuel and hold capacity need not be great.

The aim is to deliver the herring to market very fresh, so life on a drifter consists of a series of short sorties, as opposed to the

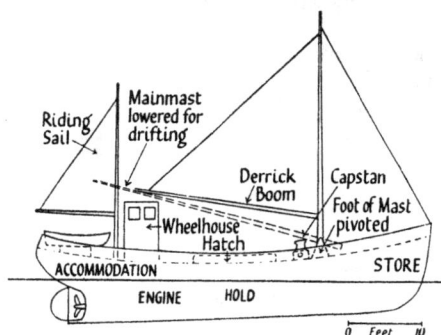

*Fig. 34.* Small English motor drifter

fairly long voyages of the steam trawler. This fundamental fact accounts for the marked difference in size between the two types. The steam drifter is nevertheless by no means a tiny craft, and the demands of sturdiness and stability have given it a draught which limits it to ports which, though small, must have adequately deep harbours and proper unloading quays.

Motor drifters, of which an English one is shown in Fig. 34, are often somewhat smaller, although in the past few years craft of over 90 ft. length have become common. Motor drifters can be employed out of the herring season in Danish seining for ground fish, as the capstan is suitable for this. Vessels broadly similar are found also in Scandinavia, Germany, and Holland, though the modern type of motor drifter is most characteristically an east coast English and Scottish type.

Drift nets are a very common form of gear in the less advanced areas of the world. They do not require large vessels, and power for towing a net through the water is not needed. The variety in size and shape of the drift nets used is very great; they can be set from one-man canoes as well as from large sailing craft. The

*Plate IIIa.* BRITISH STEAM DRIFTER

*Plate IIIb.* MODERN BRITISH DISTANT-WATER STEAM TRAWLER

Valai valai of the Coromandel coast is an important form of drift net. Many small Japanese inshore-fishing craft also use drift nets. In western Europe, drift-net sailing craft are still significant. The flat-bottomed Dutch vessels are well known. Fig. 35 illustrates a botter, once one of the common classes. The influence of the type of deltaic coast zone of shallow water and few natural harbours is very marked here. The boats originally operated from exposed beaches, though those still working use artificial harbours. The shallow draught was essential to enable the craft to be floated up the beach and left when the tide receded. The flat bottom keeps her upright and facilitates unloading. Stout stem and stern posts and other hull framework resist damage due to pounding upon the beach when not fully afloat. Complementary to the shallow draught is the broad beam for stability and adequate load capacity, the low sail height to prevent capsizing in high wind, and the leeboards, lowered when

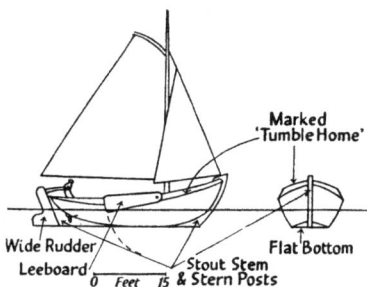

*Fig. 35.* Dutch botter

the boat is away from the beach to give it the necessary 'grip' on the water for sailing into wind. An average botter is about 38 ft. long, 13 ft. beam, and 3 ft. 6 in. draught. There is an open cockpit aft. The upper parts of the sides have a 'tumble home' or inward turn which increases rigidity and protects the cockpit.

In striking contrast to the Dutch vessel is the Breton sardine lugger. It is designed for the same method of fishing, but works from a very different coastline: the ria type of deep sheltered natural harbours. Its average length is little more; about 45 ft., but its draught is 6 or 7 ft. As the boat can be built to this draught it does not need to be so broad in proportion to its length, and its beam is about 13 ft. Construction is robust, but less so than that of the Dutch vessel. Sail area is greater, and there are two masts. Leeboards are not required. Both the botter and the French lugger are commonly fitted with small motors in these days, but the sail remains an important driving force because of its economy.

Other forms of gill nets are used in many parts of the coasts of Asia and North America. There are numerous variations in size, shape, and detail, but the principle of trapping the fish in the meshes of a static net wall remains the same. Such nets are frequently used in shallow water. The attendant craft often do not remain attached to them, but the nets are anchored to the bottom and visited by the boats at intervals.

*Ring Nets.* This group of methods involves the surrounding of the school of fish with a net hanging, like the drift net, in a manner similar to a curtain from the surface of the water. The net is laid by a vessel on a circular course, or by two vessels towing the net on parallel courses and then turning to meet. It is then drawn closely round the school. The fish do not become enmeshed in the net, which is made of too small a mesh. They are hauled aboard by a 'brailer', a dip net lowered from the vessel. To prevent some of the fish escaping under the net, some types are made to 'purse', like the purse net described next. In some forms the middle portion of the net is made in the form of a bag or 'bunt' in which the fish collect. Ring-netting in one form or another is widely used in the world, but in few areas is it dominant. In Britain it is much used in the Firth of Clyde area.

An advantage of ring-netting over drifting is that it is an active, not passive method. The fish are hunted out, instead of being waited for. Also, the length of net required is much less. On the other hand, fuel costs are naturally greater, and these are an increasingly important item in total cost. In some forms of the technique two vessels are needed, thus considerably increasing expense. For the main part of the pelagic catch in Britain, drifting remains dominant, as the advantage of local mobility attached to ring-netting is not of great importance in the North Sea herring fisheries. In these the herring are usually either absent from a particular spot at a given time, or are present in great numbers. In the former case, the localized mobility of ring-netting is of small advantage, while in the latter drift-netting is as effective as ring-netting. Ring-netting is used to best effect by small vessels in restricted coastal waters, particularly where there are shipping lanes and there may not be enough room or opportunity to lay the long drift nets.

The boats may take a wide variety of forms despite being within the same functional class, because the method of ring-netting differs markedly from place to place, according, for example, to whether one boat or two is used. Further, the ranges at which ring-netting is practised also vary greatly. The craft may be conversions from other types, and may be motor drifters adapted to use the technique when not drift fishing.

*Purse Seines.* Akin to the ring net is the purse seine. It is another 'curtain' type net, hung between surface floats and weights along its foot. It possesses a purse line, which is a stout rope threaded through eyes along the foot of the net. When the school is surrounded, this purse line is hauled on by a winch,

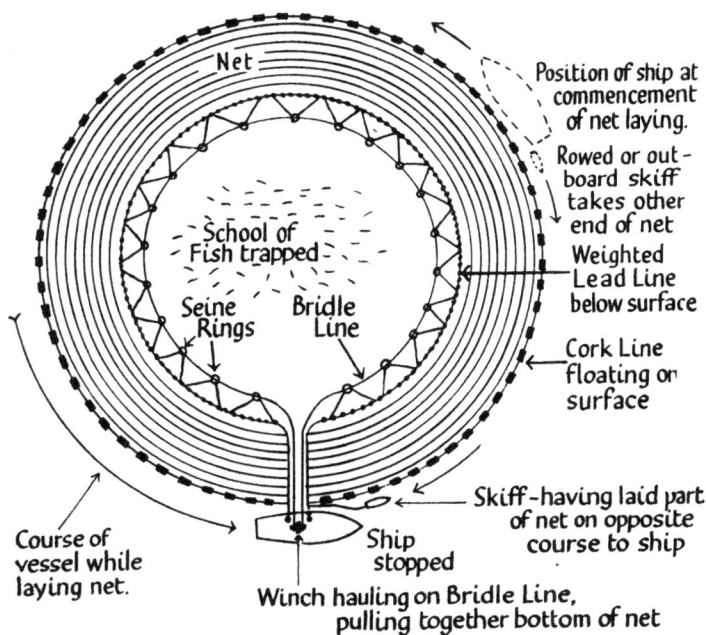

*Fig. 36.* Purse seine net, of type used off British Columbia for salmon. Simplified diagram showing net at commencement of pursing. Net approx. 1200 feet length and 70 feet deep

thus closing or 'pursing' the bottom of the net at the same time as it draws it in to a small area beside the vessel. The fish are thus trapped completely. The net is made of small mesh, as the aim is not to entangle the fish, but to lift them out of it by a dip net lowered from a derrick on the vessel (see Plate IV).

The purse seine is very popular in North American waters, where it is used chiefly for catching menhaden, herring, mackerel, sardines, and salmon. The normal method of laying the net is shown in Fig. 36. The net is up to 1,200 ft. long and 70 ft. deep.

9

The technique lends itself particularly well to use in the numerous inlets and channels of the northern Pacific coast. Other countries in which the purse seine has become important, chiefly for herring, are Iceland, Norway, and Sweden.

In general appearance and hull type the American Pacific coast purse seiners are quite like the tuna clippers, already discussed, although rather smaller, as the range needed is less. Like them, they are low and wide at the stern, to offer a satisfactory platform for fishing operations. The net is usually carried on a turntable on this after-platform, so that it can easily be swung to the best position for shooting. The superstructure, as in the tuna clipper, is crowded forward. The bait tanks are normally omitted, but may be fitted, as many of the larger purse seiners now go tuna fishing in the off-seasons for their normal types of catch. The average-sized modern American purse seiner is about 80 ft. long, 20 to 22 ft. beam, and 12 ft. draught. Power is from the usual diesel engine, and is normally between 250 and 400 h.p., giving a maximum speed of 11 to 12 knots. General characteristics of these craft vary little from California to Alaska. Other countries where the use of this type of craft is spreading include Australia and South Africa.

*Lampara Nets.* These are used, like ring nets and purse seines, to surround the school, but are different in shape, the lower edge or lead line being shorter than the floating edge or cork line, so that the net is partly pursed by the mere action of laying it in a circle. It has no pursing mechanism. This type originated in the Mediterranean, where it is particularly used on dark nights, a bright light being shone on the water to attract the sardines, anchovies, or other fish. It is also used by Californian fishermen for mackerel and sardine, and in Australia and other areas. Lampara nets are sometimes weighted sufficiently along their lower edges to sink them, so that they can be used on or near the sea-bed in shallow water.

*Beach-hauled Seines.* As these were discussed in the previous chapter, no further description need be given here.

*Vertically-hauled Nets.* These are rarely important in Western commercial fisheries, although they are used in the Lofotens, but they are important in many less advanced areas, particularly along the Madras coast, where they are known as 'madi valai'.

Such nets are often used, as in India, in conjunction with fish lures, which attract the fish to the desired point. The net, lying submerged in the horizontal plane, is then brought under the fish and hauled quickly to the surface, as shown in Fig. 37. The method is, of course, limited to use by small boats in the vicinity of the shore, and may be used for demersal as well as pelagic fish. It lends itself well to use by such small craft with no other power available than human hands.

*Bottom Trawls.* As the normal trawl is designed to move along the sea-bed, it is not usually of much significance in pelagic fisheries, but there are certain exceptions. For example, at certain times the mackerel and herring on the North-west

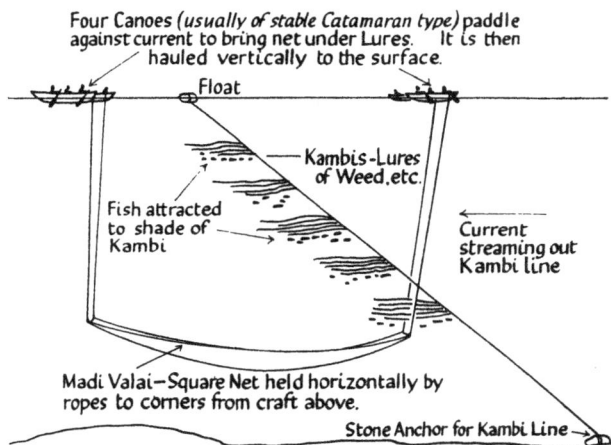

*Fig. 37.* Fishing by madi valai on the Coromandel coast

European shelf take to the bottom, when they can be caught by trawl. The German and Dutch North Sea herring trawlers are important users of this method of catching pelagic fish. Their trawls are often modified by the attachment of a third board, or 'kite', to the top of the net in such a way as to open its mouth wider than the normal vertical distance, so as to catch fish a little above the sea-bed. Other countries carrying on bottom trawling for fish normally classed as pelagic include Sweden, Denmark, Belgium, and Russia.

*Floating Trawls.* Recently, trawls have been developed capable of being adjusted to work in mid-water at any required depth. They are chiefly the work of Scandinavian and Icelandic inventors, and are now quite important in the herring fisheries of these countries, while they are being tried out in other areas. The devices themselves are not particularly complicated and would doubtless have been evolved earlier had there been a demand for them. As with many inventions, however, they were themselves stimulated by a demand created by another invention, in this case the echo sounder, which for the first time enabled the precise depth of shoals of fish to be registered. Fishing by mid-depth trawl without the help of the echo sounder would in most cases be unprofitable, so that net fishing had hitherto confined itself chiefly to devices operating in the surface or sea-bed layers, two planes in which fish tend to congregate.

The floating trawl opens up new possibilities of catching fish at times or seasons when they congregate in mid-water. A typical Scandinavian type is a roughly conical net, about 180 ft. long and 50 ft. wide at the mouth, towed behind and midway between two vessels steaming abreast on parallel courses. The depth of the net can be adjusted by the length of tow-rope, by varying the speed, by weighting, or in some cases by adjusting vanes. There seems no reason why its use should not spread widely about the world. It may find a valuable application, for example, in sardine as well as herring fisheries, while it may also be useful in catching demersal fish in areas where trawling right on the bottom is impossible owing to rocks.

*Stationary Traps.* Large permanent traps, usually known as pounds or weirs, are important in the salmon fishery of Alaska, British Columbia, Washington, and Oregon, and in the Mediterranean tunny fishery, but they are most characteristic of Asian fisheries. Trapping methods have already been discussed in connexion with demersal fishing, and are therefore not considered in detail here.

It can be seen that all the methods outlined in these chapters have evolved in response to specific local physical and economic conditions. It is interesting to note how, in widely separated areas until recently lacking much contact in fishing matters, very similar techniques have arisen when conditions resemble each other. This is a good example of the influence of environmental factors. The successful response to the basic problem posed by natural conditions can only lie within a certain range of possibilities. Within this range, however, there is considerable scope for differentiation due to human factors: the manner of working of the minds of one people may have tended it towards one solution, whereas another will naturally follow other lines of thought.

The methods of catching the fish, with their necessary vessels

*Plate IV.* TRANSFERRING MENHADEN BY DIP-NET FROM THE PURSE SEINE TO THE HOLD OF THE FISHING CRAFT. (ATLANTIC COAST OF U.S.A.)

and apparatus, are of course the most immediately striking aspect of a fishery. The organic aspect of a fishery is thus frequently overlooked, but this is the essential one. The fishery is only the harvesting machinery in a process of which the sowing and growth of the crop, because it takes place without man's aid, must not be forgotten. Without a satisfactory organic condition of a fishery, without suitable opportunity for reproduction and the growth of young fish, it is a wasting asset comparable to a mine rather than a farm. A fishery operated by high-powered craft with complicated equipment may be unhealthy if its yield is steadily being reduced, while a fishery operated by primitive methods may yet be basically healthy. This is not to suggest that primitive methods are better than advanced methods, for they may be economically inefficient. When advanced techniques are introduced, however, a careful watch must be maintained against their abuse.

# CHAPTER VIII

# PROCESSING AND TRANSPORT METHODS, AND ANCILLARY INDUSTRIES

TRANSFERENCE of fish from the place of landing to its ultimate point of consumption is an important aspect of the fishing industry. Frequently it is not given due importance in discussions of fisheries. A balanced view of the industry cannot, however, omit the distribution of the product, because the conditions under which this is done react markedly on the fishing activities themselves. Fish, like meat, is distinguished from the majority of commodities in that, unless specially processed, it is very quickly perishable. Certain methods of processing have therefore long been used, and the requirements of these, which are in turn largely conditioned by the tastes of the consumers, frequently affect and are affected by the type and seasonal timing of the fisherman's work. The British herring fishery, for example, depends to a great extent on the demand at home for kippered herring, and abroad for pickled herring. The yearly migration of much of the drifter fleet from the north of Scotland progressively southwards to East Anglia has an essential complement in the migration of the Scottish women and other workers to supply the extra demand for labour in processing at the ports.

Where fish is marketed fresh, it is either limited to an area close to the coast, as in primitive economies, or it requires a complex service of fast transport with cooling facilities, as is found in Britain and other advanced countries. Fresh fish naturally commands a higher price, and in advanced countries is the generally favoured type for consumption, but in large areas in Asia, Africa, South America, and southern Europe the average inland consumer cannot regularly afford fresh sea-fish, more expensive because of the need for rapid distribution facilities. Dried fish is a common form for these areas; fish dehydrated in the sun until it may become almost as hard as wood, but which, on soaking in water, fills out and becomes soft again. In addition to the locally produced fish, there is also an important international trade to these areas in dried, salted, or smoked cod, the main exporters being Norway, Canada (particularly Newfoundland),

and Iceland. Before the war certain Asian countries, particularly Malaya, Indo-China, and Thailand, were important exporters to their less favoured neighbours, but since the war and its succeeding political and economic troubles these Asian exports have shrunk very greatly.

On landing, fish may be disposed of in a number of forms, of which the following are important:

1. Fresh, usually packed with ice for transit.
2. Frozen, and maintained frozen in transit by refrigeration apparatus.
3. Dried by the sun or other agency.
4. Dry-salted: another form of dehydration.
5. Smoked: also a form of partial or full dehydration, but imparting a popular flavour.
6. Pickled in brine.
7. Canned.
8 Reduced to: (*a*) Animal feeding-stuff.
                (*b*) Fertilizer.
                (*c*) Fish oil (from certain parts of the fish).

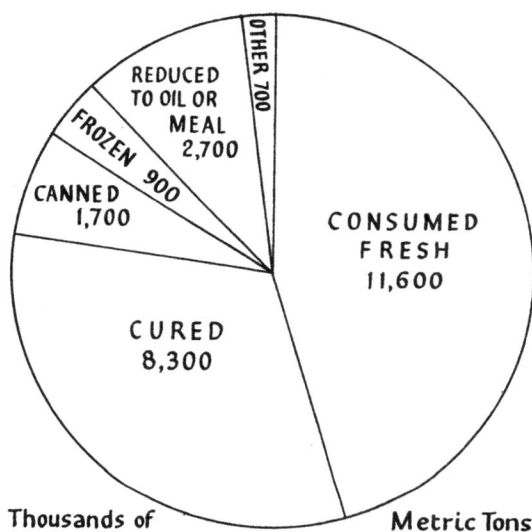

*Fig. 38.* Relative disposition of world catch, 1951.
(*F.A.O.* estimates)

Fig. 38 shows the relative importance of these in the disposition of world catches. 'Cured' embraces groups 3 to 6 above.

Reduction to animal food or fertilizer is normally less profitable than sale for human food, although there are certain species, such as menhaden off the United States middle Atlantic coast, which are caught primarily for this purpose. Most large ports, however, now have reduction plants which handle the excess fish when there is a glut and landings are too high to be disposed of quickly for human consumption. Such excess is sold to the plants at much below the price to the human consumer.

All of the methods of dealing with the fish listed above make their demands on equipment, labour, and administration, and directly and indirectly account for an important part of the population of fishing ports in advanced countries. The economies of scale in these operations have been a potent factor in centralizing the industry in fewer but larger ports in recent years.

The chief ancillary industries, not all of which are found at the ports, which contribute to these methods of disposal of fish, can be summarized thus:

Ice-making plants.
Salt mines and refineries.
Factories making barrels, boxes, cans, cartons, greaseproof paper, etc.
Establishments for drying, salting, smoking, pickling, and freezing.
Canning factories.
Animal feeding-stuff factories.
Fertilizer factories.
Oil extraction plants.
Laboratories making medicinal and specialized food products from oil.
Railway and road networks for inland distribution. (In some areas, such as eastern Canada and North-east U.S.A., small-scale but significant ventures in the air transport of fresh fish have also been started.)
Inland cold-storage centres.
Engineering works making and maintaining the specialized equipment required by the above factories and services.

A really large fishing port will usually have practically all of the appropriate types of activity listed (save, of course, salt mines, though even in this case the presence of the large demand for salt of such a port will stimulate the development of the nearest suitable sources of salt). Smaller ports may tend to concentrate on one or a few related types of fish products, being unable to furnish the labour and other requirements for an economic development of several types. The variety of fish landed at the port also affects the number of activities. Some fishing regions produce a wide and balanced variety of fish, others have one dominant species, such as cod in Newfoundland or Iceland, herring in Holland, or sardines in Portugal. In such cases one type of plant tends to dominate the processing scene: cod salting, herring pickling, and sardine canning respectively in the above cases.

The least economically advanced areas of the world, where life is still mainly on a subsistence basis, as in some islands of Oceania, eat all their fish freshly caught. Areas slightly more advanced (in the orthodox view) supplement their fresh fish with the less palatable and nourishing form of rehydrated dried fish. Drying fish flesh in the sun is the natural and very cheap method of preservation for the tropics (see Plate V). Areas rather further advanced, and where the appropriate materials are available, will also resort to salting and smoking. Such methods are also necessary in temperate zones where the sunshine is insufficiently strong or dependable, though drying by sun and wind may still form part of the preserving process. Even in advanced areas such as North-west Europe and North America, salting, and particularly smoke-curing, remain important aspects of preserving, though relatively they are declining in favour in many parts of these areas.

As a country reaches the most advanced stage, stress is once more put on the advantages of fresh fish. Fast inland transport, and apparatus for cooling, make a fresh fish supply possible, though 'freshness' is often rather broadly interpreted. The simplest method of transporting fresh fish, packed surrounded by ice chips in boxes or on shelves, is not completely satisfactory, for the temperature is appreciably above freezing-point, and certain forms of decay can still proceed, particularly if the fish are bruised or cut in transit. Provision of full refrigeration equipment in the railway vans and storage places is much more expensive and still not resorted to on a very large scale. It will doubtless ultimately become the general practice, in conjunction with quick freezing on board the catching vessels themselves, so that from the time of its catch until it leaves the retail shop the fish can be kept continuously at an adequately low temperature. The need for keeping the fish at a low temperature on board the catching vessel is of course equally as important as keeping it so after landing. At present, storage amongst crushed ice in a cooled hold is normal practice. With long-distance trawlers, well over a fortnight elapses between the time of catching the first fish and their landing at the port, by which time their quality has tended to deteriorate. Plant on the catching vessel for filleting and quick freezing is thus needed, though expensive. An alternative solution is the carrier vessel system which has been practised by some German firms, whereby a special vessel not engaged in fishing, but equipped with full refrigeration plant for maintaining a temperature below freezing, is employed to shuttle between the fishing fleet and the ports, landing the fish soon after their capture.

Canning of fish is a process that has developed rapidly in this century, but has probably now reached its maximum relative importance in advanced countries, because of the increasing desire for really fresh fish. Canning grew with the cheap large-scale production of tinplate in South Wales and other centres. It enables food to be packed in a neat, easily handled form, often in an appetizing sauce or liquor, and, once canned, the food will keep for a considerable time at a normal temperature. The system is naturally more expensive than the older methods of drying, salting, or smoking, but it produces a food that is normally more pleasant and also more hygienic, for, once packed, it is free from further possibility of contamination. The fairly low price of tinplate, coupled with conveyor-belt methods of packing, have enabled certain species of canned fish to be marketed at prices within the range of the bulk of the consumers in the more advanced countries (see Plate VI). Not all types of fish lend themselves to the canning technique; suitability depends on such matters as bodily structure, and the texture and precise chemical composition of the flesh. Some of the most suitable and popular are the sardine, salmon, and tunny, though widely different in size.

Because canned fish is more highly priced than dried or salted fish, poor countries which catch a good deal of fish suitable for canning often find a more profitable market abroad than at home for their canned produce. Thus Japan exports a large amount of canned tunny, while Portugal exports large quantities of canned sardines, using part of the proceeds to import cheap salted cod for its population of low purchasing power. Canned fish lends itself well to international trade because of its keeping and easy handling qualities. The chief world exporters of canned fish are Japan (in normal years, to which she now appears to be starting to return), Canada, Portugal, U.S.A., Norway, and French Morocco. The exports are widely dispersed, but the chief importers are Britain, France, U.S.A. (though remaining on balance a substantial exporter), Italy, Belgium, and Australia. Less developed countries are less important individually, though important in the aggregate. The Philippines and Indonesia are in normal times substantial importers of canned fish, although these imports have dropped in the immediate post-war period. While it is likely that the amount of canned fish consumed in advanced countries will not increase much further, a considerable relative expansion is possible in the less advanced countries as more of their masses move from the ability to purchase only dried, salted, or smoked imports to the ability to pay for the canned product.

Fig. 39 shows graphically the relative proportions, by weight, of their own catches of fish devoted to various uses in some representative fishing countries for which such information is collected. Reasons for the differences can be found in the local tastes of consumers, the degree of technical advancement, the types of fish caught, the relative advantage of exports to national economy, and the availability of the ancillary raw materials and fuel. The latter point is important. All methods of processing, save simple sun-drying, require raw materials. Salt is important for the salted, pickled, or smoked group, while smoking also requires a supply of a suitable type of wood. Canning requires tinplate, preserving oil or sauce, and fuel, normally coal. Even simple freezing needs appreciable amounts of fuel or electric power. If these requirements are not adequately available in an area, and the balance of trade situation does not permit their import, plainly the particular method cannot be developed. The expansion of canning in the under-developed countries is undoubtedly retarded by these factors.

The countries given in Fig. 39, though widely different in many respects, are classified there according to their utilization characteristics into groups within which certain features are similar. The most convenient standard is the proportion of the total landings marketed fresh, either at home or abroad. Group A, with a very high proportion marketed fresh, contains countries which are not particularly rich in fishing resources, and therefore

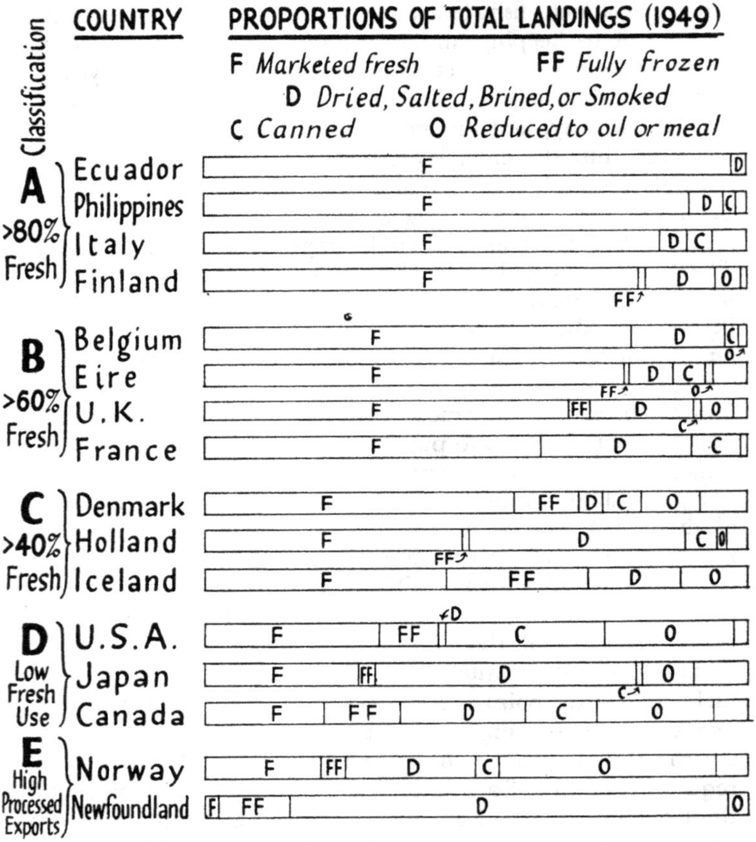

| Classification | COUNTRY | PROPORTIONS OF TOTAL LANDINGS (1949) |
|---|---|---|

F *Marketed fresh*       FF *Fully frozen*
D *Dried, Salted, Brined, or Smoked*
C *Canned*      O *Reduced to oil or meal*

**A** >80% Fresh
- Ecuador — F ... D
- Philippines — F ... D C
- Italy — F ... D C
- Finland — F ... FF D O

**B** >60% Fresh
- Belgium — F ... D C O
- Eire — F ... FF D C O
- U.K. — F ... FF D C O
- France — F ... D C

**C** >40% Fresh
- Denmark — F ... FF D C O
- Holland — F ... FF D C O
- Iceland — F ... FF D O

**D** Low Fresh Use
- U.S.A. — F FF D C O
- Japan — F FF D C O
- Canada — F FF D C O

**E** High Processed Exports
- Norway — F FF D C O
- Newfoundland — F FF D O

*Fig. 39.* Fish utilization by representative countries

concentrate on supplying the home market, having negligible exports. They are also countries where the centres of densest population are on the coast or easily accessible from it. There is thus small requirement for the locally produced fish to be processed, although, particularly in Italy and Finland, there is a substantial *per capita* import of processed fish.

Group B countries, with a fairly high proportion of their own landings marketed fresh, include typically those densely or moderately densely populated parts of Europe which, although having access to rich sea resources, do not have any appreciable surplus available for export. The United Kingdom's exports

*Plate V.* DRYING FISH IN THE SUN AT ABERDEEN, HONG KONG

are now far below the pre-war average, partly due to increased demands of the home market, partly to economic and political difficulties in the trade with the once large markets in eastern Europe. Nevertheless, a considerable proportion of the present British output of salted, brined, or smoked fish, particularly herring, is accounted for by exports to Europe; sporadically to Germany, Russia, and elsewhere according to the fortunes of government negotiations. France nowadays has very little export trade left. Her appreciable output of dried, salted, and allied types is accounted for particularly by the protracted voyages of her Grand Banks cod-fishing vessels, which must perforce use salting as the method of preservation.

In Group C, marketing but a moderate amount of their landings fresh, we find countries with important exports. Denmark has expanded her fishery exports considerably since the war, although a good deal of her exports are sent fresh or frozen because of the nearness of her main markets such as Britain and Germany, and because of the stress of her industry on high-grade products. Holland, on the other hand, has traditionally always been a big exporter of brined, salted, and smoked fish, and factors of industrial inertia have kept this one of her major fishery activities. Iceland has what at first sight seems a rather low proportion of dried and similar fish in her exports, when her distance from markets is considered. During and since the war years, however, the high prices of fresh and frozen fish in her nearest market, Britain, have caused a radical change in her patterns of utilization. The year 1949 shows a ninefold increase in her fresh and frozen fish exports as compared with 1938, while dried and similar forms have fallen to less than half of the 1938 output.

The substantial proportion of landings reduced to oils and animal meal in Denmark and Iceland is significant, and typical of some other countries. The reason is primarily a shortage of agriculturally produced feeding-stuffs relative to the requirements of their livestock, though this shortage arises from varying reasons. In Denmark's case, of course, it is due to the large demands of the major exporting dairy, poultry and pig-raising industries, and the post-war short supply and high prices of imported maize and other animal foods. In Iceland, whose livestock exists solely for the home market, climatic and soil conditions are nevertheless deficient even for the agricultural production of these limited feeding-stuff needs. Iceland is also an important exporter of meal, and of oils for medicinal or chemical uses.

Group D, with less than 40 per cent of landings marketed fresh, includes the two major countries of North America. Their large area is an important factor in this, with the consequent remoteness from the sea of important consuming centres. Some form of preservation was thus inevitable for many inland markets in the past, although nowadays fast freight trains, and even aircraft on a very small scale, have made fresh sea-fish easily available well in the interior. A considerable proportion also is frozen for distribution and conveyed long distances by railroad refrigerator cars. Nevertheless, the habit of using processed fish is now ingrained, and, indeed, processed food of all kinds is more commonly used in these two countries than anywhere else in the world. In the U.S.A. the main form of processed fish is, of course, canned, and the dried and similar forms have fallen in recent years to very small amounts. Fully frozen fish is also an important item. A large amount is also reduced to animal food for the large livestock population, or to oils; these are derived mainly from species of fish, such as menhaden, abundant at certain points around the American coast and which do not find favour for human consumption. Again, the U.S.A. is only a moderate consumer of fish in *per capita* terms, because of the abundant supply of meat, but is a large consumer of industrial chemical products derived from fish oil.

Canada (excluding Newfoundland) also has a substantial consumption and export of canned fish, and a large reduction to oil or animal food. There are also traditional exports of dried and salted cod to South America, the West Indies, Mediterranean countries, and other consumers of cheap fish. Canada's proportion of fish marketed frozen is also considerable, because of the long haul to her middle-interior markets.

Japan has canned and other processed exports which are substantial in absolute terms but small in proportion to her enormous landings. The bulk of her dried, salted, and smoked fish is consumed in her own territory, particularly since the war. The low proportion marketed fresh is presumably due to the inertia of tastes developed in days before Japan had her present well-knit rail network, together with the fact that in a country very hard pressed for food and strongly averse from waste, there is the desire to avoid the proportion of spoilage inevitable in the distribution of fresh fish.

Group E principally includes two countries which, like Iceland, export the bulk of their landings. Norway and Newfoundland, however, differ markedly from Iceland in various respects, particularly in their low proportion of utilization fresh. Newfoundland still concentrates on the old-established dried and salted cod exports through her traditional channels to Latin America, southern Europe, and Africa. The Newfoundland fisheries on the whole are not particularly progressive. This method of disposal of her catches is, of course, the least lucrative available, but it calls for little in the way of skill or capital. Interference with traditional channels during the war, however, coupled with an expanding market for frozen fish in the United States, has led to an increase in the production of the latter type. It is still not relatively large, but markedly expanding. In 1948 exports of frozen and fresh fish were nearly three times the 1938 level.

Norway utilizes a higher proportion of her catch fresh or frozen, but in her exports the dried and salted group is of equal importance to the fresh and frozen, and supplies largely the same markets as Newfoundland. Canned production is increasing and now important, and goes mainly to the markets of higher purchasing power, such as Britain. A significant feature of the Norwegian utilization, however, is the very substantial proportion of catches going for reduction to oils and animal food, while an important proportion of the remainder is made into fertilizer. The size of these 'indirect' uses of fish is due to a number of factors. A large proportion of Norway's fishery output must, of course, be exported because of the rather small home market. Certain types of indirect uses, such as medicinal oils, particularly cod-liver and halibut-liver oil, were developed on a large scale by Norway as a source of valuable exports, and from these has grown a large industry using other parts of fish. Unlike Newfoundland and Iceland, Norway has had for some time sufficient technical skill, capital, and labour supply to develop a group of factories carrying out fairly complex processes. Again, she has a by no means negligible home agriculture, with an appreciable demand for feeding-stuffs and fertilizer.

Transport methods for fish may next be discussed. They vary considerably according to the degree of development of the area concerned. In the more primitive areas in Africa and South-east Asia, transport by cart, or even by human porterage for short distances, is common, so that here the range to which fresh sea-fish can penetrate inland is clearly very limited. Preservation by drying is therefore important if inland markets are to be supplied, though often the effect of transport difficulties is virtually to prevent any appreciable consumption of sea-fish at all away from coastlands. The deficiency may be made up partly by freshwater fish where large rivers and deltas are situated, but the products of these are of course similarly confined to their own districts.

The development of efficient railway networks in the Indian sub-continent, Java, and to a lesser extent in some other backward countries, has considerably extended the consumption of fresh sea-fish in their inland areas. The limiting factors on further improvement in their still generally low *per capita* consumption tend to be matters other than transport. Many other regions, however, such as much of China, and Africa outside the Union and the Mediterranean fringe, have important areas of inland population away from the rail network. Current fairly rapid development of motor roads, the modern substitute for railway branch lines, will gradually extend the hinterland for fresh sea-fish in these regions. Meanwhile the *per capita* consumption of fresh fish, and indeed of all types of fish, is undoubtedly much lower in the inland parts of such areas than it is on the coast, though statistics of internal differentiation of consumption are lacking.

By contrast, in a country such as Britain with a dense rail and road network, the consumption of fresh fish *per capita* differs little between the coast and the most inland parts of the country. Goods trains are sufficiently fast to deliver the fish fresh to such centres without the aid of refrigerator cars, packing in ice being normally sufficient. Larger countries such as the United States and Canada, although possessing good transport systems, are naturally compelled by their size to use refrigeration during transport to areas well inland, but as has been seen above, these countries are also large consumers of canned fish.

Transport of fish by sea, after initial landing, is mainly in the dried and salted group and the canned group. Fresh and frozen fish are exported in appreciable quantities from Iceland and Norway to nearby markets with which there is in any case no alternative means of communication. An increase in the number of vessels specially equipped as refrigerated fish-carriers is, however, to be expected with the changing emphasis of demand from the dried and salted group to frozen fish, the next best thing to fresh fish. Refrigerator ships, of course, are nevertheless expensive in both initial and running costs. The remaining method of transport, air, is at present of negligible importance in moving fish products, yet it has considerable possibilities. Its most likely large-scale application will be in the flying of fresh fish of high value-to-bulk varieties to markets of high purchasing power, such as inland cities of North America and the capital cities of many other countries. An important aspect of this trade may be the moving of fish in season at one place to other places where it is out of season.

In discussing the question of transport, it should be stressed that the type of inland transport facilities available is a force in the moulding of the fishing vessel itself. A fishing industry, as has been pointed out before, is an organic whole composed of many interdependent parts ranging geographically ·from its most distant fishing grounds to its most inland market. Development of an efficient railway or road transport network alone makes possible a market sufficiently large and resilient to absorb the catch of a large modern long-range trawler within a short time after she docks. Were the market for fresh fish limited to the district of landing, say to Yorkshire for Hull, the docking of a few large trawlers with good catches within a few hours of each other would heavily depress prices. Large fluctuations of prices paid to the trawler firms, automatically militating against the larger vessels' catch, would make large vessels uneconomical. The growth of the large modern trawler is thus complementary to an efficient inland transport system. It is notable that Britain possesses a far higher proportion of large fishing vessels than any other country. The most important single factor behind this is undoubtedly her large, compact population, well served by a dense transport network.

It may be seen that a modern fishing industry, with all its ramifications, employs a great number of people besides the actual fisherman. Some detailed statistics are available for Scotland, from which the following percentages have been calculated.

Employment in ancillary occupations here outnumbers the fisherman proper by two to one. Scotland, however, is an area where fisheries are in an advanced stage. Vessels are nearly all fully or partly power-driven, and embody labour-saving devices such as power winches for handling nets. This cuts down the requirements for men on the boats. On the other hand, the highly developed curing and .allied industries have a large direct

EMPLOYMENT IN THE SCOTTISH FISHERIES AND ANCILLARY INDUSTRIES, 1938

Total: 54,000 (railwaymen and employees of road transport
firms not solely connected with fish are not included)

*Percentages employed in various sections:*

| | |
|---|---|
| Fishermen | 33·0 |
| Fishmongers and fryers | 16·0 |
| Gutters, curers, kipperers, packers | 13·0 |
| Employed on vessels regularly carrying fish for home and export markets, and in mobile curing (includes foreigners) | 7·0 |
| Unskilled labourers, porters, and carters | 6·5 |
| Employed on vessels regularly importing salt, wood, etc. (includes foreigners) | 4·6 |
| Making and mending nets | 3·3 |
| Boatbuilders and repairers | 2·8 |
| Hawkers | 2·8 |
| Clerical staff | 1·7 |
| Coopers | 1·7 |
| Bait gatherers and preparers | 1·3 |
| Makers of boxes, barrels, staves, baskets, etc. | 1·0 |
| Other occupations | 5·3 |

and indirect demand for labour. Again, as in most modern
Western economies, division of labour has been carried far, so
that many tasks, such as net-making, often carried out by the
fishermen themselves in many less advanced countries, are left to
specialized workers here.

By contrast, Japan may be quoted. Detailed figures are not
available, but 80 per cent of the total engaged in Japanese
fisheries (excluding aquiculture) and related manufacturing
were fishermen proper in 1938. This means, of course, that
many of the functions discharged in Scotland by specialized
workers are here carried out by the fishermen. It is likely that
Japanese ancillary industries will also develop a higher degree
of importance and specialization, and employ more workers,
while, with increasing mechanization of their vessels, the number
of actual fishermen will decline. It is unlikely, however, that this
process will reach the stage of western European and North
American countries, and this holds true, indeed, for all Asian
countries, and much of Africa and South America. Where
labour is cheap and relatively plentiful, but capital is short, it is
neither economically nor socially desirable to create a technically

*Plate VI.* CANNERY IN DOUARNENEZ, FRANCE. WORKERS SIT ALONG
CONVEYOR-BELTS

over-developed industry, which makes less than optimum use of the labour resources of the country, but burdens it with a high rate of capital repayment and interest. True technical progress does not necessarily lie for all countries in increasing mechanical complexity of the industry. There is an optimum degree of technical advance which must be related to the stage of social organization reached.

# CHAPTER IX

# FISHING COMMUNITIES AND PORTS

THE fisherman tends to have a number of attributes which distinguish him from the rest of his countrymen. This is true even in modern urban societies where mass-produced clothing, newspapers, radio programmes, and other influences have largely succeeded in standardizing the appearance, mannerisms, and idiom of the bulk of the workers, irrespective of their occupation. Most machine-minders and clerks do not differ essentially in outlook or mode of life, whether they work in textile mills, motor factories, or plants producing material for nuclear fission. The operations they perform, in the manipulation of levers, switches, or typewriters, are quite similar, even though directed to widely different ends: indeed, the relation of their duties to their ultimate product often appears to be vaguely understood by many industrial workers. After the day's work, the same spate of bicycles and small cars pours from the gates of innumerable plants on the instant of the hooter, with an urgency that belies the stereotyped nature of the evening to follow. Changes in the weather, unless it rains or becomes uncomfortably cold, are barely noticed, despite frequent references in casual conversation. Perhaps less than one town-dweller in ten is aware of the wind direction at a given moment.

On the other hand, the fisherman is not so effectively insulated from natural forces. From a third to three-quarters of his time is spent on the sea, and even when ashore he normally spends much of his leisure in the company of other fishermen. Changes in the weather are of immediate personal interest, as they closely affect the conditions and profitability of his work. When at sea each man's job is clearly related to a purpose. A bored coil winder in an electrical factory may well feel that one coil more or less will not affect anyone much, but a man handling a trawl net on to the deck knows that any slip may have serious consequences in loss of gear or catch, or injury to shipmates.

By its nature, fishing must be carried on by small groups of men, and personal relationships cannot be submerged to the extent they are in most modern industries. This personal aspect of the work in turn colours the life even of large fishing ports.

There is more scope for 'characters', who tend to be frequent in such communities. Fishing centres usually have an atmosphere that distinguishes them clearly from the usual urban settlement, and indeed from the normal commercial port. They are concerned with one of the few remaining industries which has its own distinctive idiom. It is true that in Britain many of the smaller fishing centres are predominantly holiday resorts, and some of the larger, such as Hull and Leith, are also important commercial ports, but in such places the fishing element still forms a community, often clearly limited geographically, usually within the older part of the town.

Even where this geographical homogeneity of the community has been broken up, there still remains a social homogeneity. Fishermen tend, to a greater degree than most occupational groups, to congregate in their own clubs, pubs, and other institutions. They cultivate a jargon which may be only partly comprehensible to the layman. Despite the fact that the fisherman is often temperamentally an individualist, he has an underlying sense of unity with other members of his occupation, of belonging to a group which is fairly sharply differentiated from the rest of society. There are, of course, other occupational groups which tend to isolate themselves in this manner; miners are a notable example. However, the fisherman differs markedly from the miner. Notwithstanding his strong sense of belonging to a group, his individualism has made him very much slower to acknowledge this by entering into formal organization. It is striking, for instance, that in Britain, where the trade union movement is perhaps the most developed in the world, there is no specifically 'Fishermen's Union'. The trawler fishermen's interests are among those of a comprehensive union, the Transport and General Workers, while employees in some important fisheries have little or no organization. Trawlermen's unionization has inevitably come as a result of the centralization of the bulk of their industry in the hands of large firms of owners, but fishermen do not appear to have been in the forefront of the trade union movement. In the same way, co-operatives of fishermen have made little progress in many countries, though government-sponsored co-operatives have been successful in some backward countries where they are essential to provide capital for modernization.

Fishermen generally are unimpressed by grand titles and conceptions, and are not very good soil for militant political faiths of any complexion. Although their work is hard, they rarely harbour for long any sense of persecution or grievance such as has been common among miners. This lack of mass movement and emotion is not solely a matter of temperament. There is, of course, the physical fact that the work demands that a considerable proportion of the fisherman's time must be spent away from the shore community, when he remains insulated from much social pressure and political argument. This effect is enhanced by the need to compress into his limited time in port activities that other men can spread over a longer period. The stay in port for a long-distance British trawlerman may only be three or four days in a month. There is thus little time left for the concerted thought and action needed for the development of large-scale economic or political movements.

A key point in evaluating the outlook of the fishermen of any country is the degree to which ownership of the boats is by the men who work them. Growth in the size of craft employed, as more complex gear is introduced, tends to lead to ownership by business organizations, and the gradual proletarianizing of the fishermen themselves. This is sometimes a definite factor in reducing the characteristic independence, initiative, and self-reliance of the fishermen. Its effects are, however, considerably modified by the common system of giving bonus shares to the crews in the proceeds of the catch, so that incentive to personal effort, and the sense of being directly concerned in the fortunes of the boat, is retained. This is the system generally prevalent in Britain. In other countries, such as Norway, the increased capital required for more expensive boats and gear has sometimes been raised by the formation of producers' co-operatives.

There are undoubtedly opportunities for such movements in many parts of the world, notably in the East. They can serve the twofold purpose of financing the fishermen and of marketing the catch on conditions more favourable to the fishermen than when they sell their catches individually. Because fish is a perishable commodity, a fisherman, with no reserves of capital, is inherently at a grave disadvantage when faced with a buyer, backed by ample capital, who may have a quasi-monopoly of the immediate channel of distribution, and can force down the price paid to the fisherman and retain an excessive part of the proceeds of the final sale. In the East this has led to the characteristic situation of fishermen being deeply in debt to the moneylenders, who may also be merchants. Since the war an interesting large-scale experiment has been encouraged by the government of Hong Kong, in the creation of a fishermen's co-operative, with good results in increase of income and general improvement of conditions and economic security.

The inshore fisherman, operating one small boat by himself, or with a small crew often drawn from his own family, has often been a difficult person to interest in co-operation or large-scale organization of any kind. He may only be induced to join, and surrender some of his personal economic sovereignty, when competition from the catches of more advanced craft is threatening his livelihood, and he is forced to look beyond his own resources for capital to modernize his methods. Organization of fishermen may take place again, not from a desire to modernize methods, but to meet on equal bargaining terms with buyers' monopolies or rings. The initiative in each case, however, may have to come from the government.

We may now consider the ways in which fishermen form settlements, and their detailed aspects of location, size, and degree of complexity. The location of a fishing port is strongly dependent on physical controls determined by the type of coastline, as was discussed in Chapter IV. A submergent coastline provides many suitable natural harbours, and often has many fishing settlements. If the region is mountainous, however, gaps permitting easy transport of the fish to the interior markets may be the main determining factor in the location of the port, unless it is mainly concerned with production for export. Norway, Iceland, and Newfoundland are the chief examples of coasts with poor inland communications which nevertheless have many fishing settlements. Alaska and British Columbia also have very poor inland communications, yet are important fishing areas, again mainly for export by sea to other regions. In Alaska, however, there are few true fishing settlements. The majority of them are fully occupied only during the fishing season, and are largely used by a transient population whose homes are in Seattle and other towns to the south. The mobile or temporary type of settlement is important in world fisheries, and will be discussed in more detail in this chapter.

The main geographical factors controlling the location, size, and type of fishing settlement are:

A. *Earth Features*

    1. Type of coastline, controlling the frequency, extent, and depth of natural harbours.

2. Nature of the land behind the coast, controlling the routes to interior markets.
3. Form of continental shelf, determining the extent of the adjacent fishing grounds for demersal and neritic (shallow water) pelagic fish, which are the most abundant and commercially important types.

B. *Water and Air Conditions*
   1. Conditions of sea temperature, currents and nutrients which determine the fertility of the area.
   2. Climate and weather conditions which may hinder fishing, or may particularly favour certain sites for ports.

C. *Human and Economic Influences*
   1. The density of population of the area, determining both the size of the adjacent market and the numbers available for fishing activities.
   2. The skill, enterprise, and organizing ability of the inhabitants.
   3. The availability of suitable fuel.

The factors listed in Group A and Group B 1 have already been discussed in their general effects in earlier chapters. In Group B 2 weather conditions are mentioned, and these are often of importance in the siting of ports. In areas of high onshore winds, the chief harbours tend to be on the lee side of an island or promontory with respect to these prevailing winds. Most of the main fishing centres of West Scotland and the Islands, for example, show this feature. They include Lerwick, Stornaway, Portree, Tobermory, and Campbeltown. Exposure to strong winds may, even in these days of powered craft, still render a place unsuitable for a fishing port, particularly if the type of fishing is that using small craft. Especially difficult are places where the winds and tidal currents are often in opposition, so creating steep, turbulent seas. Frequency of fog is another aspect of weather which bears on suitability of location for fishing ports. It is rare for prevalence of fog actually to prevent the development of fishing ports, but it has the effect of making certain sites particularly desirable, such as those with deep-water approaches free of obstructing reefs, rocks, and islands.

Of the more basic elements of climate, a long season of ice-blockage is the chief condition deterring growth of fishing ports, and has operated markedly along the north coasts of Eurasia and North America. It should be noted that, whereas the sea itself may remain open for fishing, the shore may be blocked by ice, particularly the otherwise best sites for ports in such areas, the estuaries of rivers. The higher freezing-point of fresh water, the greater loss of heat from the land mass, and the piling up of ice in bays by wind and current, all combine to make these coasts unsuitable as ports. The development of large modern ice-breakers, particularly by the Russians, has made it possible to shorten the ice-blocked season greatly in some ports such as Archangel, but these are primarily large commercial ports which can afford the cost. This would not be economic for the normal fishing settlement.

The important fishing areas of Labrador, East and West Greenland, Bear Island, and South Spitsbergen therefore possess no substantial fishing settlement. The large-scale fishing is all done by vessels based on St John's, Lisbon, Hull, Grimsby, Fleetwood, and other such towns. In northern Norway and North-west Russia the residue of the warm North Atlantic Drift enables ports such as Tromsö, Hammerfest, Pechenga, and Murmansk to remain open, but farther east all the coasts and the seas themselves remain blocked for a considerable season. The recent improvement in northern climate seems just to have passed a critical point at which the outer Arctic seas have become less completely blocked by ice, so that the North-East and North-West Passages have been completed by Russian and Canadian vessels, though at very slow and uneconomic speeds. For commercial fishing purposes, however, where unrestricted movement is essential, these passages are of small significance, and possibly quite well stocked Arctic areas remain the preserve of the sparse populations of native subsistence fishermen.

The physical controls we have listed may not, of course, be considered in great detail by a primitive community when it first sets up a fishing settlement. What is more likely is that a number of settlements will start, some in good and some in bad places. As the fishery develops, the size of craft increases, and the general demands of the fishery become more critical. Unsuitable sites are then eliminated by a process of natural selection, because of the more successful competition from the better ones. Their inhabitants must either give up fishing or migrate to a better port. The process may take a long time because of the conservative nature of fishermen. Those in unfavourable circumstances may continue where they are by concentrating on work such as inshore shell-fishing, for which the disadvantage of their port is not great, or they may develop additional sources of income, particularly from holiday-makers. This has happened in many parts of Britain, especially along the south coast.

This leads us to a study of the human influences in fishing port development. The density of population in a region is important. It is obviously the most convenient, though not necessarily the only, market. In some major fishing areas it may even be almost insignificant, as in Iceland and Newfoundland. We can say, however, that although a fishery may develop without a large local market, the presence of such a market ensures development when it might otherwise not take place. In discussing the size of the market we are naturally referring to the effective market; that is, one to which there are adequate communications, and which has purchasing power to satisfy its needs. The effective market provided by a million Londoners will differ very greatly, for example, from that provided by a million Bengalis, in weight, and still more in value.

The density of population also affects the numbers available to man a fishing industry and its ancillaries, although the proportion available will vary greatly according to the counter-attractions of the other resources of the region. In Argentina a history of relatively cheap land and expanding markets for its produce has led to the neglect of a large fishery resource; in Norway poor land has forced interest to the sea, and the development of the world's greatest fish-exporting economy.

Degree of maritime skill also varies widely between regions, due partly to innate racial aptitudes, partly to influences of environment. The coast dwellers of much of India, despite their long contact with the sea, have not evolved a particularly large sea-fishing industry, and their methods are still backward.

Maritime skill and enterprise, however, are not the only kind of human ability important in fishery growth. In modern fisheries large-scale financial organizing abilities are needed. These can only flourish in a country in a generally advanced state of capital and technical resources. The great technical development and complexity of British fisheries is the maritime projection of the general industrial development of the past century and a half. Conversely, there are no large modern fishing industries based on otherwise backward countries. Growth and modernization of Asian fisheries, outside Japan, cannot take place on a large scale in the absence of an industrial base to sustain it. India is slowly creating such a base, and China is belatedly trying to force the pace, with what sustained progress can hardly yet be assessed. The broad truth of the above principle is, of course, not invalidated by occasional 'show pieces' in the way of modern craft or canning plants, which represent only a small fraction of the total industry.

One important feature of increasing technical advance and capitalization is increasing centralization of the industry in fewer and larger ports, as we have already mentioned. This might be formulated as 'the principle of cumulative growth of the best sited fishing ports'. There is a certain critical utility of site. Ports above this tend to grow, ports below it to decay. In the most primitive areas this level is at its lowest, so that practically all sites can continue successfully because they serve only their immediate neighbourhood and suffer no competition from others. Hence the typical distribution of ports in such areas: a string of small settlements. As technique advances, and as transport facilities improve in the land behind, differentiation of the suitability of sites becomes more marked. Some prove too shallow for the larger craft evolved. Others lack land suitable for buildings for storage and curing. Some are too far from larger inland markets which could furnish the profits to enable expansion. So the critical utility rises, and ports below this decay. Fish landings, therefore, must be canalized through fewer ports, whose size increases. As technique advances still more, the critical utility rises further, and the bulk of the trade, which is growing in total amount, is gathered by the increasingly fewer ports that remain above this level.

The process is cumulative because the bigger ports are at an advantage over the smaller in attracting further capital and man-power. They have a higher degree of organization, a greater reputation, and a greater industrial and social capital on which to base new enterprises. The process continues until each marketing region is dominated by a major port, although there may be a number of ancillaries for specialized purposes, and a number of decaying ones developing other non-fishing industries. The size of the marketing region dominated by a port will be the larger, the better the inland transport system. At their edges regions will overlap, and indeed for specialized types of fish one port may dominate several marketing regions. For this reason there is small point in attempting to define precisely the limits of a port's marketing region, although the limits within which the bulk of the fish sold come from a given port can be drawn quite easily. The limit between two regions will lie along points at which the cost of similar fish is the same from both ports, after inland transport charges. This economic line may be distorted in detail by institutional factors, such as bulk-buying from one port by a chain of retail shops which overlaps the limit, but the general principles must in general be followed if there is to be economic distribution.

In a small, densely populated country, with good rail communications, we may thus expect only one main fishing port, such as Ostend for Belgium. In Britain, larger in area, we have but a few. The large fishing ports are sited on good positions for deep-water harbours, and approximately on lines drawn between their main industrial conurbation market and their chief fishing grounds. There are two ports landing over ten million pounds' worth of fish per average year, another two landing over four million, while no other port approaches anything like these figures.

The annual initial values (which are considerably increased after packing, transport, wholesaling, and retailing) of landings at those British ports landing over £500,000 worth are tabled below. English figures are for 1951, Scottish for 1948.

|                | £          |
| -------------- | ---------- |
| Hull           | 11,700,000 |
| Grimsby        | 10,600,000 |
| Aberdeen       | 4,580,000  |
| Fleetwood      | 4,290,000  |
| Milford Haven  | 1,990,000  |
| Lowestoft      | 1,890,000  |
| Leith          | 1,860,000  |
| North Shields  | 1,070,000  |
| Fraserburgh    | 890,000    |
| Peterhead      | 780,000    |
| Yarmouth       | 680,000    |

Hull, Grimsby, Aberdeen, and Fleetwood provide about 67 per cent of the total British catch, and the remainder is shared by some 130 other fishing stations. The dominance of the large ports is evident.

Hull and Grimsby are the chief channels between the northern fishing grounds of the Barents Sea, Iceland, Bear Island, and Greenland, together with the adjacent North Sea, and the West Riding, East Midlands, and south-eastern England. Fleetwood is the chief channel between the northern grounds and the

Lancashire and North-west Midlands conurbations. Milford Haven dominates the South Wales area of dense population. Lowestoft and Yarmouth lie between the southern North Sea and London. North Shields supplies the densely populated area of the Northumberland-Durham coalfield. Aberdeen, Fraserburgh, and Peterhead lie between the northern fishing grounds, together with the nearer grounds of the northern North Sea, and the densely populated Midland Valley of Scotland, while Leith is sited within it.

There are, as we have mentioned, overlaps of hinterland, and certain types of fish found especially in waters near a certain port may be sent far into other regions. For example, Yarmouth and Lowestoft have an enormous catch of herring in their near waters in the autumn, and supply much of the country. Milford Haven and Fleetwood dominate the hake market of England and Wales because these fish are quite abundant on the shelf to the west and south-west of Britain, but sparse to the north and east.

It might be considered that Hull and Grimsby are too close together for the best spacing of large ports to serve the country. This is certainly a valid contention. If, instead of Grimsby, there was an equal fishing port farther south, perhaps on the Thames estuary, inland transport costs of the bulk of the fish eaten in the south-east could be reduced. The presence of Hull and Grimsby so close together does not disprove our theory of the forces operating to develop a number of large ports, each supreme in one region. The basic tendency is there, but other forces may sometimes modify it. In this case a purely human factor, the especial enterprise of municipal authorities, merchants, and fishermen of both Hull and Grimsby, enhanced by a local rivalry, has maintained the expansion of both Hull and Grimsby, whereas in most circumstances one or the other would have become dominant. It must also be noted that, from the point of view of inland transport, Grimsby and Hull are much farther apart than appears at first sight, as the Humber is not bridged below Goole. There is thus less overlap of hinterland than there seems. North of the Humber, Hull has a marked advantage over Grimsby, and vice versa.

The lack of a first-rank fishing port on the Thames estuary can be explained partly by the large tidal flats along much of the shores of the lower estuary, making the construction of any major fishing outport for London an expensive undertaking.

There is further the congestion of shipping in the Thames channels, already considerable, and which might become severe if a large fishing fleet were added to the regular traffic. It was chiefly this congestion, together with the demand for waterfront space by shipping and other interests able to pay more than the fishing industry, that caused the decay of the once flourishing fishing bases along the Thames.

Again, the advent of steam power for fishing vessels naturally tended to favour the development of ports near to coalfields. The higher price of coal fuel in the southern English fishing ports was an important factor retarding their rate of conversion to power. Brixham, and other ports far from coalfields, retained substantial sailing fleets for many years after the northern ports had converted to steam. The relative decline of the south coast ports was partly due to their lower catching power than the northern ports, whose bigger output enabled them to offer lower prices and so expand sales still more: a cumulative process.

Hence the south coast ports generally retained sail until they converted to internal combustion engines in the early part of the century. The advent of this form of power has to some extent neutralized the advantages of the big northern English ports as regards fuel, but the trawlers still cling to steam. Of more immediate significance is the introduction of oil-fired steam boilers. Nevertheless, Hull, Grimsby, and Fleetwood have already reaped the reward of a siting near sources of coal; industrial momentum will help them to maintain their dominance. The internal combustion engine may help to retard further centralization in certain areas of this country, but its main effects in this respect are in areas abroad which were slow to adopt the steam engine for fishing.

One further point must be considered regarding the siting of fishing ports. While it is true that the port should not be far from its hinterland, because the cost of inland transport is much above that of sea transport, it also remains true that fish is perishable. For good-quality fish, therefore, a shortening of the sea journey and the transference of the fish to fast rail or road transport is advisable. London is on the whole a wealthy market, and can afford to pay rather more for its fish to cover the cost of such fast rail freight.

The centre of effort of the British fishing industry lies north of the country. It is therefore to be expected that the main fishing ports lie to the north of the centre of population. If there were

*Plate VII.* AIR VIEW OF A FISH PIER AT BOSTON. THE BUILDING AT THE NEAR END IS THE AUCTION MARKET; OTHERS CONTAIN OFFICES AND PROCESSING PLANT; RAILWAY SIDINGS LIE CLOSE BEHIND

not such a good inland transport system this could not be the case, and the London area would be served, as it once was, by nearby ports. The system of fast, ice-cooled fish trains and long-distance lorries further enables such ports as Aberdeen to flourish despite their large production in a relatively sparsely populated region, by sending their supplies, particularly of certain specialized species, to distant populous markets. From the point of view of good-quality fish from northern grounds, Aberdeen actually has an advantage over Grimsby in the London market. Fish going from, say, the Faeroe grounds by trawler to Aberdeen at 9 knots, and thence by rail to London at an average speed of about 30 m.p.h., would reach Billingsgate in some sixty hours, excluding unloading time, whereas the same fish going at the same speed via Grimsby would take over eighty hours. Needless to say, the cost of the fresher Aberdeen fish would be more.

The good rail and road communications along the coast plain of eastern Scotland have sustained its fishing ports in competition with those farther south. The west coast of Scotland, on the other hand, with on the whole poor communications, has not developed like the east coast, and has a total landed value of under a fifth of that of the east.

The siting and growth of fishing ports will thus be seen to be the product of complex, often conflicting forces, and too ready explanations may prove wrong. A physically suitable site that is well placed both in regard to markets and fishing grounds should develop well, but there are also places where, due to unusual enterprise, or by concentration on types of fish that can stand the cost of longer inland transport, development has occurred in less favourable locations.

In considering the various types of fishing port or settlement we may distinguish five main categories. There are, of course, border-line cases, but the classification still serves as a criterion for comparative study. While we are not attempting here to list and classify the very great number of ports and settlements in the world, some representative examples are given in each category.

*Major Comprehensive Ports.* These may be defined as fulfilling the following requirements. The annual landings must, of course, be large, but it is difficult to state a precise figure because of variations in local conditions of value-to-bulk, tonnage of craft required for a given catch, and so on. The minimum figure for this category would be of the order of 70,000 tons per year. This is little more than a quarter of that of Hull in a typical year, but is still a great figure, enough to provide about seven million people with a moderate consumption of fish by western European standards. A major comprehensive port should also provide full facilities for unloading large trawlers or other vessels used in its fisheries, and for supplying all the requirements necessary to maintain these ships in seagoing order. Normally it will also provide full ship-repairing and even shipbuilding facilities. These are not essential to our definition, so long as the port provides running repairs and has a shipbuilding centre reasonably close. Such a port will also command a first-rate transport network to inland markets, by fast goods train, road, and in some cases also by inland waterway for the less perishable products. This transport criterion is an essential one, and such major ports are found only in or near to areas of dense population, providing the large market which has brought them into being.

Ports of this type will normally have an array of curing, canning, meal, fertilizer, and other processing factories, but we cannot make the employment of a large number of workers in these an essential criterion, because some such ports may have as their primary aim the dispatch of fresh fish.

Examples of major comprehensive fishing ports are Hull, Grimsby (see Fig. 40), Aberdeen, and Fleetwood in Britain; Geestemünde, Hamburg-Altona, and Cuxhaven in Germany; Boulogne in France; and Boston, U.S.A. (Plate VII). The fish and cargo docks are usually clearly separated. The major modern fishing port has, however, sometimes found a large cargo port to be a valuable close neighbour, because of its command of fast rail and other routes to interior areas of dense industrial population. The fishing port will thus tend to serve mainly, though not entirely, the hinterland of the cargo port. Fishing activities of certain cargo ports have thus expanded in recent times, while other fishing ports without their good rail communications have languished. The economic advantage of the cargo-*cum*-fishing port is not limited to transport. Large modern fishing craft have many needs in common with cargo vessels, for fuel and equipment, while there is some interchange of crews between the two kinds of ship. Hence there are economies of scale in combining the supply of the various requirements in one place.

There are exceptions; there are many large cargo ports, such as London and Liverpool, which do not have fishing activities because congestion in the approach channels and docks would

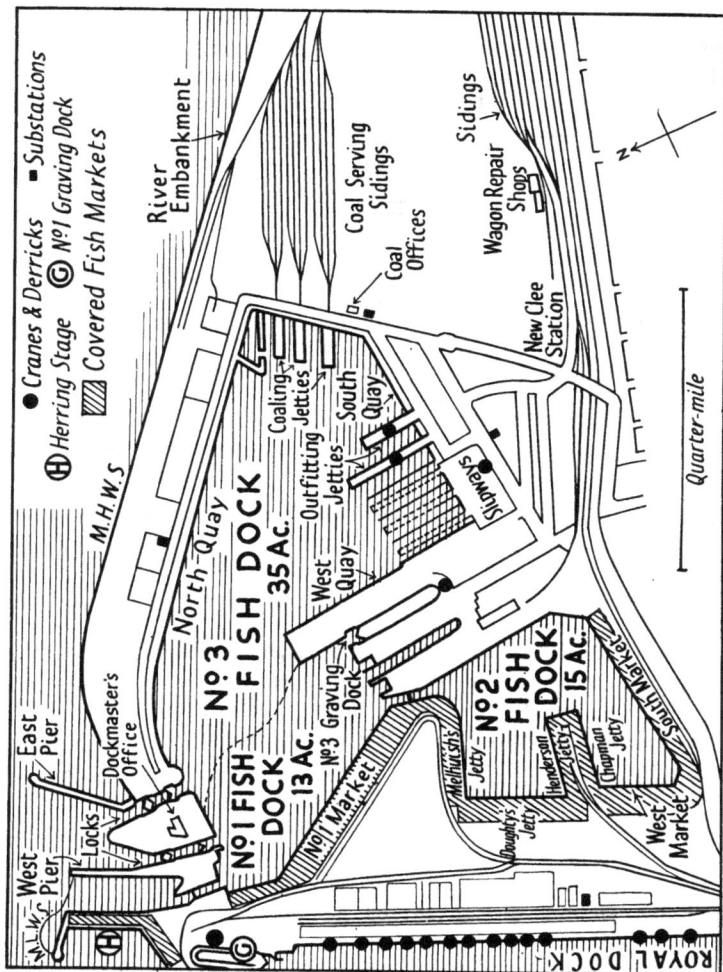

*Fig. 40.* Grimsby fish docks. The chief railway lines are indicated, but the number of tracks is considerably more than is shown

Labels within the figure:

● *Cranes & Derricks* ■ *Substations*
Ⓗ *Herring Stage* Ⓒ *Nº1 Graving Dock*
▨ *Covered Fish Markets*

River Embankment

Coal Serving Sidings

Coal Offices

Sidings

Wagon Repair Shops

New Clee Station

*Quarter-mile*

M.H.W.S

North Quay

No 3 FISH DOCK
35 Ac.

Coaling Jetties

Outfitting Jetties

South Quay

West Quay

Sidings

No 1 FISH DOCK
13 Ac.

Nº3 Graving Dock

Nº1 Market

Melhuish's Jetty

Doughty's Jetty

Henderson Jetty

Chapman Jetty

No 2 FISH DOCK
15 Ac.

South Market

West Market

East Pier

Dockmaster's Office

West Pier

Locks

M.L.W.S

ROYAL DOCK

II

be too great, and there are major fishing ports like Fleetwood whose cargo activities are small. (Fleetwood operates an Irish Sea passenger service, but these vessels operate from wharves outside the docks.) It may be noted, however, that Fleetwood is significantly close to Liverpool, and serves particularly the hinterland of Liverpool.

*Fishing Entrepôts.* This term is perhaps the best to describe those fishing ports which do not handle the ultimate dispatch to market, but are essentially points of bulk transhipment from

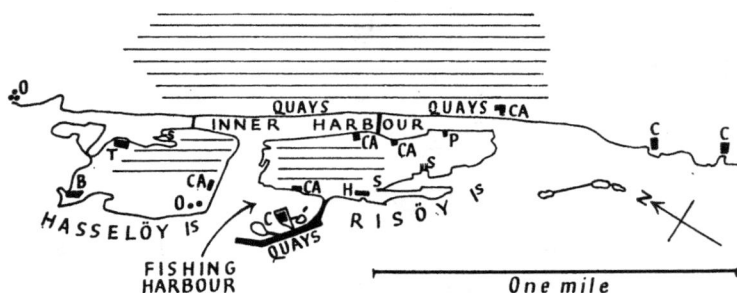

*Fig. 41.* Haugesund, Norway

≡≡≡ Approximate extent of built-up areas. B. Barrel factory. C. Coal store. CA. Cannery. H. Herring oil plant. O. Oil fuel tanks. P. Packing case factory. S. Slipways and repair facilities. T. Tin can factory. There is no railway

fishing vessels to cargo vessels, which then take them to cargo ports for final distribution. In the course of transhipment the fish may undergo various degrees of processing, and some fishing entrepôts may therefore employ a substantial number of workers. Nevertheless, they differ from the comprehensive port in their inadequacy of inland distribution channels, with their attendant railway marshalling yards, and so on.

Fishing entrepôts are usually good harbours located near fishing grounds in sparsely populated regions, whose main markets are overseas or in distant parts of their country with which they are connected wholly or mainly by sea transport. Their annual tonnage of catch may sometimes be of the same order as that of major comprehensive ports. Their populations, however, are usually fairly small.

Norway has many such ports. Typical examples are Svolvaer, the chief port of the Lofotens, Tromsö, Kristiansund, and Haugesund, of which some features are shown in Fig. 41. The main ports in Iceland and Newfoundland also come into this

*Plate VIII.* PART OF LORIENT FISHING HARBOUR

category. Britain, with its large inland markets and transport network, naturally has few examples, although Lerwick in the Shetlands is quite a good one.

*Full-scale Ports*. This term may be used for those ports offering a fair range of facilities to medium- or large-sized vessels for unloading and supplying with essentials, and having adequate inland transport channels for their size. Their tonnage of landings may lie within a wide range, from about 5,000 tons to 70,000 tons a year. In many such ports the interests may centre mainly on one species, and the dock or harbour facilities may be limited to those needed by a more or less standardized size and type of craft, though this is by no means always the case. Examples of full-scale ports are Yarmouth, whose large annual landings of about 33,000 tons (1951) are almost entirely of herring; Milford Haven, the chief Welsh fishing port, with landings of a wider variety, though dominated by hake; and Leith, the largest fishing port within the densely populated Midland Valley of Scotland. In the advanced countries there is a considerable number of such ports. In France, for example, we might quote Dieppe, Fécamp, Lorient (Plate VIII), and La Rochelle; in Belgium, Ostend, which handles the bulk of its country's landings; in Holland, Ijmuiden; in Denmark, Skagen and Esbjerg.

*Minor Ports*. These are found in large numbers in countries of moderate fishing advancement. In more advanced countries they are tending to decay because of their lack of adequate facilities for handling of modern craft, or of good communications with interior markets, or merely because they lack the economic advantages of large-scale operation. As the process of decline of the fishing activities is relatively slow, hardship is usually avoided by a shift of the disposition of the town's labour force. The older men continue fishing, the younger ones either join vessels of a nearby large port or turn to other industries. Often the village or small town will develop into a holiday resort with hotel, catering and entertainment businesses taking the place of fishing as the chief employment. The chief difficulty is in the seasonal nature of this work, though if it dovetails with winter fishing it may help to maintain the fishing industry in being, because the fishing no longer has to bear the expense of supporting the population throughout the year.

In Britain there are still a good number of places worthy of mention as minor fishing ports, though in nearly all cases fishing does not employ, either directly or indirectly, more than a small proportion of their populations. To rank as a minor fishing port we may say the qualifications to be the possession of a small harbour, jetty, wharf, or other suitable unloading place, and to have a few small craft in more or less continuous employment catching a total of over £5,000 initial landed worth of fish a year. On the east coast of England alone there are over thirty such places. On the Mediterranean coasts such small fishing villages produce a substantial proportion of their countries' catches, while in many areas of Asia, Africa, and South America they produce the bulk of the catch.

At the lower end of the scale in these continents such ports fade into small settlements thinly but fairly evenly spread over the length of a coast. They may offer nothing in the way of port facilities save a suitable beach for hauling up craft, and little in the way of transport facilities to marketing areas, which may be confined to a few miles radius from them. At this stage we can hardly speak of 'ports', yet such settlements cannot be dismissed when they may form the chief means of landing fish in their region. Provision of better port facilities, to take larger and perhaps motorized craft, is one of the essential requisites of increased fishing production in many parts of the world.

*Mobile or Temporary Settlements.* Those form a special case, but one which logically should be mentioned as a port category, as they exist to fulfil some or all of the functions of ports. Mobile ports or mother ships are used in areas where sparse settlement or generally inhospitable nature of the coasts near the fishery makes it more convenient to keep the port facilities afloat. Such vessels will perform the duties of a port in conveying stores and fuel for the catching vessels or coastal trapping installations, in receiving, processing, and storing their catches, and ultimately transporting these to market, and acting as a centre of administrative, recreational, and medical services for the crews of the dependent craft, and in some cases as their living quarters. The mother-ship system lends itself particularly well to seasonal fishing, where the fishery may last only a few months out of a year, so that the overhead expense of keeping a shore settlement going for the rest of the year would be high. The mother ship can return to her home port during the off-season, and her crew be discharged. The whaling factory ships of Britain, Norway, U.S.A., and Japan in the sub-Antarctic are examples of this method, as are the Russian and Japanese salmon and crab cannery ships operating in the Sea of Okhotsk and Bering Sea.

Temporary shore settlements are another solution of the problem of the seasonal fishery in an out-of-the-way area, and are nowadays chiefly confined to areas where the bulk of the catch is obtained close to land or in rivers. Such is particularly the case with the salmon fisheries of Alaska. There are a number of small nucleus settlements along the south coast of Alaska, inhabited throughout the year, together with many cannery stations which are practically deserted out of season. For the summer and autumn seasons, when various types of salmon make their spawning runs into the rivers, thousands of men and great quantities of cans and other equipment are shipped up to these settlements and canneries from Seattle and other bases to the south. At the end of the season these return home again.

As an area becomes more developed, especially if so in ways other than fisheries, temporary settlements may ultimately become permanent ones, as happened long ago, for example, in the case of Newfoundland. The permanent population of Alaska is steadily increasing, with the development of mining, military establishments, forestry, and even some agriculture. Gradually, therefore, an increasing proportion of the labour, materials, and services required by the salmon canning industry may be supplied locally, and seasonal movements decline while the permanent settlements grow in importance. It seems likely, however, that some seasonal migrations to supply the peak labour needs during the season will continue indefinitely. Man is here dictated to by the salmon.

In this chapter we have been considering a traditional form of human settlement: one that in many areas may be the oldest of any. Changes of techniques have rarely brought sudden upheavals and shifts as in some other industries, and this state of affairs is likely to continue. The essential features of relationship of the port to its markets and its fishing grounds are fixed.

## SOME BOOKS AND PERIODICALS DEALING WITH SUBJECTS TREATED IN THIS SECTION

*Fishing Boats of the World.* An F.A.O. symposium. (Heighway Publications, London, 1955.)

*Fishing in Many Waters.* James Hornell. (Cambridge Univ. Press, 1950.)

*Sea Food Ships.* A. C. Hardy. (Crosby Lockwood, London, 1947.)

*Mast and Sail in Europe and Asia.* H. Warington Smyth. (Blackwood, Edinburgh, 1929.)

*British Fishing Boats and Coastal Craft: A Historical Survey.* E. W. White. (Science Museum, London, 1950.)

*An Account of the Fishing Gear of England and Wales.* F. M. Davis. (Fishery Investigations, Series II, vol. xv, No. 1, London, 1937.)

*Fishermen and Fishing Ways.* P. F. Anson. (Harrap, London.)

*The Quest of the Schooner 'Argus'.* Alan Villiers. (Hodder and Stoughton, London, 1951.)

*Marine Products of Commerce.* D. K. Tressler. (Chemical Catalog Co., New York, 1923.)

*Fish and Fish Inspection.* John D. Syme. (H. K. Lewis, London, 1949.)

*Salted Cod and Related Species.* (F.A.O., Rome, 1949.)

*The Technology of Herring Utilisation.* Ed. Mogens Jul. (F.A.O., Rome, 1935.)

*The Freezing and Cold Storage of Fish.* (D.S.I.R., London, 1950.)

*The Care of the Trawler's Fish.* (D.S.I.R., London, 1949.)

*Conditions of Work in the Fishing Industry.* International Labour Office, Geneva, 1952. A digest of data submitted by member governments.

The following English language publications are among those regularly having articles on fishing and processing techniques.

*World Fisheries Abstracts.* (F.A.O., Rome, approx. bi-monthly.)

*Fisheries Bulletins.* (F.A.O., Rome, approx. bi-monthly.)

*World Fishing.* (London, monthly.)

*The Fishing News.* (London, weekly.)

*World Fisheries Yearbook.* (Continental Trade Press, London.)

*Canadian Fisherman.* (Gardenvale, Quebec, monthly.)

*Fishing Gazette.* (New York, monthly.)

*Commercial Fisheries Review,* and

*Commercial Fisheries Abstracts.*

(Monthly periodicals of the Fish and Wild Life Service, U.S. Department of the Interior, Washington.)

*World Fish Trade.* (Copenhagen, monthly.)

*International Fish and Other Food Journal.* (Copenhagen, monthly.)

Further periodicals are listed after some regional chapters.

*Section III*

# FISHERIES OF
# THE WORLD'S REGIONS

# CHAPTER X

# STANDARDS FOR COMPARATIVE STUDY

A BASIS for comparison of the fisheries of various regions is not easy to develop, for the detailed variations in type and structure of fisheries are infinite. Nevertheless, some clear criteria are valuable in helping to reduce a mass of statistics to useful form. No single standard, such as production total, production efficiency, and so on, is adequate, for these do not vary in the same manner. A low efficiency area may yet be extremely important in total production, while an area using advanced methods may be of but minor importance. Again, matters of consumption and trade must obviously be considered in the assessment of a fishery. In evolving suitable criteria it is possible to fall into the errors both of over-simplification, using only one aspect as the basis for comparison between regions, and of over-diversification, taking so many aspects that an appreciation of the relative importance of a number of fisheries becomes blurred.

It is therefore considered that the criteria discussed below give, when taken together, the essential basis for broad evaluation of the fishing economy of a region and for comparison with others, and they will be used frequently in the regional discussions in the chapters to follow.

The first major criterion by which a fishing region can be judged is its stage of technical development in terms of craft, gear, processing methods, degree of use of available sea resources, and so on. Such a criterion cannot be measured in any one simple way, and hence cannot be defined even approximately by mathematical means as can the other standards mentioned below. For practical purposes, however, it is usually fairly easy to judge whether a region uses mainly 'primitive' or mainly 'advanced' methods, once all the relevant information has been collected. It is often less easy to estimate the degree to which the region is making use of its available resources. In many areas these are not fully known, and no really accurate method of testing an area in microcosm has yet been evolved. The only satisfactory test of resources is that by large-scale fishing itself. Nevertheless, accurate methods of assessing the resources of an area are not necessary in order to state whether it is being over-fished: this is proved ultimately by declining total catch. A sub-optimum use of resources, on the other hand, is revealed by a rate of catch that trends markedly upwards as more advanced methods are brought into operation, or, alternatively, a total catch that rises roughly proportionately as more craft of the same standard are put into operation.

The actual efficiency of catching methods may be indicated in such terms as the production per fisherman per year, per ton of craft per year, or per average ton-hour of fishing. While these are valuable standards and give clear figures, they must be used with caution, for none of them, taken alone, tells the whole story. They may be very useful for comparison between two regions using similar techniques under more or less similar conditions, but may be misleading if applied to widely different areas. Inefficient fishermen may yet produce good figures on grounds with plentiful fish. Again, production per man per year may be low in one place which uses methods demanding plenty of labour but little equipment, and high in another which uses little labour but much expensive equipment. Each may have economically the best method for the local conditions of labour supply, degree of industrialization, and so on. The extra equipment of the more mechanized region is in any case itself a demander of labour not included in the total of fishermen. Despite the above qualifications, output per fisherman per year remains a good general guide to the degree of technical advancement of a region, and will often be used here.

The next criterion is total production. This indicates the general world status of the region in terms of fishery importance, but of course gives little indication of the actual importance of the region's fisheries to individual inhabitants, or of the intensity of fishing activity. Statistics of total production are now compiled by a large number of countries, but need caution in use for comparative purposes. It is important to check, for example, the type of weight or bulk unit used, and make sure that it is used uniformly for all types of fish at the same stage of processing. Statistics for some fish may be published of weight on catching, for others of weight after heading, or when dried. Again, some figures may be marked underestimates, particularly in primitive areas of many scattered fishing hamlets where proper checking is impossible. There may also be delayed and infrequent publication of data by several countries, so that study of current trends is difficult.

For estimation of total production, weight is a better standard than value. It is, of course, open to the objection that not all fish are of the same quality or value, so that areas producing mainly high-value fish, such as most flatfish, are underestimated by comparison with areas mainly producing such fish as herring. This is true, but most regions in practice produce a composite of high-and low-value fish. In any case, the question of value can always be considered when a detailed local analysis is made. For world comparison, weight is a far more reliable guide. Value depends not only on the fishing industry but on economic tendencies only remotely connected with it. Indeed, the use of value as a comparative standard, in these days of near-autonomous national currencies whose conversion value is often determined more by arbitrary government action than by the operation of a free market, is liable to be grossly misleading. For instance, general inflationary tendencies on one country will raise its fish prices and hence the nominal value of its· output as compared with other countries, because its currency rates of exchange remain fixed by its government. Yet in reality its production remains unchanged both in quantity and quality. One is forced to the conclusion that total tonnage of fish 'in the round' (i.e. before any form of processing) is the only feasible unit for broad comparative study of production, so long as its limitations are borne in mind.

Having learned the total production of a country or region and seen its relative importance as compared with other areas, the next requirement is to determine the importance of the country's fisheries to its own economy. Fishery employment as a percentage of the total employment in all the country's industries could be used, but this is in some respects misleading for comparative studies, unless general *per capita* output and the degree of mechanization are roughly the same in the regions under consideration. This is frequently not the case. Value of fishery products in relation to value of the total output of all the country's industries is another standard. While theoretically very good, it is not always easy to apply in practice save in countries which produce detailed and accurate statistics of production and trade, making clear whether their figures refer to value on production, on wholesaling, or on retailing. As we are here concerned with criteria to be valid for most of the world's countries, whether advanced or backward, it will be seen that relative value is not generally suitable. The best and most easily applied broad criterion of the importance of a country's fisheries to it as a source of real wealth in terms of food and/or exports (and thus of imports of other goods) is in production per head of total population. This may be termed the 'production rate' and quoted in terms of kilograms per head per year.

Export and import figures should next be studied. Both value and quantity are worthy of note, as in foreign trade the value/weight ratio may vary greatly between, say, salt cod and canned salmon. In comparing quantities exported with quantities landed it should also be noted in what form the fish is when weighed, for when headed, gutted, filleted, and processed it may weigh well under half what it did in 'round' weight.

From the figures of total production, exports and imports when corrected approximately for loss of weight in processing, and the total population, may be calculated the approximate consumption rate per head in terms of original round weight. This is the best uniform standard for comparisons between regions. Dried fish recover much of their original weight on soaking in water during cooking. Consumption rate, in kilograms per head of total population per year, gives the importance of fish in a region's diet in absolute terms, while its relative importance can be judged from the region's general level of total food consumption.

Total production, production rate, consumption rate, net export or import figures relative to total production, and production per fisherman give together a quite easily appreciated picture of the essential regional characteristics. One can refer, for instance, to Norway as an advanced country of high total production, high production rate, high consumption rate, and high export ratio. India can be summarized as a country of technically backward methods but fairly high total production, and of low production and consumption rates.

The table below shows the fish and shellfish landings and exports of those countries which may particularly be classed as 'high exporters'. Their exports of fish products are large, over 100,000 tons, and form a substantial proportion of the landings. These exports are also an important (and in the case of Iceland, a dominant) element in the countries' total exports. It should be noted that catches are given for fish 'in the round' whereas exports include processed fish, and are therefore underweighted. Conversion to appropriate round weights has not been attempted, as conversion ratios are approximate, and would not be uniformly accurate for the products of the various countries. Norway's exports are an approximate figure after the deduction from her total of the estimated quantity of all mammal products.

TONNAGE FOR 1951

|  | Catches | Exports |
|---|---|---|
| Norway | 1,819,000 | 500,000 |
| Canada | 948,000 | 315,000 |
| Iceland | 418,000 | 208,000 |
| Holland | 280,000 | 144,000 |
| Denmark | 292,000 | 126,000 |

The U.S.A. exported 127,000 tons in 1951, but this was a small figure in proportion to its total catch. Furthermore, its fish imports, at 448,000 tons, greatly outweighed exports, so that fisheries products did not on balance help to pay for imports of other goods.

The majority of countries are neither high exporters nor (save for those with no seaboard) high importers of fishery products. This is primarily because of the universal nature of the sea's resources. These differ quite considerably from region to region, but nevertheless are still adequate in most areas to supply the present consumption of the neighbouring lands. Further, until fairly recently the only means of large-scale preservation of fish were drying, salting, pickling, and smoking, which produced normally low-value products. Canned fish, on the other hand, have mainly been in the semi-luxury class, and so also have not developed a very large value of trade. It is generally to be expected that, barring international currency problems, the long-term trend of world trade in fish will be upwards. There may be a development on long-distance routes of vessels for carrying, at low temperature, fish which were quick-frozen on board the catching craft. Distribution of fresh fish by air on a large scale is also a possibility.

The regional studies to follow will chiefly concern themselves with the essential contributions of the fisheries to their regional economies. Detailed study of the fisheries region by region is obviously beyond the scope of a single work; many fisheries are worthy of a book to themselves. Every region will, however, be considered from a comparative viewpoint in regard to its physical basis and the use it has made of its resources.

The chapters each deal with a continental area, for convenience in treatment. These in turn have been divided into the true regions within which fishery conditions are broadly similar, having regard both to physical and human factors.

There is, of course, some overlapping even between the continental areas, as in the case of European fishing off Newfoundland and Greenland. Realities never make too tidy a picture, and this is perhaps more the case with fisheries than with land industries.

*Note.* **1951 or 1952 are the most frequently used recent years for quoting catches in the following chapters, to permit international comparison. At the time of writing the book these were the latest years for which world figures collated by the U.N. Food and Agriculture Organization were available. While the book was in the press, statistics for 1953 have been published, and the catches for that year of most countries are therefore tabled in the Appendix.**

*Plate IX.* FISHING-BOAT OF TRENGGANU, MALAYA

# CHAPTER XI

# ASIAN REGIONS

ASIA has the largest fisheries output of any continent. At present it is computed at 13,000,000 tons per year, compared with about 8,250,000 for Europe and 3,400,000 for North America. This great output, almost exactly half the world's estimated total, is impressive when one considers that the bulk of it is obtained by small-scale and often primitive methods. It serves to emphasize a significant way in which fishing differs from most other economic activities, both agricultural and manufacturing. Until means have been perfected by which man can significantly increase the total biological output of the seas, improvement of technique does not have an effect comparable to its achievement in some other fields. If the catching power of an old-established fishery is doubled by new equipment, it may catch something approaching double its old catch for the first season, but after that the catches are likely to decline until ultimately total catches may be little above the original amount, if not below it. The exact level of stabilization depends on many factors, such as the rate of growth and sexual maturing of the fish, the period in youth when they may be absent from the catching areas, and so on. Nevertheless, the general proposition of decreasing returns holds true.

This is not to say that new methods are a waste of effort. They may reduce the costs of production of the industry, and they may improve working conditions. Where a fishery was previously catching below its optimum amount, they may permanently raise total output, so long as their use is controlled when symptoms of over-fishing appear. In Asia there is thus still great scope for such improvements. Costs of production are not high, because of the low wages, but they are often high in relation to the purchasing power of the consumers, as is shown by the fact that fish consumption is low in many areas where fish are available, even when under-nourishment is prevalent. India and Pakistan fall within the very low consumption group of countries which eat less than 5 Kg. of fish per head per year. This, it is true, includes also countries with a high standard of living, like Switzerland and Argentina, but here abundant supplies of other

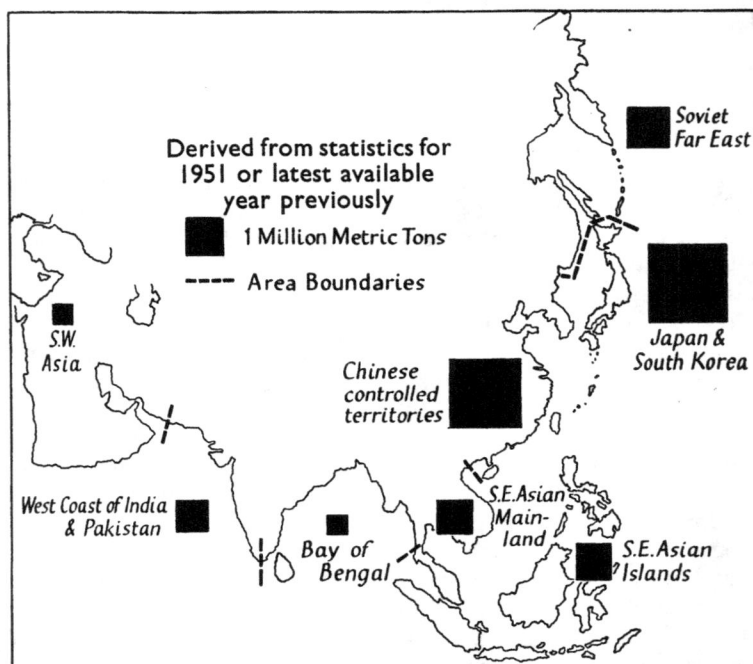

*Fig. 42.* Asia. Annual catches by major areas

protein foods are available. Annual fish consumption levels of some important Asian countries are shown below:

| Very Low (Below 5 Kg.) | Low (5–10 Kg.) | Moderate (10–20 Kg.) | High (Over 20 Kg.) |
|---|---|---|---|
| India | China | Philippines | Japan |
| Pakistan | Indonesia | Siam | Malaya |
| Turkey | | Indo-China[1] | |
| | | Ceylon | |

The two largest countries in Asia, it will be seen, have low or very low consumptions. Those headed 'Moderate' fall within the same group as Sweden, Germany, Holland, and several other European countries regarded as having good nutritional standards, but it must be remembered that fish is generally regarded there as an occasional substitute for meat, whereas in Asian countries it usually forms a much higher proportion of total flesh

[1] Before civil war.

food. In the densely populated areas of Asia there is greater need than elsewhere to bring in the sea to redress the failings of the land. Japan is the one large Asian country that has grasped the idea, and this is one of the factors contributing to its recent history as the most formidable nation in Asia. Fig. 42 illustrates the comparative importance of fisheries production among Asian areas.

From the physical and human points of view we can divide Asia into five main fisheries regions. As in all such divisions, there are no exact lines of demarcation. The regions 'shade' into each other at the edges, and the attempt to draw a precise line is an arid exercise. This does not, however, detract from their essential individuality as regions. They are listed below.

1. The North-east. This is comprised of the Sea of Okhotsk, the Bering Sea, and the adjacent waters of the Pacific.
2. The Mid-Latitude East, comprising the Sea of Japan, the Yellow Sea, the East China Sea, and the adjacent Pacific.
3. The South China and adjacent seas.
4. The Northern Indian Ocean.
5. The Western Landbound Seas.

The Arctic Ocean, although producing small quantities, chiefly for local consumption along its sparsely populated coasts, is not at present worth detailed consideration. However, vigorous Soviet interest in the North Siberian coasts, together with the present warming-up climatic phase, may lead to significant developments in due course.

*The North-east.* This is a region where the water temperatures, coastal, and other conditions are favourable to a large salmon production, and this industry is important, as it is on the other side of the Pacific. There is also a substantial area of shelf, particularly in the northern Bering Sea, and this may lead to the growth of an important demersal fishery. The region is sparsely populated, another resemblance to the north-west of North America. This is one of the reasons that the two chief fisheries, for salmon and crab, make much use of floating canneries, which act as mother ships to the catching vessels.

The Oya Shio current, moving southwards from the Bering Straits, carries cold water far along the Asiatic coasts. Winter drift ice nearly reaches the northern coast of Hokkaido. All the area of the Okhotsk and Bering seas has a yearly mean sea surface temperature of below 40°, save for a small belt of water off southern Sakhalin. Temperatures are decidedly lower than for the same latitudes on the North American Pacific coast. Cold-water species are therefore prominent in the catches over a greater zone on the Asiatic side.

The bulk of the Bering Sea shelf is on the North American side, but there is a considerable shelf area along the coast of the Sea of Okhotsk. However, shelf area is not a major consideration in salmon fisheries, which are the most important at present carried out in this region. The coasts are endowed with numerous size-able rivers up which the salmon proceed for spawning, and at whose mouths the main catches are made by means of fixed nets.

Russia's fisheries in these waters accounted for something approaching a quarter of her total production in the immediate pre-war years. The Five Year Plan of 1946–50 aimed at increasing the total fish output of the U.S.S.R. by 1950 to 48 per cent above the 1940 figure, but the Far East output was to be increased by no less than 240 per cent. This should have proved perfectly feasible in view of the richness of the area, and its former relatively light exploitation, so that now the Far East must account for about half the total production of the U.S.S.R. Earlier development was hampered by distance from the main Russian centres of population, and by poor communications. These handicaps still remain, but have partly been counteracted by a concentration upon processed fish. Shortage of salt for curing herring and other fish has been overcome by the opening up of large salt deposits by the Khatanga River in northern Siberia. The salt is shipped eastwards in summer from the port of Nordvik. Large catches of herring have lately been reported from the Sea of Okhotsk. Spotting aircraft and echo sounders are used, with factory ships for processing the catch.

The mainstay of the production in terms of value, however, has for some time been canned salmon (*Oncorhynchus* species) and crabs. Many canneries are situated along the coasts of Kamchatka, Sakhalin, and the northern and western Okhotsk shores, chiefly on or near major river-mouths. Much use is also made of floating canneries, which have the advantage of mobility and self-sufficiency in a sparsely populated region. Some of the chief shore canning centres are Nizhni Kamchatsk, Petropavlosk, Vladivostock, Nikolayevsk, and Sovietskaya Gavan. Vladivostock is also the chief centre for the growing fleet trawling for flatfish, some of which is consumed locally, and some frozen for dispatch by rail westwards. Freezing plants have also been erected at several points on the Kurile islands.

Canned crab and salmon form an important export, chiefly by sea, to western Europe and elsewhere. They are commodities of high value in proportion to weight, and can stand the cost of transport for long distances. They make an important contribution to the Soviet supplies of foreign currency. A specialized product of the region, chiefly consumed within Russia, is red caviare, or salted salmon eggs. Fur-sealing is also important, particularly on the Komandorskie Islands off eastern Kamchatka. A survey of some general features of the U.S.S.R.'s fishing industry is given in the chapter on Europe.

The Japanese also have a considerable interest in these waters, although they have been subject to restrictions as a result of the war. They have, of course, lost to Russia their important fishing bases in southern Sakhalin and the Kuriles. Russia's attitude to Japanese fishing in waters near her coasts appears to have hardened. Nevertheless, the Japanese, with their dense population, cannot neglect these seas, and are again gradually intensifying their efforts. Now that they have lost their land bases they must rely on long-range mother ships, equipped with canning or other plant, and with attendant catcher fleets, for fishing in waters off the Russian and Alaskan coasts. The main Japanese salmon-catching area lies between the east coast of Kamchatka and about 170° W., and extends both north and south of the Aleutian chain. The Japanese have normally exported appreciable quantities of salmon and crab from the north-eastern region. The foreign currency so obtained helps in the purchase of cheaper foodstuffs.

Considerable development of the demersal fish resources of the large shelf area on the eastern side of the Bering Sea, by Japanese long-range ships, equipped to refrigerate or cure the catch, is also possible. This area, which might well prove rich, is at present little used because of its remoteness. However, it is not too far away from Japan, by modern standards, and the more than eighty million underfed Japanese provide a much larger potential market than the relatively sparsely distributed and well-fed inhabitants of the Pacific coast of North America. A good deal depends, of course, on the American attitude towards Japanese fishing in waters near Alaska.

We may conclude, however, that the seas off north-eastern Asia will form one of the chief areas of expanding production in the world in the coming decades.

*The Mid-Latitude East.* This is the most important fishing region in the world. It has a very large output, both of pelagic and demersal fish, while Japan is the base also for fishing activities ranging for thousands of miles over the Pacific, and into other regions.

A large area of continental shelf (Fig. 43) is here adjacent to the world's most compact belt of dense population, stretching from the island of Honshu to the northern shores of the South China Sea. Intensive exploitation of this shelf was inevitable.

The fish caught in this region are mainly warm-water species. The isotherm of 55° mean annual surface temperature cuts southern Hokkaido, and roughly bisects the Sea of Japan. Tuna are caught in quantity south of the latitude of central Hokkaido. The chief tuna types landed, with their Japanese names, are:

> Kihada or Yellowfin tuna (*Neothunnus macropterus*)
> Katuwo or Skipjack tuna (*Katsuwonus vagans*)
> Binnaga or Albacore (*Germo germo*)
> Maguro or Bluefin tuna (*Thunnus orientalis*)
> Mebati or Big-eyed tuna (*Parathunnus sibi*)
> Yaito or Little tuna (*Euthynnus yaito*)
> Sujigatuwo or Bonito (*Sarda orientalis*)

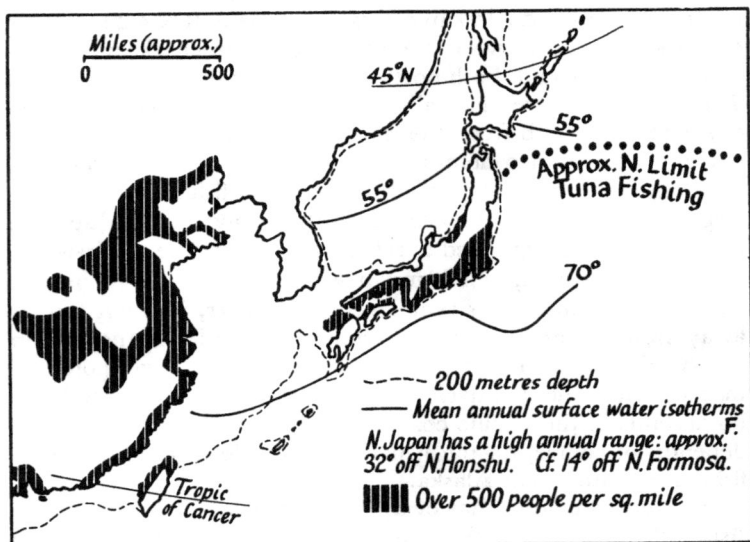

*Fig. 43.* Mid-latitude East

In the northern waters of the Sea of Japan, tara or Pacific cod (*Gadus macrocephalus*) and suketodara or wall-eye pollack (*Theragra chalcogramma*) are landed. In Japanese and East Korean waters flatfish are also important. Some of the chief species, with their Japanese names, are:

> Ohyo or Pacific halibut (*Hippoglossus stenolepis*)
> Same-garei (*Clidoderma asperrimum*)
> Usinosita (*Phinoplagusia japonica*)
> Meita-garei (*Pleuronichthys cornutus*)
> Matukawa-garei (*Verasper moseri*)
> Hosi-garei (*V. variegatus*)
> Musi-garei (*Xystrias grigorjewi*)

Great quantities of sardines, known as maiwasi (*Sardinella melanosticta*), mizun (*S. mizun*), and yamato-mizun (*Sardinia okinawensis*) are landed in Japan. Other fish important in various parts of the region are herring, mackerel, anchovy, yellow-tails (*Seriola*), sea breams, sharks, rays, grey mullet (*Mugil cephalus*), sea eels (*Anago anago, Astroconger myriaster*, and *Muraenesox cinereus*), horse mackerel (*Trachurus* species), croakers, and flying fish (*Cypsilurus agoo*). Squid (*Loligo* species), cuttlefish (e.g. *Sepia esculenta*), and octopus (*Polypus* species) are very important, being popular in East Asia. There are also large landings of crabs, clams, oysters, cockles, prawns, shrimps, spiny lobsters, and other shellfish, and appreciable quantities of such delicacies as sea slug or bêche-de-mer (*Stichopus japonicus*). Edible or industrially useful seaweeds are also important.

In 1951, Japan's output of fish, shellfish, and other non-mammalian aquatic products was about 3,800,000 tons.

The leading species groups were:

| | Tons |
|---|---|
| Molluscs (cuttlefish and allies, and smaller shellfish) | 877,000 |
| Sardine, herring, and allies | 852,000 |
| Tuna and mackerel | 338,000 |
| Sea bream and allies | 230,000 |
| Cod and allies | 211,000 |
| Pompano (Carangidae) and allies | 144,000 |
| Flatfish | 100,000 |
| Sharks and rays | 86,000 |
| Crustaceans | 56,000 |
| Salmon and allies | 25,000 |

The great total figure exceeded the 1938 output, which was 3,520,000 tons. Recovery was complete from the slump in output during and immediately after the war. The 1952 output was no less than 4,674,000 tons. There is undoubtedly over-fishing in some home waters, but any falling-off in output here is likely to be more than counterbalanced by greater use of distant waters. High landings of fish are indeed essential to Japan, particularly now that she has lost control of the Manchurian food surplus lands. Her population continues to grow rapidly. Meat production in Honshu is small, as most arable land must be used for growing rice and other food for direct human consumption. Manufactured exports are not high enough to pay for as much as Japan really needs in food imports. The greatest dietary deficiency is in fats and proteins. When the large amount of direct and indirect American aid ultimately ends, the food problem will be still more pressing.

Well over three-quarters of the output has in recent years come from home waters, followed in importance by the seas off South Korea, despite occasional conflicts with the South Korean government on the matter. A wide variety of methods is used in these near waters, such as purse-seining and drift-netting for pelagic fish, and lining, otter, and pair-trawling for demersal fish. The other chief fisheries are for salmon and crab off the Kuriles and Kamchatka (depending partly on the Russian attitude, as already mentioned), otter and pair trawling in the Yellow and East China seas, and catching skipjack, bonito, and others of the tuna group by pole fishing and other methods in the western and central Pacific, in latitudes from Japan to the Tasman Sea. Regular whaling expeditions are once more sent to the Antarctic, while a considerable amount of whaling has long been carried on in home waters.

In 1952 Japan's production rate of non-mammalian aquatic products was about 55 Kg. per head, easily the highest of the world's major countries, being well over double that of the U.K., and well over three times that of the U.S.A. Consumption rate is roughly similar to production rate, as foreign trade in fish is only a small proportion of the catch. In 1951 the country exported 78,000 tons, chiefly of canned tuna and sardine, and fresh or cured shellfish. Imports were negligible. Before the war, Japan was important in world fish trade as an exporter, her exports in 1938 being 257,000 tons. While an increase on the present levels is likely, possibly in high-priced types of fish finding a sale in such countries as the U.S.A., exports may not reach the pre-war amount because of the increasing demands of the home market.

Japan has a vast number of fishing craft, the majority being of small size. Nevertheless it has a considerable number of modern diesel craft for longer-range work. A steady technical development has been proceeding for many years, hindered, of course, by the war. Progress in post-war years can be seen from the following table (which excludes freshwater craft).

| Type of Vessel | 1947 Number | 1947 Gross Tonnage | 1951 Number | 1951 Gross Tonnage |
|---|---|---|---|---|
| Engined steel craft | 848 | 173,770 | 944 | 210,363 |
| Engined wooden craft | 86,743 | 455,857 | 126,352 | 655,541 |
| Craft without engines | 301,102 | 288,099 | 305,009 | 297,876 |

There are about a million fishermen in Japan, of whom over a quarter are females. In addition, about 130,000 are engaged in aquiculture on ponds and inland waters, and over a quarter of a million in processing. The rate of catch per fisherman in 1952 was about $4\frac{1}{2}$ tons per year, little over a sixth of Britain's. Considerable improvement in this figure will undoubtedly take place, but labour is cheap, and prepared to work hard, while capital is short, so that it is likely that the degree of mechanization and catch per fisherman will lag well behind that of advanced Western countries. This will not denote inefficiency, but the response to a different set of conditions.

Because of its small area and good inland communications, the country uses a fairly high proportion of the catch fresh. Utilization of the catch in 1951 was as follows:

| | Tons |
|---|---|
| Sold fresh | 1,690,000 |
| Cured | 1,287,000 |
| Reduced to oil and meal | 255,000 |
| Frozen | 106,000 |
| Canned | 96,000 |
| Other purposes | 362,000 |

The small amount canned is noticeable, but the quantity is increasing, and likely to continue to do so, with a growing export of canned tuna to the U.S.A., and possibly of canned sardines and salmon to other countries.

Japan also makes great use of the seaweeds which grow, and

are in some cases cultivated, about her shores. Seaweed is eaten both by humans and animals, while one of its products, agar agar, was once exported in large amounts for industrial and confectionery uses. This may once again become a substantial export.

The Japanese Government and the American occupying authorities are well aware of the need for still further expansion in the country's fisheries, and for an improvement in the efficiency of catching, processing, and distribution. In certain directions American technical help can undoubtedly be of value. Japanese canneries, for example, have the same total costs of operation per unit of output as those in the U.S.A., although the Japanese cannery worker is only paid a fraction of the American's wages.

The most important question, however, is the extent to which other countries will permit the Japanese to encroach upon their waters, even when these waters are well outside the present legal territorial limits. At the time of writing, Australia is claiming territorial rights over the whole of her great northern shelf, while in 1952 the Chinese confiscated well over a hundred Japanese fishing vessels, and killed a number of fishermen.

Turning to China, we find a country for which precise detailed statistics and information are lacking. While the country has never been renowned for its administration, the events of recent years have made accurate collection of such information impossible. The new government now appears to have a close enough control to do so, but may, like the Russians, prefer not to publish much detail.

It is certain, however, that the Chinese industry is of very great importance. The F.A.O. estimates its annual production as about 3,000,000 tons. With its long coastline bordering large shelf areas, and its great home demand, such a high figure is to be expected. Aquiculture in ponds, lakes, rivers, and paddy-fields also contributes a great amount of fish to this total. The scattered nature of the freshwater production, and the fact that it is consumed in the immediate locality of production, makes an estimate of its relative importance very difficult.

Even with its great total production, China has an average yearly production rate of only about 6 Kg. As foreign trade is small, the consumption rate must be similar, so that the Chinese are far worse off than the Japanese in this important flesh food. They also are not in a position to increase meat production very much. In a country of generally poor inland transport, there are of course great local differences in fish consumption. In the neighbourhood of fishing ports consumption is high, but there are extensive inland areas where fish consumption is very small.

Average production per fisherman is undoubtedly less than in Japan, so that the number of people engaged in fishing or aquiculture must be two million or more. A great variety of fishing methods is used, a common method in the open sea being

*Fig. 44.* Southern Chinese pair trawler

pair-trawling by junks. (Shortly after the end of the Second World War, China was estimated to have about 53,000 junks or other sizeable craft engaged in fishing. Of these only 1,100 were fitted with engines.) Motorization and modernization programmes are bound to remain relatively slow because of the country's shortage of capital, manufacturing capacity, and foreign currency with which to import equipment.

In the case of Korea, the time is not ripe for an appraisal. It is, nevertheless, a very important fishing country, and both northern and southern catches must still be substantial, in spite of the effects of the civil war. It is likely that the north has suffered relatively the most. In 1938 Korean production was as high as 1,955,000 tons, giving it a production rate of about 80 Kg. per head, approaching double that of Japan, and easily exceeding that of Canada. The South Korean production in 1951 was about 280,000 tons.

*The South China and adjacent seas.* Figures of the landings along the tropical coast of South China are approximate, and matters are further complicated by the Nationalist possession of Formosa. The annual contribution of this coast to the total Chinese landings is probably of the order of half a million tons.

This is a region of really warm water. Mean annual sea surface temperatures are everywhere above 75° F., and usually above 80°. Seasonal changes in temperature, and migrations of fish, are small in extent. With the South China Sea we may include bordering areas continuous with it, such as the Gulf of Siam, the Java Sea, Malacca Straits, Sulu Sea, and the closely adjacent parts of the Pacific and Indian oceans. Physical and human conditions are fairly uniform throughout this zone.

The tonnage of annual catches in representative years is given below. As with most of tropical Asia, these official figures are more likely to be underestimates than overestimates.

| | | |
|---|---|---|
| Indonesia | 420,000 (1949) | 472,000 (1940) |
| Philippines | 296,000 (1951) | 270,000 (1940) |
| Siam | 196,000 (1948) | |
| Malaya and Singapore | 177,000 (1951) | 87,000 (average, 1936– |
| Cambodia | 157,000 (1951) | [40) |
| Hong Kong | 34,500 (1952) | 29,000 (1938) |
| Macau | 9,000 (1947) | |

It will be seen that these catches are substantial. The Indonesian catch, for example, is about equal to that of France. Large numbers of fishermen are employed, and methods are generally traditional, giving low catches per fisherman. Freshwater fish raised in ponds and paddy-fields are important, particularly in Indonesia and Siam.

A great variety of fish are found, as in most warm seas. They include mackerel, anchovy, sardines, bonito, and other tunas, groupers (*Epinephelus*), threadfins (Polynemidae), meagres (Sciaenidae), sharks, rays, and flying fish. Shellfish and other creatures are also important, particularly prawns, shrimps, cuttlefish, squid, octopus, bêche-de-mer, crabs, clams, and oysters.

Catching methods are similarly varied. In the Philippines, for instance, the chief methods are the bag net, beam trawl, and haul seine, though newer devices, such as the otter trawl and purse seine, are gaining ground. In Indonesia a traditional form of purse seine has long been important, used chiefly in conjunction with an anchored or floating lure. Fish traps are also very important here. In Malaya, purse seines, haul seines, drift nets, set gill nets, lift nets, and barrier nets are important, while for individual use in shallow water hand-cast nets and push nets are popular. As elsewhere in tropical Asia, many forms of line, spear, and trap are also common.

Much ingenuity has often been shown by the local fishermen in evolving the techniques of capture, and many methods do not need much further development. A major impetus to greater output will, of course, come from increasing motorization of the fishing craft, so that time taken in proceeding to and from the grounds can be shortened, and the catching of fish made less dependent upon vagaries of wind. Various governments are encouraging the installation of motors by publicity and sometimes by loans.

The post-war motorization programme of the British colony of Hong Kong has already been mentioned. The motorized junks have demonstrated a considerably increased catching power. In 1947 the colony had no motorized fishing craft, but by 1952 the figure had reached 145. Boats without engines, however, numbered some 5,880, so a fair time must elapse before the bulk of the suitable vessels are converted.

In some places, such as Singapore, the expedient is being tried of using a motor boat to tow strings of other craft to the grounds. In some conditions this may prove to be the most economical use of power. Fisheries officers in British colonial territories in this region are fostering such developments.

The work of the Indo-Pacific Fisheries Council, under United Nations auspices, may be mentioned here. It is valuable to the fisheries development of many countries in tropical Asia. Fisheries experts from U.S.A., Australia, Europe, and the more advanced countries in Asia give technical advice, and arrange courses and conferences at various centres. Equipment is also given or lent to countries, but, of course, the main aim of the Council is to stimulate governments and private enterprise into action themselves.

There is still considerable scope throughout the region for motorization of the larger craft, while great numbers of small craft are without engines. In Malaya (excluding Singapore), craft with inboard or outboard motors increased from 327 in 1949 to 1,228 in 1952, although over 20,000 or so remained unmechanized. Outboard motors have many advantages for small craft in simplicity of installation, portability, and ease of maintenance.

In the Philippines, in 1951, of the fishing vessels above 3 tons gross, 828 were powered and 354 without engines. In Siam, of those above 6 tons gross, 395 were powered and as many as 3,260 without engines. Rates of output per fisherman in Southeast Asia are generally low. In Malaya (including Singapore), about 75,000 fishermen averaged about 2½ tons each in 1951.

Production rates, in proportion to total population, differ considerably. Indonesia as a whole had an average of only about 6 Kg. per head in 1951, but this differed a good deal between localities. The Philippines and Siam had moderate rates, with 15 Kg. and 11 Kg. respectively, while Malaya, including Singapore, had a really high rate of 28 Kg.

Average overall consumption rates for these countries do not differ greatly from average production rates, although consumption rates are naturally decidedly higher on the coasts than inland, because of the general poorness of inland communications, save in Java and Malaya. International trade is on a moderate scale, but does not affect matters greatly. In 1951 Indonesia imported about 54,000 tons, mainly of cured fish from Siam and Malaya, and exported some 24,000 tons of miscellaneous sea products such as offal for fertilizer. The Philippines imported 47,000 tons, mainly of canned sardines from the U.S.A., and exported a negligible quantity.

Siam is the chief fish exporter of south-eastern Asia, in net terms. In 1951 she exported 21,000 tons, chiefly of salted fish, and imported only 3,300 tons. Although Singapore is a major entrepôt, through which pass many fish products, Malaya and Singapore are essentially an importing unit in net terms. In 1951 they imported 98,000 tons, in which the chief items were salt fish from Siam, offal fertilizer from Indonesia, and canned sardines from the U.S.A. Exports and re-exports were 47,000 tons.

Although the South China and subsidiary seas are at present quite heavily fished, they do not yet appear to show signs of general over-fishing. Gradually increasing output can be expected with improved marketing and inland transport, better techniques, and more available capital.

*The Northern Indian Ocean.* We may now consider the Bay of Bengal and Arabian Sea areas. The lands bordering them have much in common with those of the region just discussed, from the human and economic point of view, but they are much poorer in the area of adjacent continental shelf (Fig. 45). In spite of the much greater population, the total production of this area is therefore lower, as the following table of computed outputs shows.

|  | *Tons* |
|---|---|
| India | 763,000 (1951) |
| E. Pakistan | 77,000 (1950) |
| W. Pakistan | 40,000 (1950) |
| Burma | 43,000 (1950) |
| Ceylon | 37,000 (1951) |

There is much room for expansion, but the Indian Ocean as a whole will be unlikely to approach the outputs of the North Atlantic or North Pacific. Its densest bordering populations are near its less productive areas, the warm seas which, for reasons already discussed, have generally less abundant fish than the temperate ones. The distance from India to the southern parts of the ocean is considerable, but should not present an insuperable obstacle. The fishery potentialities of the temperate and cool southern areas have not yet been fully assessed. While plankton production is abundant, the large stocks of whales compete with fish for this food.

In shelf area the ocean is not well provided, and this fact militates against large demersal stocks, and to a lesser extent against the pelagic stocks. Only in the regions of the Straits of Malacca, North-west Australia, the Gulf of Cambay, and the nearly separate Persian Gulf and Red Sea are there substantial areas of shallow water. There is no single area of such water to compare with the North Sea, Yellow Sea, or East and South China seas. Traditionally, the peoples about the Indian Ocean have usually been less enterprising in the use of the seas than those of Europe or East Asia.

Although Arabs and other Moslems have made good seamen and sea traders, they have not, save in the East Indies, developed fisheries to any major importance, while the Hindus, forming by far the largest population group about the ocean, never seem to have taken much to the sea. Orthodox Hindus may suffer loss of caste if they leave inshore waters, or 'green' waters, for the darker waters of the deeper sea. Though the caste system is weakening, such proscriptions must have had a powerful effect in past centuries in retarding the evolution of Indian fisheries, a delay which has not yet been made good.

For both physical and human reasons, then, the Indian Ocean has not become an area of really great fisheries. A phase of more intensive development is undoubtedly beginning now, and may be one of the main factors in any solution of the chronic problem of insufficient food in South Asia. This process will fall into three main parts:

(*a*)  More efficient and intensive use of existing fisheries on shelves adjoining the mainland coasts.

(*b*)  Development of virtually new demersal fisheries in mid-oceanic shelves such as those about the Seychelles, Chagos, Amsterdam, and other islands.

(*c*)  Development of long-range oceanic pelagic fisheries for bonito and other such types.

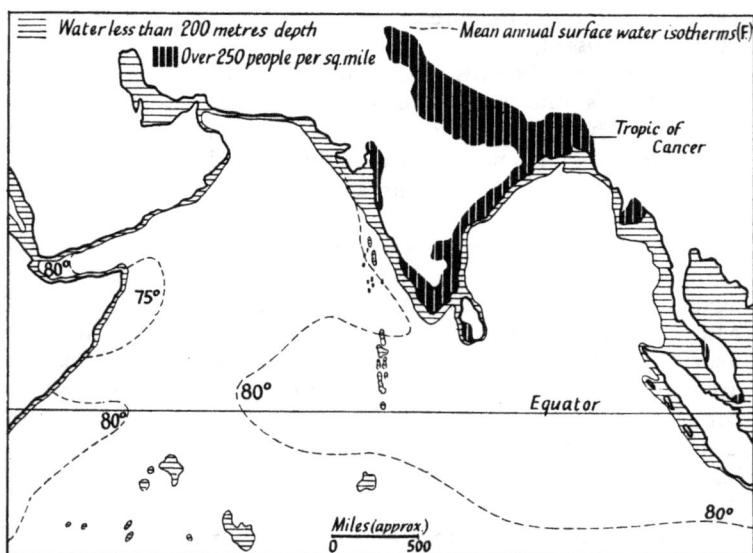

*Fig. 45.* South Asia

For group (*a*), existing methods may be improved but not radically changed; the short-range fisheries remaining mainly as small economic units in the hands of owner-fishermen. Craft will probably remain small, though increasing numbers will become motorized. The developments under headings (*b*) and (*c*), on the other hand, may well be with large modern vessels of the trawler and tuna-clipper type, at first employing partly non-Asian crews. There may also be scope for an intermediate form of vessel, such as the dory-carrying auxiliary schooner for line fishing on mid-ocean shelves. This type is less demanding of fuel but more demanding of man-power, and may therefore lend itself well to local conditions. Another important aspect of increasing fish production will be the further growth of fish culture in lakes, paddy-fields, and other areas of fresh water.

The chief sea and estuarine fish landed in India are:

|  | *Percentage of total weight (1951)* |
|---|---|
| Mackerels (e.g. *Rastrelliger* spp.) | 18·2 |
| Sardines (e.g. *Sardinella longiceps*) | 16·6 |
| Prawns | 14·2 |
| Anchovy and herring types | 11·4 |
| Jewfish (*Sciaena* spp.) | 5·9 |
| Shark and ray | 4·4 |
| Silverbelly (*Leiognathus* and *Gazza* spp.) | 3·3 |
| Ribbonfish (*Trichurus* spp.) | 3·3 |
| Catfish (Siluroids) | 3·0 |
| Flatfish types | 2·9 |
| Sea perch | 2·6 |
| Bombay duck (*Harpodon nehereus*) | 2·0 |
| Carangids | 1·5 |
| Pomfret (*Parastromateus, Stromateus,* and *Pampus* spp.) | 1·3 |
| Seerfish (*Scomberomorus* and *Cybium* spp.) | 1·3 |
| Tuna types (*Euthynnus* and *Sarda* spp.) | 0·5 |

Needless to say, these proportions do not closely reflect the relative abundance of the species in the northern Indian Ocean. For example, the catch of tuna could be greatly increased if suitable longer-range craft were used.

The west coast of India, with its wider shelf, accounts for about 80 per cent of the republic's total annual catch, although the rough weather of the south-west monsoon brings fishing practically to a standstill on this coast in June, July, and August. The chief landings of mackerel, prawn, oil sardine, and jewfish are made on this coast.

The fishing industry of India is highly dispersed. There are about 1,270 settlements classed by the government as 'marine fishing villages', possessing some 74,250 boats. In 1951, the average catch per fisherman was about 0·7 ton. The production rate per head of population was a mere 2 Kg., and consumption rate was identical.

These very low figures can be increased greatly, and should be, if India's serious food situation is to be improved. The total yearly food intake of an average Indian is only about 250 Kg., compared with 680 Kg. for the average Englishman, and 730 Kg. for the average Swede. Making all allowances for the difference in temperatures, it is still evident that the Indian is grossly underfed. To make matters worse, only a very small proportion of the Indian's diet is of animal protein. Pressure on the land, as well as religious objections to various meats, mean that increase of meat consumption can only take place slowly. There must therefore be an enormous latent demand for fish in India. It must be transformed into effective demand by improvements in distribution, and by reducing the cost of production and distribution of fish to the minimum. This is a great task, but one in which there is hope of success. The existing railway network is good by Asian standards.

However, a great increase in production, with lowered costs per unit, cannot come about unless the local traditional fisheries are supplemented by completely new and longer-range fisheries using modern techniques.

While India may increase its fish imports from other countries, this cannot make a major contribution to its nutrition, for the country is only a minor exporter of goods in relation to its population, and likely to remain so. The pressure on the better land prevents any great expansion of agricultural exports, while backward industrial development and unimpressive known mineral resources cannot produce any great flow of exports.

At present India's foreign trade in fish is relatively almost negligible, and exports exceed imports. Exports, in 1951, were 19,700 tons, chiefly of dried fish from the south coasts to Ceylon. Imports were 5,200 tons, the chief item being dried fish from Muscat and Pakistan.

More fish are consumed fresh than in other ways, chiefly because the main consumption zone is near the coasts. Large quantities, however, are cured by drying, or, where salt is sufficiently available, by dry-salting. The standard of curing is often low.

The great majority of craft are small and without motors, and operate within 7 miles of the coast. Methods vary in importance between localities, and include various forms of lift nets,

*Plate X.* DEALERS IN SMALL BOATS TAKING CATCH FROM FISHING CRAFT; TRENGGANU, MALAYA

haul seines, set gill nets, traps, drift and ring nets, cast nets, long lines, and hand lines.

The fishermen generally are poor, and their calling has never been regarded highly in the country. Financial control of the catching side of the industry is decentralized, often with members of the crew having shares in the proceeds of the catch in proportion to their shares in the ownership of the boat and fishing gear. This arrangement is, of course, common throughout Asia. Another common feature is the tendency of fishermen to become indebted to moneylenders who are also fish buyers and suppliers of equipment. This places the fishermen in a weak bargaining position, and reduces his share of the ultimate selling price of the fish, which in turn limits his accumulation of capital with which he could improve his equipment and rate of catch.

Government action is being taken to improve the lot of the fishermen, but progress can hardly be fast. In addition, experiments in the development of modern type fisheries are being made in certain areas, such as Bombay. This province had fifty-four powered vessels in 1951, compared with nine in 1939. The provincial government is making loans and giving subsidies for the construction and improvement of curing yards and cold-storage plant. The province's daily output of ice was 700 tons in 1951, compared with 300 tons in 1939. The Bombay government is also encouraging the development of a fisheries co-operative association, of which the number of affiliated branches reached forty-eight in 1951. These associations give technical advice on catching, assist in marketing, and advance subsidies and loans for improvement of boats and gear.

The other countries of this region have much smaller populations and production. As they present broadly the same picture, and have generally similar conditions and problems, they may be considered briefly.

Pakistan's production rate in 1950 was even lower than India's; only 1·1 Kg. per head. Efforts at least as great as India's are called for, if the standard of nutrition of the seventy million Pakistanis, and particularly those of East Bengal, is to be improved. There is a fair area of shelf off the Ganges and Indus deltas, and survey work has been carried out in both areas by experts, including those of the F.A.O. Expanded Technical Assistance Programme. The government has recently approved a project for the construction of a specialized fish harbour at Karachi.

Burma's production rate in 1950 was 2·5 Kg., very similar to

India's. The war and the civil war following it had not given the country much chance to apply its energies to fisheries development. Ceylon's production increased from 24,000 tons in 1948 to 43,000 tons in 1950, although it fell to 37,000 tons in 1951. The latter figure gives a production rate of 6½ Kg. Imports considerably outweigh exports so that consumption rate in 1951 was 12 Kg. per head, easily the highest for the major countries of this region.

With a fairly high export of tea and other goods in relation to its population of under seven millions, Ceylon is able to afford comparatively substantial fish imports. In 1951 import tonnage of fisheries products was 42,600, mainly of cured fish from India and Pakistan, whose populations, incidentally, are in greater need of the fish. Other imports were canned fish from the U.S.A. and South Africa, and substantial amounts of fish fertilizer. Fish exports were negligible.

The country's 45,000 fishermen average a catch of about a ton each per year. This figure can, of course, be increased by improved methods. Advances have been made in local methods in some areas, with government encouragement, while experimental fishing has recently been carried out on various banks with trawlers and Danish seiners. Longer-range fisheries, such as trolling or pole-fishing for the tuna group, should also be capable of development by modern craft. Ultimately, Ceylon should export to India rather than vice versa.

The remaining part of this region, the southern coast of the Arabian peninsula, is at present of relatively minor fishery importance. Oman has an important pearl fishery, of which the main grounds are within the Persian Gulf. Dried fish, wet-salted fish, and fish fertilizer are exported from Muscat, chiefly to India. This sparsely populated land, on the fringe of the desert, has long had its attention forced to the sea, and produces good seamen. Exact assessments of its production are lacking, but there is no doubt that the production rate is high by Asian standards.

The Aden colony and protectorate, a rather similar land, also has fishing interests. The F.A.O. estimates its annual production to be rather more than 50,000 tons. Its small but growing exports of dried or dry-salted fish go chiefly to Ceylon and East Africa. There is no doubt that the Gulf of Aden and the southern Arabian coast are well stocked with fish. For part of the year, during the south-west monsoon, they form an upwelling zone rich in nutrients. Fish of the sardine and tuna groups normally occur in abundance. Large-scale development of local fisheries for export to India and elsewhere primarily depends upon the attraction of capital and enterprise from abroad.

*The Western Landbound Seas.* South-western Asia contains or touches a number of enclosed or nearly enclosed seas. The Red Sea and the Persian Gulf have unimportant fisheries, save for the pearling industry of the latter, as they are surrounded by sparsely populated countries, and, like most enclosed seas with restricted circulation, are not organically rich. More intensive exploitation of their edible fish stocks is now likely. Saudi Arabia is increasing her interest in the Red Sea, while Egypt's interest will be discussed in the chapter on Africa. Asian countries concerned with these seas have very low production, as is shown by the following table of F.A.O. estimates of annual catches:

|              |         | *Tons* |
|--------------|---------|--------|
| Iran         | approx. | 30,000 |
| Iraq         | ,,      | 7,000  |
| Saudi Arabia | ,,      | 4,000  |
| Bahrein      | ,,      | 2,000  |
| Trucial Oman | ,,      | 2,000  |
| Kuwait       | ,,      | 1,000  |
| Qatar        | ,,      | 1,000  |
| Yemen        | ,,      | 1,000  |
| Jordan       | ,,      | 500    |

The greater part of Iran's production is from the Caspian, which is nearer to its main centres of population. Conditions in this sea are referred to in the chapter on Europe. The pearling industry of the Persian Gulf is in the hands of local craft with native divers. Britain, which has long played a generally protective role in the Gulf, forbids the use of modern diving gear and the entry into the producing side of the industry of craft and men from outside the area. Over-fishing has thus been generally prevented, and the livelihood of the local areas and divers protected. Foreign buyers enter the Gulf, however, and dispatch their purchases chiefly to Paris and Bombay, the international centres of the pearl trade.

Pearling is done mainly from a string of small ports along the west and south sides of the Gulf, of which the best known is Kuwait. The competing demand for labour of the rapidly growing oilfields in Kuwait and Saudi Arabia has, however, destroyed the ancient local dominance of the pearl fishery.

Neither the Mediterranean nor the Black Sea is rich in fish, and none of the Asiatic lands bordering them is a major fish producer. Turkey, however, has made advances in recent years as part of its generally forceful development. Annual production is now over 100,000 tons, compared with only 23,000 tons in 1935. The country's imports are negligible. Exports in 1950 were 5,500 tons. Production and consumption rates are about 5 Kg.

Israel has also been making vigorous efforts to expand its fisheries. This expansion is particularly important to a country with heavy immigration and poor land resources. Production has increased from about 1,700 tons in the area in 1938 to 4,200 tons in 1949, and 7,700 tons in 1953. Modernization of the fishing fleet is proceeding, as is the development of aquiculture in inland waters. Imports, however, have also greatly increased. They were 21,900 tons in 1949 and 25,200 tons in 1950, compared with 5,700 tons in Palestine in 1939.

Lebanon (1,500 tons in 1951), Syria (approx. 1,000 tons), and Cyprus (approx. 400 tons) have unimportant fisheries.

The consideration of Asia in this chapter has shown it to be a continent having several very large fisheries, yet it remains the continent in which lies the greatest world market for more fish. In the further expansion and technical advance of its fisheries there lies one of the main hopes of raising the general standard of nutrition of the continent to acceptable levels. This development will also provide a great field of opportunity for Western manufacturers of engines, boats, catching gear, and processing plants.

## REFERENCES

*Yearbooks of Fisheries Statistics, 1947, 1948–9*, and *1950–1*. (F.A.O., Rome.)

*Reports on the Proceedings of the Indo-Pacific Fisheries Council.* (Singapore, 1949; Cronulla, N.S.W., 1950; Madras, 1951 and 1952.)

*Recent Fisheries Developments in Asia, the Far East, and Oceania.* (F.A.O. Fisheries Bulletin, May/Aug. 1952.)

*Production of Fish in the Colonial Empire.* C. F. Hickling. (Colonial Office, London, 1949 and 1954.)

*Fisheries Programs in Japan, 1945–51.* W. C. Nevill. (Allied G.H.Q., Tokyo, 1951.)

*Illustrations of Japanese Fishing Boats.* (Fisheries Agency, Tokyo, 1952. In Japanese and English.)

*Systematic List of Economic Aquatic Animals and Plants in Japan.* T. Indo. (Report No. 151, Natural Resources Section, Allied G.H.Q., Tokyo, 1951.)

*Review of the General Conditions of the Trawling Grounds of the South China Sea.* Liu Fah-Hsuen and Chen Gin-Chen. (Ministry of Economic Affairs, Taiwan. Series commenced 1952. In Chinese, with English summary.)

*Annual Reports of the Hong Kong Fisheries Department.*

*Annual Reports of the Malaya and Singapore Fisheries Department (Singapore).*

*Malayan Fisheries.* Ed. G. L. Kesteven. (The Malaya Publishing House, Singapore, 1949.)

*Administrative Report of the Acting Director of Fisheries for 1951 (Colombo).*

*Ceylon Fisheries; Recommendations of Experts, 1951 (Colombo).*

*Annual Reports and Statistics of the Madras Fisheries Department* (and those published by various other Indian provinces).

*The Common Food-Fishes of Madras Presidency.* D. W. Devanesen and K. Chidambaram. (Department of Industries and Commerce. Madras, 1948.)

*A Preliminary Report on Trawling in Pakistan.* M. R. Qureshi and M. A. Burney. (Ministry of Food and Agriculture, Karachi, 1952.)

# CHAPTER XII

# EUROPEAN REGIONS

MANY countries of Europe have large-scale and efficient fishing industries. The western part of the continent is well endowed with shelf area, and seas of the right temperatures and other conditions for good organic production. Nations with many centuries of maritime tradition line its shores. Prosperous fisheries, indeed, were an essential basis of their early mercantile and naval prowess, providing the training ground and reservoir of man-power. Long use of the fishing grounds has led to a stage at which production is fairly stable, with signs of over-fishing in some areas such as the North Sea. On the other hand, some specialized fisheries are still capable of expansion. Norway's production, for instance, has increased substantially in the past few years, partly because the use of echo sounding has enabled her purse seines to catch herring profitably in open waters to the westward.

Total output of Europe (excluding the U.S.S.R. and the small production of European Turkey) was about 7,000,000 tons in 1953, as compared with 5,450,000 tons in 1938. European Russian production is now probably about 1,250,000 tons per year, a considerable advance on the pre-war amount. Fig. 46

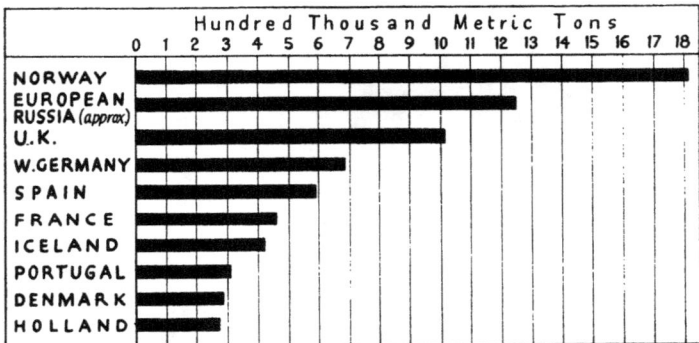

*Fig. 46.* Catches in 1951 (France, 1952), of the ten chief European producers

shows the production by European countries in 1951, while Fig. 47 shows the production rates.

Consumption rates of most northern and western European countries are high by world standards, while those of central and eastern Europe are fairly low. Consumption figures, in round fresh weight, of some representative countries in 1949 are given below:

|  |  | *Kg. per head* |
|---|---|---|
| Norway |  | 53·4 |
| Iceland | approx. | 50·0 |
| Portugal |  | 45·0 |
| U.K. |  | 23·7 |
| Sweden |  | 20·0 |
| W. Germany |  | 16·1 |
| Denmark |  | 15·5 |
| Greece |  | 13·0 |
| European Russia | approx. | 10·0 |
| Belgium |  | 8·2 |
| France |  | 8·1 |
| Italy |  | 7·5 |
| Austria |  | 2·9 |
| Rumania | approx. | 2·0 |
| Switzerland |  | 1·9 |

There is clearly room for expansion in the markets of some countries, but tariffs, import quotas, and the conservative tastes of the consumers are all obstacles to this. Again, maintenance of fish in good condition during transport is a problem to which more attention needs to be paid. It has been estimated by O.E.E.C. food experts that about half of the white fish sold to consumers as fresh fish, even in western Europe, is over fifteen days from catching. Increased development of freezing, as opposed merely to cooling, the catches would greatly improve the condition of the fish. Denmark is probably the most advanced European country in techniques of fully refrigerated fish transport.

In the long term, however, the European market for fish should expand. It is likely that prices of the competing meat will tend to rise relatively to fish prices. The European livestock population cannot be increased rapidly, and imported meat and animal feeding-stuffs will, in the long run, become more difficult to obtain as exporting countries such as Argentina and Australia become more industrialized.

For the regional study of European fisheries, we may make the following divisions:

1. The Barents Sea.
2. The North-west European Shelf.
3. Iceland and The Faeroes.
4. The Baltic.
5. The Warm Atlantic.
6. The Mediterranean and Black Sea.
7. The Northern Caspian.

*The Barents Sea.* This large area lies north of the northern coasts of European Russia and Norway, and is bounded on the east by Novaya Zemlya and on the north by Spitsbergen and Franz Josef Land. The main area of shelf lies in the south, and includes the large gulf forming the White Sea. The other main shelf area lies about Spitsbergen and Bear Island, and for purposes of fishery statistics is usually treated separately from the Barents Sea. Only the southern and south-western coasts of Spitsbergen are regularly fished, as ice obstructs the other coasts. Even so, it is surprising how far north the trawlers penetrate. This is the most poleward extension of fishing in the world, and is made possible by the long northwards travel of the North Atlantic Drift before its warmth is finally dissipated. The 40° mean annual isotherm of sea surface water reaches far inside the Arctic to 76°N., almost to the southern tip of Spitsbergen.

The chief fish species are cod, haddock, herring, redfish (*Sebastes marinus*) and coalfish (*Gadus virens*), while there are smaller quantities of other cold-water fish such as plaice, halibut, and dab. The region is used by several nations besides Russia and Norway. It is a very large source of British fish landings. Hull, Grimsby, and Fleetwood are the dominant British ports sending ships to the Barents Sea and Spitsbergen area. The vessels are all large trawlers, nearly all powered by steam. The average duration of voyage is about three weeks. In 1951 the southern Barents Sea provided about a quarter, and the Spitsbergen-Bear Island shelf about a seventh, of the total fish landings in England. The southern Barents Sea English catches were about 150,000 tons, and the Spitsbergen-Bear Island English catches were about 90,000 tons.

Scottish ports are relatively much less interested in the Barents Sea area, although nearer. The reason is chiefly that the Scottish industry is dominantly one of small- and medium-sized craft.

Western German trawlers carry out a moderate amount of fishing in these waters. In 1949 the German catch here was about 19,000 tons in the southern Barents Sea and 10,000 tons in the Bear Island area.

Russian catches in the region are now considerable, although the region is less important to them than the Pacific. Precise recent statistics are difficult to obtain, but the Russian catch here is annually over half a million tons. The chief fish landed are cod and herring, while haddock, redfish, and plaice are also caught in substantial quantities. There is also a scattered salmon-trapping industry along the coasts and estuaries.

Murmansk is the chief trawler port, followed by Archangel, which is, however, hampered by several months of ice-blockage per year because of its more continental climate and the fresher water at the mouth of the North Dvina River. Pechenga (the

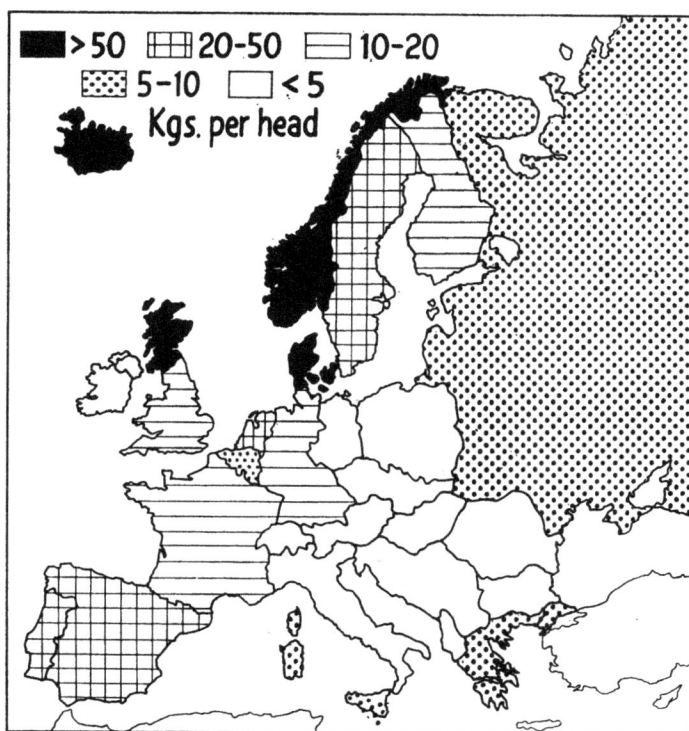

*Fig. 47.* Production rate in 1951 by country or part of country

ex-Finnish Petsamo) is also a fishing base. Kandalaksha, on the north-western arm of the White Sea, has for some years been an important fishing and canning town. Naryan Mar, at the mouth of the Pechora River in the eastern and colder part of the Barents Sea, is a base for summer fishing only.

The Russian fishing industry is widely dispersed in Europe and Asia. A survey of some of the general features may be given here. The fourth Five Year Plan (1946–50) called for an increase in fish production of 48 per cent over 1940, and in this plan, unlike the agricultural plan, the Russians appear to have succeeded. The F.A.O. estimated production in 1951 to be about 2,500,000 tons, compared with about 1,600,000 tons in 1947 and about the same figure in 1940. This is yet another example of the truth that, in an under-developed area, fisheries can be expanded far more quickly than agriculture. The exact figure of 48 per cent for the planned increase, however, tends to show a rather rigid outlook, for fishing is an industry with too many unpredictable factors for the catch in any one season to be so accurately forecast.

The industry is organized into State Trusts for each region, which supply boats and equipment, and carry out marketing, repairs, training, and welfare work. The degree of independence of the individual fisherman varies according to the type of fishery, being greatest in small-scale inshore and river fisheries where the catching unit is small. In this type of work the effect of incentive bonuses on catch is to make the fisherman's status not very different from that of a small independent fisherman outside Russia. Fishing is not an activity that lends itself well to detailed state control. A planning authority can set a norm for the work of a miner or steel worker, and to some extent with reasonable accuracy for a farm worker, but in a fishery he cannot completely control the fisherman, for he is far from able to control the fish.

There are about 300,000 fishermen and 200,000 processing and ancillary workers in the U.S.S.R. Production per fisherman is about 8 tons per year, or about a third of that in the U.K. Consumption rate is moderate, on the national average, but varies considerably between regions, the highest consumption naturally being near the areas of production. The great land distances and the relatively slow railways limit the areas of fresh fish consumption, so that some 80 per cent of the fish landed in Russia is salted. Of the rest, a good deal is canned, chilled, or reduced to oil and meal. The accessibility of suitable sources of salt is one of the chief factors in the location of fishing bases.

Production rate of the country as a whole in 1951 was about 13 Kg. per head, quite a high figure for a country with most of its areas of densest population well inland. This rate is almost equal to that of the U.S.A., and about four times that of Brazil. One of the causes contributing to the fairly high rate is the considerable extent of freshwater sources of fish, such as the Volga system and Lake Ladoga, to be found within or near important centres of population. Before the war, over a quarter of Russian production was from fresh waters, though the proportion has since decreased. In 1939 there were 830 kolkhozes (collectives) for sea production, and as many as 810 for river and lake production. The rivers in the coniferous forest belt produce chiefly sterlet, perch, salmon, and burbot, while those flowing to the Caspian and Black Sea produce mainly sturgeon, carp, and barbel.

Foreign trade in fish takes a relatively small proportion of the total catch, although the Pacific coast exports substantial quantities of canned salmon and crab in most years. European Russia, on the other hand, once more imports a good deal of cured herring from Holland, Britain, Norway, and elsewhere.

There seems little doubt that total Russian fish production will continue to expand. Output from the Caspian, Black Sea, Baltic, and the lakes and rivers of European Russia is probably incapable of much increase. The Barents Sea region, however, shows no very clear signs of over-fishing yet. Russian herring craft are now also voyaging to the Norwegian Sea and Iceland areas. Again, there is scope for expansion of summer fisheries along the Arctic coasts of Asiatic Russia. Improvements of sea and land transport to markets is here the dominant concern. It is in the Far East, however, that the most rapid further increase is likely. This area has been discussed in the chapter on Asia. Technically, Russian fisheries are making headway in methods of catching and processing fish, and in some respects are in the forefront of advance. For instance, they appear to be experimenting with large-scale electro-fishing, the use of electrically charged plates to direct fish into a catching device.

We may now consider the Norwegian fisheries of the Barents Sea region. No hard and fast line can be drawn, of course, between the Barents Sea and the Norwegian Sea. The ports of northern Norway are concerned with both.

The large Varanger Fiord forms the easternmost coast of Norway. The small port of Vadsö is mainly concerned with fishing, and has factories for the production of herring and other fish oils and fertilizer. Transport of the products to collecting centres in southern Norway is by coasting steamer. At the mouth of the fiord is Vardö, again also chiefly concerned with fishing. There is a factory producing fish oil.

Farther west lies the slightly larger settlement of Hammerfest, the chief centre for the important Finnmark cod-fishing season in April, May, and June. It is also a base for fishing for cod, haddock, and coalfish off Bear Island and Spitsbergen. There are several plants for drying and salting cod and the production of cod-liver oil. Substantial quantities of herring are also landed. The town is a base for the northern whaling, and is an important collecting centre for whale oil. Northern Norway suffered severely from the 'scorched earth' policy of the retreating Germans, but the region has had priority in the country's energetic rebuilding programme.

The general features of Norway's fishing industry will be dealt with in the discussion on the next region.

*The North-west European Shelf.* One of the world's largest areas of shallow sea here lies close to densely populated and enterprising nations, so that large-scale and intensive development was inevitable. The heart of the area is the North Sea, but we may define the area as that lying within the 250-fathom line and stretching from Tromsö, where the shelf is narrow, southwards to Brittany, where again it becomes fairly narrow, and where also the 55° isotherm of mean annual sea surface temperature meets the coast. This isotherm may be taken as the approximate dividing line between regions of characteristically cool or warm water species. Pilchard, anchovy, and tuna, which are not really typical of the landings of the north-western shelf, become important south of this line.

Trawling is common in European waters down to 250 fathoms. In some places it occurs at greater depths, but the continental slope is then so steep that the increase in area of ground trawled is small. The depth contour of 250 fathoms is a convenient one for general demonstration purposes. Fig. 48 shows the bulk of the North-west European and Icelandic shelves, with the important ports and the dominant species in each area.

The two main countries fishing the north-western shelf are Norway and Britain, though several other countries catch substantial amounts there. Since the war Norway has well surpassed Britain in total landings. In 1938 Norway caught 1,150,000 tons of fish and shellfish, rather less than the U.K. figure of about 1,200,000. After the end of the war-time dislocation of both countries' fisheries, Norway's production increased rapidly to reach 1,820,000 tons in 1951, falling slightly to 1,799,000 tons in 1952. Britain's catch in 1952 was about 1,100,000 tons. The Norwegian expansion is mainly accounted for by herring. The country's catch of this fish rose from 600,000 tons in 1947 to 1,200,000 in 1951. Use of the echo sounder for locating shoals, and in opening up new fishing areas well away from the coast, has contributed to this great increase.

*Fig. 48.* Main European shelf and Iceland

The production of the chief Norwegian fish types in 1951 was as follows:

|  | Tons |
|---|---|
| Herring | 1,200,000 |
| Cod and allies | 490,000 |
| Sharks and rays | 66,000 |
| Mackerel | 24,000 |
| Salmon and allies | 11,000 |
| Flatfish | 10,000 |
| Crustaceans | 7,000 |

The great dominance of the first two groups is evident.

With a population of only some 3,200,000, Norway is among the greatest fish-producing nations of the world, ranking higher than many countries with ten times its population. The reason for this can be seen clearly when the geographical controls are considered. Human factors are, of course, very important, but the Norwegian maritime skill and zest must itself be largely a product of environment, operating over a long period of time.

A country of short growing season, rugged topography, and generally poor soils, it was never able to develop a dense inland rural population. The farming population itself was concentrated along the narrow southern coast plain, and some of the fiords, where scattered areas of suitable and accessible land were to be found. Most farmers were therefore forced into intimate contact with the sea, and the farmer-fisherman became a very common type. Even today there are as many part-time as full-time fishermen; about 40,000 of each. In addition, there are about another 40,000 spare-time fishermen mainly employed in other occupations.

The poverty of the Norwegian soil is counterbalanced by the richness of the sea. Temperature conditions off Norway are ideal for herring, and cod and its allied species. The mean annual sea surface temperature is about 47° in the far south of the coast and 40° in the far north. This very small difference for so great a change of latitude is due to the northward movement of the warm North Atlantic Drift.

The Norwegian shelf does not have much area of really shallow water. The 100-fathom line is normally close to the coast. The numerous fiords and islands of the strongly submergent coast have, however, provided a considerable area of sheltered grounds for intensive fishing. The early Norwegian fishermen did not need to go far afield, and even today the country has a far larger proportion than most advanced countries of landings from inshore grounds.

The 100-fathom line cannot, however, be taken as the approximate shelf edge in Norwegian waters. The slope between the 100- and 250-fathom contours is gentle here. Off Namsos the 250-fathom contour is about 150 miles offshore. Beyond this the slope is much steeper; the 500-fathom contour is only about 30 miles beyond. Demersal fishing is carried on up to the neighbourhood of the 250-fathom line, so that Norway has a large area of easily accessible shelf in waters of suitable temperature conditions for large organic production.

Much of the country's pelagic fishing was until recently concerned with the winter spawning in coastal waters, when the schools were closely packed. Study of the movements of the herring away from their spawning grounds have shown that the same 'tribe' moves westwards to arrive north of The Faeroes in May and June, and east of Iceland in July. Echo sounding by purse-seine vessels now enables these migrating herring to be found in profitable concentrations well away from the coast.

Norway's fiords provide many good natural harbours, and partly account for the decentralization of the industry, which is in strong contrast to those of Britain and Germany. The coast type, however, affords poor communications inland, but this is not much of a handicap because of the predominantly exporting nature of the fishing industry. The production rate, about 550 Kg. per head in 1951, is over ten times the high consumption rate. The industry is therefore heavily dependent on exports and on processors, much of whose products also go for export. This is rather a precarious position, but is tenable so long as the world demand for cheap protein foods is maintained. On the other hand, present development of production in some of the traditional importing countries, and the common post-war tendencies to economic nationalism, do not bode well for Norway.

Survival of this great industry depends on continuing improvement to keep the cost of production below the world level, so that both tariffs and the cost of transport to distant foreign markets can be met successfully. Energetic salesmanship abroad is also essential, together with alertness in taking advantage of the demand for new industrial processes which can use fish oils and other products as a material. Fortunately for Norway, she does not lack men of enterprise.

A large group of ancillary industries is based on fisheries and whaling. They are important in the large towns, but are also widely scattered in the fishing townships along the coasts, so that most settlements of a few thousand people have at least one plant. Harstad (lat. 68° 48′ N.), for example, with a population of only 3,800, has several canning plants and a large herring meal and oil factory.

The country's processing industries include those for canning and curing, reduction to meal and oil, production of cod and other liver oil, glue and seaweed products. There are also important plants refining whale oils and fats, and making margarine and industrial materials from them. Fertilizer and animal meal are made from parts of the whale carcass. Seal-oil products are also a substantial industry. Sandefjord and Tönsberg, both on Oslo fiord, are the chief centres for mammal processing industries, as they are the headquarters of the great Southern Ocean whaling fleet. The southern whaling zone is discussed in Chapter XVII.

Prominent in the country's exports are the following items. Their main recipients are stated.

Fresh (iced) herring to Britain, West Germany, and other European countries.

Frozen herring, chiefly to West Germany.

Salted herring, chiefly to Germany, U.S.S.R., Poland, and Sweden.

Canned herring to a wide range of countries.

Fresh (iced) cod to Britain.

Dried salted cod to Brazil, Portugal, and other Latin American and Mediterranean countries.

Cod, dried only, chiefly to Italy and West Africa.

Whale- and seal-oil products to many countries, particularly to West Germany.

Cod and other liver oil to many countries.

Herring oil to many countries.

Herring meal, particularly to Britain, West Germany, and U.S.A.

In 1951 the country's total exports of fishery and marine mammal products were 630,000 tons, valued at 1,185,280,000 kroner at the time of shipment, and a good deal more on final

*Plate XI.* FISHING FLEET AT VAERÖY, LOFOTEN ISLANDS, NORWAY

sale. Apart from the war-time interruption, exports have been rising steadily in weight, and rapidly in value, in recent years. In 1938 exports were 445,000 tons, worth only 179,000,000 kroner. Making all allowances for inflationary tendencies, there is no doubt that fisheries exports have risen sharply in their importance to the Norwegian economy.

The industry is technically advanced, both in its catching and processing aspects. Indeed, the country is a substantial exporter of fishery equipment. Average catch per fisherman (excluding spare-time men) was some 20 tons or more in 1951, a very high figure when it is considered that only half of these fishermen are true full-time workers. The bulk of the tonnage is accounted for by medium-sized oil-driven vessels. There are far fewer large long-range craft than in Britain. Of the 94,000 fishing craft in 1953, 12,400 were medium-sized, fully-decked motor boats, while as many as 27,000 were small open motor boats. There were some 54,000 small open boats powered only by sail or oars, for inshore work.

Some large steam and diesel vessels are concerned with trawling for cod, haddock, and coalfish on the Bear Island-Spitsbergen grounds, or for cod, ling (*Molva molva* and *M. byrkelange*), and cusk (*Brosmius brosme*) off Iceland. Large vessels also long-line for halibut, cod, and shark off Greenland. The largest motor purse-seiners go to Icelandic waters in June and July for the herring season there. Coastal waters are fished by various types of line and net from medium- and small-sized vessels, chiefly for cod, ling, flatfish, cusk (tusk), halibut, dogfish, and skate. Cod are most plentiful in winter and spring, and the greatest concentrations are found about the Lofoten Islands during the spawning from February to April. Medium- and small-sized boats also fish intensively for pelagic catches. There are various seasons for herring corresponding to their development towards maturity, and for brisling or sprat from June to September, and mackerel from May to October. Finally, there is a fair amount of trawling by medium-sized vessels in the northern North Sea for cod, ling, and other demersal fish, and for herring during the period from June to August when some of them concentrate on the sea-bottom by day.

A detailed account of Norway's many fishing ports cannot be given here. The great latitudinal range of the fishing grounds along the coast, the large number of harbours, and the small-scale financial units involved in the ownership of vessels, which

14

are often owned or part-owned by their skippers, leads to the decentralization we have already noted. Nevertheless, since the war, centralizing tendencies have been noticeable, particularly in areas where retreating Germans wrought much destruction. The rebuilding programme for dock facilities and processing plants has tended to concentrate on fewer and larger installations. The increasing complexity and capital needs of these installations will hasten centralization, but it is never likely to approach that of most other advanced countries. As the main grounds stretch along an extended coastline, vessels operating from ports along it can have a greater ratio of fishing-time to spend at sea than can vessels based on widely separated ports.

Ports with a good harbour which can accommodate small cargo vessels for the export of the catch, and with a population of a couple of thousand or more, to supply an adequate amount of labour for a processing plant, should therefore continue to prosper.

The chief ports for cod landings are Alesund (population about 20,000), Kristiansund North (population about 15,000), Svolvaer (Lofotens), Tromsö, Hammerfest, and Vardö. All these have plants of various types concerned with fish processing. Bergen, although primarily a commercial port, is also an important fishing centre. It has several fish canneries, meal and oil plants, and salteries, and is an important collecting and exporting entrepôt. Building of fishing and other vessels is also a major industry. Oslo, Trondheim, and Stavanger also have important fish-processing industries and are large exporters.

Norway has been discussed at some length as it is a classic example of a country which catches far more fish than it can itself consume. Turning to nearby Denmark, we find a country which also has a long maritime tradition, but is endowed with conditions generally well suited to intensive agriculture. Fishing is here much less important to the economy, but it is prosecuted with characteristic efficiency and has expanded greatly since pre-war years, partly because of stimulation by the high price of meat. Feeding-stuffs and fertilizers made from fish are also important to Danish farming, and help to cut imports of these essential requirements, which have risen sharply in price in recent years. Denmark's catch was 324,000 tons in 1952 and 292,000 in 1951, compared with 96,000 tons in 1938. The industry has concentrated particularly on high-quality fish from home waters, and takes little part in long-range fishing. The shallow waters of the south-eastern North Sea are still quite rich in plaice. These are obtained chiefly by seine-netting, which can be used successfully on these level, sandy grounds, and minimizes bruising of the fish. The short journey to port also prevents any deterioration.

Other important fish are herring (of which a good deal is reduced to oil and animal feeding-stuff), cod, and mackerel, caught mainly in the adjacent area of the North Sea, Skagerrak, and Kattegat. The chief fishing ports are Skagen and Esbjerg, while substantial quantities are also landed at Tyborön, Fredrikshavn, Copenhagen, Grenaa, Hundested, and Hirtshals.

The country has a good rail network to inland markets and now has a fairly high *per capita* consumption of fresh fish. Its agriculture has a large demand for meal, though consumption of fish meal cannot exceed a certain proportion of the total meal consumption, because of the danger of affecting the taste of the meat and eggs. After home demand for fish products has been

1. Bear Island and Spitsbergen.

2. Barents Sea.

3. North and Central Norwegian coast.

4. Iceland.

5. Faeroes.

6. North Sea.

7. W. Scotland and Rockall.

8. Irish Sea.

9. S. and W. Ireland, and Bristol Channel.

10. Channel.

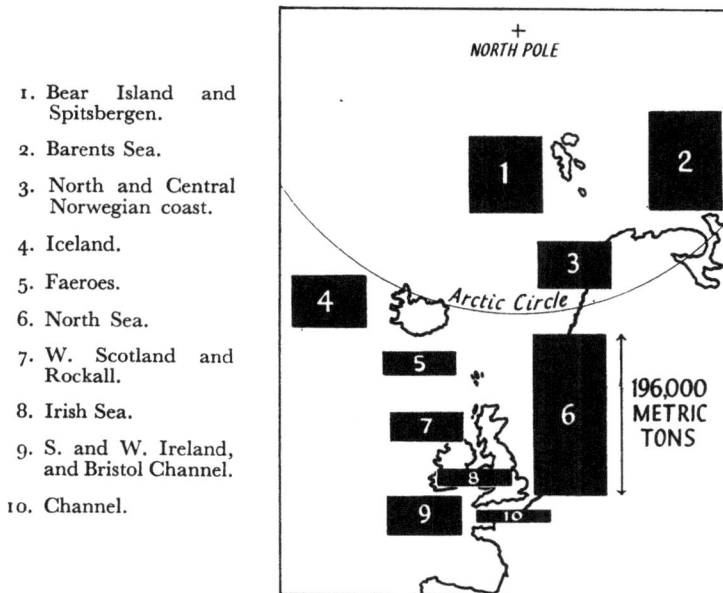

*Fig. 49.* Chief regions (excluding Greenland) of catch of vessels from England and Wales.
Areas of rectangles are proportionate to weight landed from their regions in 1947

met, there is still a large amount available for export. In 1938 exports were 61,000 tons; in 1951 they were 126,000 tons. The chief exports are fresh plaice to Britain, with which country there are short and fast sea communications, and fresh herring to Germany, with which there are fast rail communications. Substantial quantities of salt cod and haddock and canned shellfish are also exported.

Production rate was about 70 Kg. per head in 1951, roughly the same as Canada. In 1948 there were estimated to be about 19,700 fishermen, having an average production per head of about 12 tons, only about half that of Norway. It must be borne in mind, however, that Danish grounds are less prolific than the Norwegian. On the other hand, the fish have a higher value-to-weight ratio.

There were about 16,000 fishing boats in 1951, of which about half were motor boats of up to 50 tons gross. There were only eighteen motor vessels above this size, and there were no steam vessels. The rest of the craft were mainly small rowing boats or sailing boats for work close inshore or in the sheltered waters of the Belts. As in Norway, the bulk of the craft are owner-skippered.

Many features of the British fishing industry have already been mentioned in previous chapters. The industry depends to a marked extent on distant waters, particularly the Barents Sea and Bear Island area, the shelves off Iceland and, recently, off West Greenland (see Fig. 49).

The relative importance of the main species groups in the catch of the U.K. is indicated below:

TONNAGE OF CATCH

|  | *1938* | *1953* |
|---|---|---|
| Cod and allies | ·735,300 | 708,800 |
| Herring and allies | 284,400 | 246,600 |
| Flatfish | 64,700 | 66,200 |
| Elasmobranchii | 33,500 | 31,600 |
| Shellfish | 30,000 | 26,100 |
| Mackerel | 10,200 | 4,500 |
| All species | 1,197,800 | 1,121,600 |

Cod itself dominates its group, due to the heavy landings from distant northern waters. Others of importance in the group are haddock, coalfish or saithe, hake, chiefly from south-western waters, whiting (*Gadus merlangus*), and ling. Herring is far the most important of its group, but pilchard is of local importance in the south-west peninsula. The Elasmobranchii are dominated by skate and dogfish.

In England the industry is markedly concentrated at the major ports of Hull, Grimsby, and Fleetwood, which have good rail communications to the inland industrial areas. A lower proportion of the fish is cured than in Scotland, as disposal fresh is easier. The English herring fishery, with its main production in the autumn, is chiefly based on Yarmouth and Lowestoft. The other second-rank ports are Milford Haven, whose chief interest is in the hake fishery in south-western waters, which has recently been declining in importance, and North Shields. The restricted waters of the Channel have given rise to no major south coast port.

Fishing is more important to the economy of Scotland than it is to England. The Scottish industry is also less centralized in large ports, and has a larger proportion of small- and medium-sized craft owned by their skippers. There is more dependence on near and middle waters. In an average year Scottish production weighs about 40 per cent of that of England and Wales. Scotland therefore has a much higher production rate. In terms of value, the Scottish output is at a less superior rate, as low-priced herring form well over a third of it, by weight. The other chief fish in Scottish landings are haddock, cod, and whiting. Flatfish, hake, and lobster are also of substantial value. In order of value of landings, the chief ports are Aberdeen, Leith, Fraserburgh, and Peterhead, but there are also many quite substantial smaller ports.

Northern Ireland has no large fishing port. The chief fisheries are for herring in the Irish Sea, between May and September, and seine-netting for whiting on the Irish Sea between October and April. There is also an appreciable freshwater fishery on Lough Neagh and the rivers.

Long-term production trends in the United Kingdom show no pronounced movement. Catch in 1952 was about 1,105,000 tons, compared with 988,000 in 1950, and a post-war peak of 1,206,000 tons in 1948, when the fishing fleet had virtually returned to full strength and the fishing grounds still derived some benefit from their partial rest in war-time. Post-war output level is therefore of a similar order to the 1938 catch of 1,197,000 tons. Recent landings (weight after gutting or other treatment at sea), in the U.K. by British fishermen are:

|                                        | *1952*        | *1953*        |
|----------------------------------------|---------------|---------------|
| *England and Wales*                    |               |               |
| Fish, exc. shellfish                   |               |               |
| Tonnage on landing                     | 690,000       | 670,000       |
| Value on landing                       | £32,281,800   | £30,322,350   |
| Shellfish, value on landing            | £874,150      | £931,350      |
|                                        |               |               |
| *Scotland*                             |               |               |
| Fish, exc. shellfish                   |               |               |
| Tonnage on landing                     | 310,000       | 325,000       |
| Value on landing                       | £11,418,900   | £10,678,100   |
| Shellfish, value on landing            | £309,600      | £297,700      |
|                                        |               |               |
| *Northern Ireland*                     |               |               |
| All fish, tonnage on landing           | 5,400         | 5,700         |
| Value on landing                       | £148,875      | £137,360      |

Foreign fishing vessels land a certain amount of white fish directly from the fishing grounds. The amount fluctuates according to relative price movements. In the year ending on 31 March, 1953, 42,500 tons were landed.

Although fish has lost a little ground as a favourite food since meat became more plentiful in the country, there seems no reason for any real pessimism in the fishing industry. A substantial demand should continue, if greater stress is put on providing good-quality fish, well displayed by the retailer. Much depends on whether prices can be kept sufficiently competitive, having regard to the continuing rise in the industry's wages, fuel, transport, and other costs. Obsolescence of near- and middle-water vessels has also become a problem, while the cost of new ships is steadily mounting. At the end of 1952, out of the 1,059 trawlers registered at ports in Great Britain, 174 had been built before 1913. The government-sponsored White Fish Authority is now successfully attempting to encourage new building by offering grants and loans to owners.

Average production per fisherman in Britain is decidedly high. Some 30,000 fishermen average about 35 tons per head, which exceeds that in Norway or the U.S.A. The industry has long been using generally advanced methods, and has a high proportion of large vessels. The following table shows the numerical composition of the fishing fleets in 1951.

*Plate XII.* PURSE SEINING BY THE NORWEGIAN COAST

| | England and Wales | Scotland |
|---|---|---|
| Steam trawlers | 729 | 236 |
| Other steam vessels (drifters, etc.) | 113 | 116 |
| Motor vessels (above 15 tons) | 440 ⎤ | |
| Small motor boats (above 18 ft. keel length) | 4,808 ⎦ | 2,156 |
| Sailing boats | 90 | 885 |

The still considerable number of sailing craft in Scotland is, however, falling steadily, and is mainly composed of small boats, so that in terms of tonnage they are relatively unimportant.

British production rate was about 22 Kg. in 1951. Consumption rate of food is higher, at about 25 Kg., because of the country's substantial imports. For 1951 these are given as 464,500 tons (including whale oil), compared with exports of only 75,250 tons. The country has lost its pre-war importance as an exporter, in the face of strong competition from expanding exporters such as Norway and Denmark, and under the influence of the good prices obtainable on the home market. No post-war year has exceeded 100,000 tons in exports, whereas the 1938 figure was 239,000 tons. Imports, on the other hand, remain roughly at the pre-war level. The chief import items are whale oils (including those produced by British expeditions in the Antarctic), amounting in 1951 to 153,000 tons, fish meal (100,000 tons), fresh cod, plaice, haddock, and canned salmon. Norway, Denmark and The Faeroes, Iceland, and Holland are the chief suppliers, although the salmon is, of course, mainly Canadian. The general post-war pattern of foreign trade has seen imports running at some five or six times the weight of exports. There are signs, however, that a revival of the traditional large export trade in cured herring to eastern Europe may develop with the present apparent easing of international tension.

Eire is unimportant as a fishing country. In 1952 production of 18,500 tons showed a fall from its 1948 peak of 26,000 tons. Imports and exports roughly balance at a low figure, and the country's low consumption rate of about 6 Kg. is presumably due to its relative abundance of meat and other foodstuffs.

Western Germany has many conditions similar to the U.K. It has a dense and predominantly industrial population, with good internal communications. Its fisheries are technically advanced, with a high proportion of large, long-range vessels.

The conditions of catching and distribution tend, as in Britain, to centralize the industry in a small number of large ports. The tendency is of course enhanced by the shortness of the coastline. The three dominant fishing ports are Wesermünde (Geestemünde), Hamburg-Altona, and Cuxhaven.

Production since the end of the war has recovered rapidly from the effects of the heavy destruction, and at 680,000 tons in 1951 was not very far short of the 1938 figure for the western German area of 780,000 tons; 1952, however, saw a slight set-back to 663,000 tons. Imports are large, at 294,000 tons in 1951. They consisted mainly of mammal and fish oils (143,000 tons), fish meal (32,000 tons), and fresh and salted herring. Norway, Denmark, Sweden, Iceland, and Holland are the chief suppliers. German exports are small.

Production and consumption rates are still only about two-thirds of the British, but seem likely to increase under the pressure of much the same forces as operate upon Britain. The loss of the more sparsely populated east, with its surpluses of agricultural products, has left western Germany with a population, area, and home food output quite similar to those of the U.K. In the expanding fleet, the emphasis is, as in Britain, increasingly on large long-range steam or diesel trawlers, capable of fishing the Barents Sea and other distant grounds, as the following table shows.

NUMBER OF FISHING VESSELS IN WESTERN GERMANY

|  | *1947* | *1953* |
|---|---|---|
| Trawlers, over 300 tons | 59 | 200 |
| Trawlers, 150–300 tons | 98 | 7 |
| Motor drifters | 60 | 96 |
| Steam drifters | 6 | 7 |
| Smaller motor craft | 2,105 | 2,026 |

As most of the large vessels have perforce been of recent design and construction, the German fleet of long-range ships is likely to have a higher average economic efficiency than the British.

Holland has a very long-established fishing industry, which nurtured the maritime prowess which gave it a great empire, and at one time made it a naval power comparable to Britain, despite the small size of the home country. However, several countries, such as Iceland, Denmark, and Sweden, which were of similar or lesser fishing importance before the war, have subsequently made relatively greater progress. Dutch catches in

1952 were 298,000 tons, compared with 279,000 tons in 1947 and 229,000 tons in 1938.

The fishing is dominantly short-range, in the North Sea, or inshore and in the Zuyder Zee. There are few large craft; in 1947 only eight were longer than 130 ft. Motor luggers are the most important type, although there are a few steam trawlers. By far the most important fish caught is the herring, by drift-net luggers from May to December, and by trawlers from December to May, when the fish are found near the sea-bed. Fishing by line and Danish seine-net vessels for demersal fish is also quite important, while there is a large production of mussels, for which the country's large area of estuarine and shallow inshore waters provides excellent grounds. The chief fishing ports are Ijmuiden, which is the main centre for the company-owned trawlers, Vlaardingen, and Scheveningen.

Holland has substantial fishery exports. By 1951 these had risen to 144,000 tons, though they were still below pre-war levels. Imports of fish and whale products, at 89,000 tons, were decidedly less than exports in weight, though not much less in value. On balance, the fish trade is not a major source of foreign currency, although the net amount gained varies considerably from year to year, and may increase if trade with the traditional East European market becomes easier. The most important export is cured herring, especially to Germany, Belgium, Poland, and Russia.

Belgium, with its short, unindented coastline, is unimportant as a fishing nation. The catch in 1952 was 68,600 tons. Although above the 1938 level of 43,000 tons, it had fallen from the 81,000 tons in 1947. Having a dense, mainly industrial population, the country (with Luxembourg) imports a good deal of fisheries products; some 86,000 tons in 1951. This included 15,500 tons of whale oil and 10,000 tons of fish meal and fertilizer for the intensive agriculture. Exports are small.

France has an old-established and important fishing industry which has, however, not made much growth in recent years. The post-war recovery reached an annual level of production in 1951 of 505,000 tons, still a little below the 1938 figure of 509,000 tons. The slow rate of increase does not lead to much hope that production will greatly surpass the pre-war level. There are relatively few large vessels, and the industry is generally not highly capitalized. In 1950 there were only some 110 steam vessels of over 200 tons, compared with about 210 in 1938. The decrease has been partly made good by a large increase in the number of medium-sized motor boats, but the total tonnage of the fleet, at 211,000 gross tons in 1953, was still below the 1938 figure of 242,000 tons. There are still a considerable, though decreasing, number of medium- or small-sized sailing boats: about 4,240 in 1950.

France does much less long-range fishing than Britain or Germany, although numbers of large trawlers make regular trips to the Grand Banks. Inshore fishing craft contribute a substantial part of the catch. An appreciable amount of fishing and shellfishing is also done without craft, from the beaches.

French production rate was $12\frac{1}{2}$ Kg. in 1951; about half the British. Consumption rate was somewhat higher than the production rate, because of the appreciable imports. These weighed 92,000 tons in 1950, of which the leading item was canned sardines from French North Africa. Exports are relatively small.

The Biscay and Mediterranean coasts are referred to under the appropriate regions. The Channel coast has the main trawler ports, such as Boulogne, Dieppe, and Fécamp, which land cod and allied species. Such ports are the best sited for serving the densely populated consuming areas of Paris and the northern coalfield, and for access to the North Sea, the waters south of Iceland, and other cool-water fishing grounds. There is also a substantial catch of herring from the North Sea and Channel, and of pilchard and mackerel in the western Channel.

*Iceland and The Faeroes.* Here are the pre-eminent examples of communities economically dominated by the fishing industry. The cool, short, and cloudy summers of Iceland, coupled with the height and ruggedness of most of its land, render agriculture unimportant. Only about a quarter of 1 per cent of the area is ploughed. There is likewise no basis so far discovered for appreciable mineral or industrial development, but the country has one major resource: the sea. This it has exploited with vigour, and it has the highest production rate of any independent country in the world. In 1951 production was 418,000 tons, representing nearly 3 tons for each of the 147,000 inhabitants. It was a marked increase on the 274,000 tons of 1938.

The island is surrounded by a considerable area shallower than 250 fathoms, and this is an important trawling ground for British, German, and other foreign trawlers as well as the Icelandic vessels. There are also substantial areas of much shallower water lying in the fiords, and between numerous peninsulas,

*Plate XIII.* UNLOADING TUNNY AT DOUARNENEZ

but these have now been denied to all trawlers, including Icelandic ones, by the government's recent action.

Demersal fish, particularly cod and haddock, are the chief catch in the Icelandic region. The country caught 225,000 tons of cod, haddock, coalfish, and related species in 1951, and 6,000 tons of flatfish. Another important species is redfish. The main demersal season is in winter. The country now has many modern steam or diesel trawlers, purchased in Britain and elsewhere with the large profits made during the war-time boom years, when most of Britain's industry was inoperative. By 1951 the country had fifty-three steam trawlers. There are also some 800 medium- and small-sized motor boats and auxiliary-engined schooners. They fish mainly with lines for demersal fish, during the winter, and mainly for herring in summer, using purse seines. Many trawlers also trawl for herring at suitable times.

The seas about Iceland have abundant herring in the summer, and many other countries, such as Norway and Russia, send vessels to fish for them. Now that the echo sounder and mid-water trawl are in common use, the herring are sought far afield in deep water. On small craft the crew usually have a direct share in the profits, with a guaranteed minimum, while on the trawlers, which are mainly company-owned, they are paid wages and bonuses. Average production per fisherman is probably the highest in the world. It is partly due to efficient working, and partly to the nearness of the ports to prolific grounds, so that time lost in transit is relatively small.

The country naturally depends almost entirely on the export market. In 1951 the chief exports, by weight, were:

89,000 tons of iced or frozen fish, chiefly to Britain, U.S.A., and Germany.

23,000 tons of wet-salted cod and other fish, chiefly to Italy and Greece.

17,000 tons of salted or smoked herring, chiefly to Finland, Sweden, and Poland.

12,000 tons of dry-salted cod and other fish, chiefly to Spain, Brazil, and Italy.

21,000 tons of herring and other oil, chiefly to Britain and Holland.

36,000 tons of fish meal, chiefly to Holland and U.S.A.

There is, of course, considerable loss of weight in processing. At the time of writing, imports from Iceland are not received in any quantity in Britain, because of the fish trade's ban, evoked by the dispute over territorial waters. Although Britain was previously Iceland's best customer, the country does not so far appear to be suffering severely, as other markets, such as Germany, can absorb increased amounts. In the long run, however, Iceland is bound to feel the effects of the closing of so important a market.

The Faeroe islands have general conditions broadly similar to Iceland and a production rate of the same order. Production in 1949 was about 100,000 tons, chiefly of cod, ling, haddock, cusk, coalfish, herring, and halibut. In 1951 it fell from this peak to 93,000 tons, but was still well above the 63,000 tons of 1938. Local fishing is chiefly Danish seining, purse-seining, long-lining, and hand-lining, from small motor boats, while there are a number of trawlers which also fish the water about Iceland, Greenland, Spitsbergen, and in the Barents Sea. The great bulk of the catch goes for export, and the dominant item is wet or dry-salted cod.

*The Baltic.* This sea is far less important than the North Sea in fisheries production. It is semi-isolated, and is not organically rich. The chief fish are herring, Baltic herring, sprat, and cod, and a certain amount of eel and salmon.

Sweden is easily the biggest producer, but much of its catch comes from the Skagerrak, Kattegat, and North Sea, and some long-range trawling in Icelandic and other waters. Most fishing is done by small-scale financial units, with the crew sharing the profits. General technical conditions are broadly similar to Norway or Denmark, and need not be discussed at length.

In 1952 the country caught 218,000 tons, compared with 200,000 tons in 1951 and 144,000 tons in 1938. The herring group easily lead the catch (107,000 tons in 1951), followed by cod, haddock, and allies (48,000 tons). With a larger population, and less productive home waters, the country had a decidedly lower production rate than Norway or Denmark, and is not, like them, a large exporter in net terms. In 1951 production rate was about 29 Kg., not greatly in excess of Britain's. Exports and imports almost balance, by weight, but in value imports are considerably the higher. Imports were 56,500 tons (including 11,400 tons of whale oil) in 1951, while exports were 57,600 tons, chiefly of fresh, frozen, or salted herring. Germany is the chief customer. A prosperous country, with no serious balance of

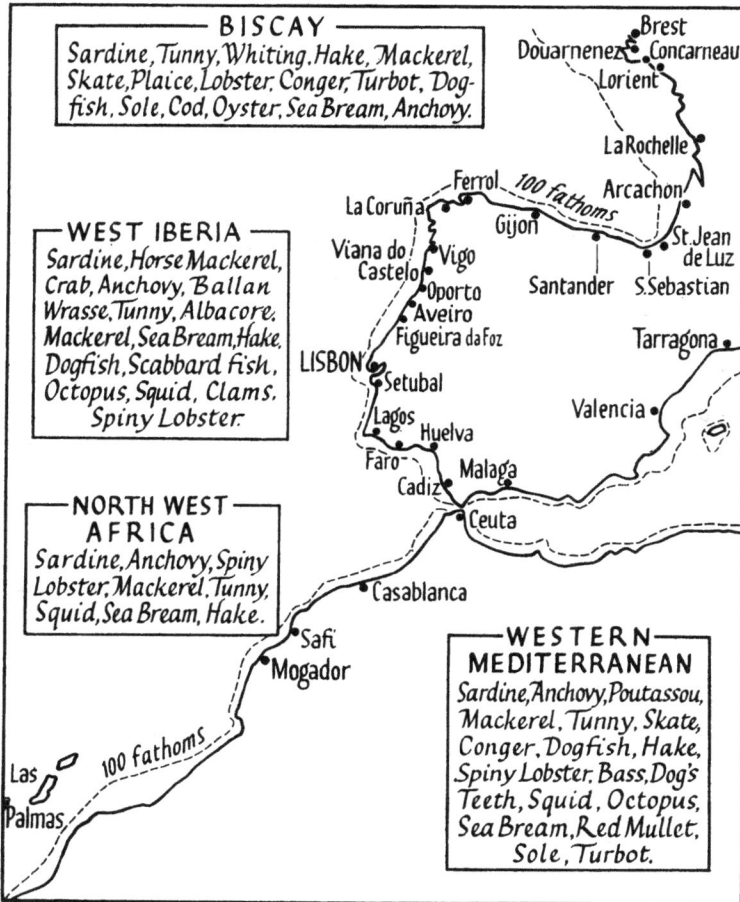

*Fig. 50.* Atlantic waters of S. Europe and N. Africa.
Some important fish, by area

payments problems, Sweden imports a wide variety of fish products, including luxury types.

The other Baltic countries are relatively small producers. Their 1951 catches are given below.

|  |  | *Tons* |
|---|---|---|
| Soviet Baltic coasts | approx. | 80,000 |
| Poland | approx. | 70,000 |
| Finland |  | 65,600 |
| E. Germany | approx. | 50,000 |

These figures include a fair amount from fishing in the North Sea, Icelandic, and other waters. These Baltic regions are also substantial importers of cured herring and other fish from Iceland, Norway, Denmark, Holland, and other countries. Trade to the Soviet Union and its satellites tends to vary in sources from year to year, according to bulk purchase agreements. In 1953 Britain had an important contract to supply herring to Russia.

*The Warm Atlantic.* The mean annual sea surface isotherm of 55° meets the French coast near Brest. In waters south of this, cold-water fish such as cod and most flatfish fall greatly in relative importance, while sardine (pilchard) becomes very important. Other characteristic fish are anchovy and the tuna and mackerel groups. Of the cod allies, only hake is plentiful. The squid, octopus, and cuttlefish group becomes quite abundant, and is caught in appreciable quantities as the local populations find it good food.

The Iberian countries are major fish producers, while the west coast of France makes an important contribution to her total catch. Before the war Iberia imported considerable quantities of cheap cured fish from northern countries. It was good value as food for the generally poor population. The war cut off several major sources of supply. As a result, Spain and Portugal energetically expanded their own industries. Production has permanently risen, and imports permanently diminished. The situation is summed up in the tables below. Figures are in thousands of tons.

### SPAIN

|      | Catch |                          | Exports | Imports |
|------|-------|--------------------------|---------|---------|
| 1934 | 400   | 1931–5 (average) approx. | 20      | 60      |
| 1951 | 592   | 1950                     | 8       | 20      |
| 1952 | 604   |                          |         |         |

### PORTUGAL

|      | Catch | Exports | Imports |
|------|-------|---------|---------|
| 1938 | 239   | 46      | 44      |
| 1951 | 307   | 38      | 24      |
| 1952 | 334   |         |         |

In shelf area Iberia is not well endowed, but pelagic fish are plentiful in adjacent waters. The main fishing is in the Atlantic, not the poorer Mediterranean. In addition to intensive use of local waters, Spain and Portugal have longer-range fisheries.

Spain has many trawlers in the hake fishery on the main European shelf south of Ireland, and also sends trawlers to the Grand Banks area for cod fishing. Both countries take part in the rich sardine fishing in the upwelling zone off North-west Africa, while Portugal sends the sizeable fleet of dory-carrying auxiliary schooners, already mentioned, to the Grand Banks and Davis Strait for cod.

The local fisheries are mainly short-range, by small boats, from many small- or medium-sized ports along the Atlantic coasts. The submergent coast of North-west Spain is an important belt of fishing ports. The bulk of the Iberian fishing tonnage is motorized, and the proportion is increasing, as the tables show.

SPAIN

|  |  | *1938* | *1951* |
|---|---|---|---|
| Steam vessels | No. | 899 | 1,049 |
|  | Tonnage | 98,500 | 95,000 |
| Motor boats | No. | 4,127 | 8,437 |
|  | Tonnage | 48,000 | 115,500 |
| Sail boats | No. | 8,887 | 12,490 |
|  | Tonnage | 24,000 | 27,500 |

PORTUGAL

|  |  | *1938* | *1951* |
|---|---|---|---|
| Powered craft | No. | 743 | 1,449 |
|  | Tonnage | 42,000 | 105,000 |
| Craft with sails or oars | No. | 12,847 | 15,047 |
|  | Tonnage | 26,000 | 26,000 |

These two countries are not normally most esteemed by the world for their technical development, yet the fact remains that, having regard to their shortage of capital and other economic difficulties, their fishery industries are in a very sound condition. State paternalism, working through various organizations, and the existence of a strong and steady home demand for fish, are important factors in this. With markedly increasing populations, and relatively poor agricultural and industrial resources, they have realized the great contribution that a healthy fishing industry can make to an otherwise weak economy.

Average production per fisherman is not high, being about 8½ tons per year for Portugal's approximately 40,000 fishermen. A lower productivity can be accepted than for such countries as Britain or Norway, with much higher wage-rates and overhead costs. In production rate per head of population, Spain, with about 22 Kg., equals Britain. Portugal has a really substantial figure of about 40 Kg. Her fish exports, chiefly of canned sardines, are a useful source of foreign currency to her. In 1951 these exports were worth nearly three times her fish imports. The sardine catch, however, is liable to fairly sharp fluctuations.

The French coast in this region has a lower production than the Iberian, partly because its hinterland is generally richer agriculturally. Nor is there a particularly strong maritime tradition, save in the submergent coast zone of Brittany. Here lie several important fishing ports, such as Douarnenez and Concarneau. The chief fish landed is the sardine, while the Brittany ports are also the bases for the large fleet trolling for tuna between June and October, at ranges of up to 400 miles to the westward. Shellfish are also valuable. Oyster cultivation is important along the lagoon coast of the south-west, particularly in the Bassin d'Arcachon.

*The Mediterranean and Black Sea.* Although there is an exchange of water between the Mediterranean and the Atlantic, it is too restricted by the narrowness and relative shallowness of the Straits of Gibraltar for the Mediterranean to share the Atlantic organic productivity. There is no access to the oceanic reservoir of deep nutrients, but even if there were such a deep nutrient supply, there are no strong vertical movements which could bring the nutrients into the euphotic zone here. Winter cooling of the surface waters is relatively small, so that there is not much overturn. Fishing experience has revealed the comparative poverty of the sea. The sea is generally fished up to its maximum capacity, while there are signs of over-fishing in western areas. Yet the production of its bordering countries is modest.

France and Spain obtain the bulk of their fish from the Atlantic. The recent and pre-war annual tonnage caught by the remaining European countries is:

|  | *Tons* | *Tons* |
|---|---|---|
| Italy | 215,000 (1952) | 181,000 (1938) |
| Trieste Zone | 4,200 (1951) | |
| Greece | 43,000 (1951) | 25,000 (1938) |
| Yugoslavia | 28,700 (1950) | 13,300 (1938) |
| Albania | 3,000 (1951 est.) | 3,300 (1938) |
| Malta | 1,000 (1951 est.) | 1,100 (1938) |

The Mediterranean is essentially a sea of deep basins, and its total area of shallow water is far less than that of the North Sea. Only the northern Adriatic has any considerable shallow area.

The chief catches are thus of pelagic fish, particularly of sardines, anchovy, mackerel, and the tuna group. Apart from these, there is a large variety of fishes, mostly caught in relatively small amounts. They include hake, sea bream (*Pagellus* and *Sargus*), horse mackerel (*Trachurus trachurus*), red mullet (*Mullus*), grey mullet (*Mugil*), skate, conger eel, gurnards (*Trigla*), bogue (*Box boops*), and croaker (*Sciaena aquila*). Some flatfishes, such as various soles (*Solea vulgaris, S. kleinii,* and *S. lascarus*), turbot (*Rhombus maximus*), brill (*R. laevis*), and flounder (*Pleuronectes flesus*) are of some significance. Squid (*Loligo vulgaris*), octopus (*Octopus vulgaris*), and cuttlefish (*Sepia officinalis*) are landed in fair quantities. On lagoon coasts in the south of France and elsewhere there is a substantial production of shellfish, especially crab, shrimp, spiny lobster, oyster, and scallop.

Most fishing is by small-scale units, with small boats, usually family concerns. Wage-earners are not a prominent feature in Mediterranean fisheries. Craft and techniques are mainly traditional. Italy had 8,100 mechanically propelled craft in 1953, and 39,000 without engines. The number of powered craft is, however, steadily increasing. Italy has a growing number of large, modern long-range trawlers fishing the Grand Banks, and elsewhere outside the Mediterranean, and these make a substantial contribution to her total catch.

In common use in the Mediterranean are lampata nets, beach seines, stationary trammel nets, gill nets and pound nets, traps, long lines, and small trawls. The use of bright lights to attract and blind the fish has long been used in conjunction with purse seines and some other nets. Fish farms are quite important, the largest being Lake Comacchio, in North-east Italy.

Average production per fisherman is low, as is production rate, which in 1951 was about 6 Kg. for Greece and 4 Kg. for Italy. These are countries which are not well fed, but they cannot substantially increase their fish output without making use of more long-range vessels to fish outside the Mediterranean.

They are traditionally importers of the cheaper types of fish, particularly dried salt cod from Iceland, Denmark, Norway, Newfoundland, and the Canadian Maritimes, but they are unable to afford sufficient quantities to increase their consumption rate very far above the production rate. Their fish exports are, of course, negligible. Italy imported 123,000 tons in 1951, giving a total consumption rate, with home production, of about 6½ Kg. Imports had increased appreciably from the

15

101,500 tons in 1938. Greece imported 29,000 tons in 1950, giving a final consumption rate of 8½ Kg. Again imports had increased; in 1938 they were 26,000.

The Black Sea is unimportant. It is a relatively small and virtually isolated sea with very little vertical circulation, so that sinking dead matter is in general not used again as nutrient in the euphotic zone. The lack of circulation keeps the lower levels short of oxygen, so that the processes of decay there make them foul and incapable of supporting life. The surface layer supports a moderate population of mackerel, bonito, anchovy, herring, and other pelagic fish, while the shallow waters in the north-west and the Sea of Azov chiefly support flatfish, particularly turbot, and also red mullet and sturgeon. Freshwater fish are caught in considerable quantities in the several large rivers entering the northern Black Sea.

The Black Sea does not, however, make a major contribution to the total Soviet catch. Average annual Russian Black Sea production is somewhat more than 100,000 tons. Rumania produces about 30,000 tons and Bulgaria about 4,000 tons.

*The Caspian.* This sea has larger areas of shallow water than the Black Sea, and is organically richer. Together with the lower Volga, it is an important Soviet producing area, averaging over half a million tons annually. Astrakhan is an important commercial centre, both for fresh- and salt-water fisheries. Sea catches include herring and sturgeon, while pike, bream, salmon, perch, and roach are caught in the river and its distributaries. Astrakhan has important canneries and other processing plants, and has good communications by rail and the Volga inland waterway system to the central Russian industrial region. It obtains large supplies of salt from the nearby Baskunchak deposits. Black caviare from the sturgeon is, of course, a renowned product of the region, although relatively small by weight.

Fishing also takes place from ports in Azerbaijan and elsewhere along the coasts, and Russian vessels cover virtually the whole of the sea. Fishing by Persian boats in the south is of small importance by comparison. It is unlikely that much further increase in output is to be expected from the Caspian. Indeed, it is possible that the increasing diversion of the Volga waters for irrigation will ultimately reduce output.

From this study of European fisheries a number of conclusions stand out. It is a continent making good use of its fishery resources. While there are contrasts in the degree of technical advance, the major producers of north-western Europe lead the world in development, as measured by the number of large long-range vessels, the average annual catch per fisherman, density of inland distribution networks, and other criteria. While North America also has fisheries of high technical efficiency, the sparser population and abundance of other foods produced there has not given the same impetus to long-range fishing.

No very great proportionate increase in total European landings is likely, although the Barents Sea and Davis Strait demersal grounds and the Norwegian Sea herring zone are likely to produce more than at present, while the pilchard output of some south-western areas is probably capable of increase if new markets were developed. Such questions involve advertising by producers' organizations and government ministries. However, despite temporary set-backs, Europe remains the world's leading consumer area in effective demand expressed in money.

## REFERENCES

*Yearbooks of Fisheries Statistics, 1947, 1948-9,* and *1950-1* (F.A.O., Rome.)

*Annual Sea Fisheries Statistics of the International Council for the Exploration of the Sea.* (Copenhagen.)

*Fish Marketing in O.E.E.C. Countries.* (O.E.E.C., Paris, 1951.)

*Lofotsfisket.* Symposium by various authors. (Trondheim, 1946.)

*Recent Developments of Danish Fisheries.* A. Strubberg. (National Danish F.A.O. Committee, Copenhagen, 1946.)

*Sea Fisheries Statistical Tables.* (Ministry of Agriculture and Fisheries, London, annually.)

*Scottish Sea Fisheries Statistical Tables.* (Scottish Home Department, Edinburgh, annually.)

*Reports of the White Fish Authority, for the years ending 31 March, 1952, 1953, and 1954.* (H.M.S.O., London.)

*Deutsche Hochseefischerei.* Otto Höver. (Stalling, Oldenburg, 1936.)

*Statistiques des Pêches Maritimes.* (Imprimerie nationale, Paris, annually.)

*Report of the General Fisheries Council for the Mediterranean.* (F.A.O., Rome, 1952.)

# CHAPTER XIII

# NORTH AMERICAN REGIONS

THIS continent ranks third in total production with an output in 1952 of some 3,400,000 tons, excluding the Caribbean countries, which are better considered with South America. The U.S.A., including Alaska, had a total production of 2,390,000 tons of fish and shellfish in 1952. This made it second only to Japan of those countries which publish detailed figures, although the F.A.O. estimates of about 3,000,000 tons for China in 1949 and 2,500,000 tons for the U.S.S.R. in 1951 exceed the American figure by fairly small relative amounts.

The 1952 American figure is almost identical with that of 1951 and of 1938. Output appears to be fairly stable in the long term. Production rate is about $15\frac{1}{2}$ Kg. per head per year, a high figure when the essentially continental nature of the country, with many large centres of population well inland, is borne in mind. Consumption rate is about $17\frac{1}{2}$ Kg., again a relatively high average figure for a continental nation. The consumption rate varies greatly within the country. Before the war it was estimated that over nine-tenths of the consumption was within 200 miles of the coast. Increased inland marketing facilities for such articles as frozen fish have probably lessened this proportion, but not yet radically so.

Exports, at 127,660 tons in 1951, are quite large, but are not much over a quarter of the imports, by weight. The chief exports are canned sardines and pilchards, particularly to the Philippines and Cuba, and fish oils to Europe. Highly diversified imports include frozen tuna from Japan and Peru, salmon and lobster from Canada, cod fillets from Canada and Iceland, salt cod and herring from Canada, Mexican shrimps and Norwegian whale oil. Fig. 51 shows recent import and export trends. Weight of exports was only about a nineteenth of the total catch, though in equivalent round weight this proportion would be rather higher.

There were about 160,000 commercial fishermen in the U.S.A. and Alaska in 1950, including those on the Great Lakes and other freshwater bodies. If to these are added those employed in canning and other processing, and in wholesaling, the total employment figure was over 250,000. Craft, equipment, shore plants, and storage places were worth over $200,000,000 in 1947. Production per fisherman was the fairly high figure of 16½ tons in 1950.

The number of fishing craft has increased from 77,300 in 1938 to 94,700 in 1951. The most important increase was in motor vessels, from 4,860 in 1938 to 10,320 in 1951, with a tonnage of 204,000. Steam vessels, on the other hand, fell steadily in numbers from 102 in 1938 to 33 in 1951, representing only

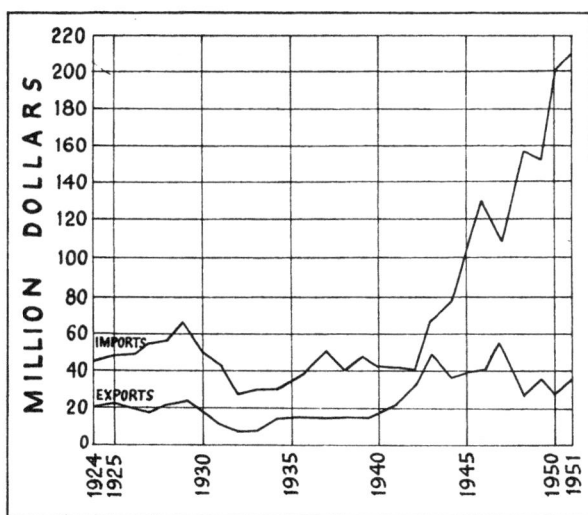

*Fig. 51.* Foreign trade of U.S.A. (inc. Alaska) in fisheries products, 1924–51.

950 tons in all. Exclusively sailing vessels similarly dropped to insignificant importance, totalling only 1,700 tons in 1951. Of smaller craft, in 1951 there were 48,000 motor boats and 36,000 sail and rowing boats, including dories. The motor boats had risen in numbers by more than a third compared with 1938. These figures all point to steady increase in total size of the fishing fleets, and progress in their modernization.

Of the 1951 catch, about a third was marketed fresh, and not far short of another third was canned. Over a seventh was frozen, and this is a method growing in importance as inland markets are extended. Salting, smoking, and other forms of curing account for only a small amount of the catch; some

43,000 tons in 1951. Of the rest of the fish catch, and offal from processing, the great bulk (about 970,000 tons in 1951) goes for reduction to oils, glue, poultry grit, other animal feeding-stuffs, and fertilizer. Great quantities of oil are produced from menhaden, sardine, and herring. These are normally the most important species in quantity landed. They are each of low value-to-bulk ratio. The other leading fish in quantity landed

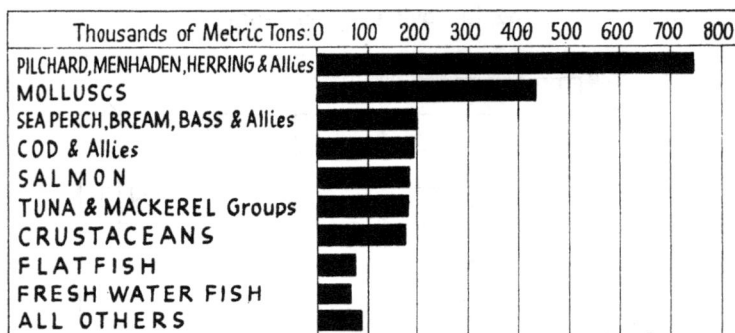

*Fig. 52.* Catch of U.S.A. (inc. Alaska) by species groups in 1951

are shrimp, pink and sock-eye salmon, haddock, yellowfin tuna, and rosefish. Fig. 52 shows the catch in 1951 by major groups of species.

Canada, though smaller in production than the U.S.A., has a much higher production rate in relation to her low population. In 1952 Canada, including the new province of Newfoundland, had a production rate of about 65 Kg. per head. Catches (excluding mammals) were 301,000 tons for Newfoundland and Labrador and 622,000 tons for the other provinces. Consumption rate is, of course, well below production rate. The national average is probably not much above the American, though the large amount of processed exports makes it difficult to calculate exactly the internal sales in terms of initial landed weight.

By the time fish is exported it has increased considerably in price, sometimes by processing, and in all cases by transport and passage through the stages of distribution. Thus in 1948 the export value of Canada's fish and fish products was $90,000,000, or more than the total value on initial landing weight of all fish. From Newfoundland, exports in 1949 were valued at $21,000,000. Fish is, of course, much more important on a *per capita* basis to Newfoundland's economy than it is to the rest of Canada. Yet even in the rest of Canada fisheries retain a significant place in primary production, as the following table shows. (Newfoundland and Labrador joined Canada in 1949. Figures quoted in this chapter for Canada prior to that year exclude them.)

CANADIAN NET VALUES OF PRIMARY PRODUCTION, 1947

|  | *Millions of Dollars* |
|---|---|
| Agriculture | 1,580 |
| Forestry | 954 |
| Mining | 552 |
| Fisheries | 110 |
| Trapping | 17 |

In terms of relative value in Canadian exports, fish is a significant but not major item, representing, in 1948, 3·4 per cent of the total. It was nearly a quarter of the value of Canada's most important export item, newsprint.

The long-term production trend is a gradual increase in quantity, but a marked increase in value, partly due to improved processing and marketing. Quantity landed in 1947 was 133 per cent of that of 1918, while value was 208 per cent. Numbers employed have fallen since the early part of the century, due to increasing mechanization. In 1947 the total number employed in fishing and processing was 84,050, as compared with a peak of 102,180 in 1915. In actual fishermen, Canada had in 1947 some 42,250 in marine fisheries and 18,200 in Great Lakes and other inland fisheries. Average production per fisherman was about 10 tons, well below that of the U.S.A. Even if one makes allowance for the substantial proportion of inland fishermen, the figure is not high.

Improvement of the fleets, however, is proceeding gradually, as the following table for the sea fisheries (excluding Newfoundland) shows:

NUMBERS OF CRAFT

|  | *1947* | *1950* |
|---|---|---|
| Diesel or petrol trawlers (draggers) | 108 | 138 |
| Steam trawlers | 7 | 5 |
| Diesel boats (over 10 tons) | 743 | 719 |
| Petrol boats (over 10 tons) | 1,142 | 1,365 |
| Petrol boats (under 10 tons) | 16,592 | 16,698 |
| Sail and row boats | 11,348 | 10,844 |

This table does not take into account the increasing size of the modern craft. It will be seen that steam vessels, always of small importance in Canada's fisheries, are diminishing to insignificant numbers, but the number of internal combustion-powered trawlers is increasing rapidly. The drop in the numbers of the smaller diesel craft is more than compensated for by their increase in size.

In order of value landed in 1948, the following were the chief Canadian species:

|  | *Millions of Dollars* |
|---|---|
| Salmon | 20·7 |
| Lobster | 9·7 |
| Cod | 8·1 |
| Herring | 6·1 |
| Halibut | 3·3 |
| [1]Pickerel | 2·9 |
| Haddock | 2·3 |
| [1]Whitefish | 2·3 |
| Sardine | 2·2 |

Of the total weight of landings in Canada, outside Newfoundland, in 1951, nearly a quarter were consumed fresh, and about a sixth each went to freezing and canning. Curing, a traditional Canadian use of fish, is decreasing, as in the U.S.A. The large remaining portion of the catch goes chiefly for reduction to oils and meal.

The waters of North America may be divided into the following main regions:

The North-eastern Shelves
The Great Lakes
The Warm Atlantic
The Gulf of Mexico
The Warm Pacific
The Cool Pacific

We will now consider these in turn.

*The North-eastern Shelves.* These have the oldest large-scale commercial fisheries of the Americas and still the greatest total catch of the regions. They were visited regularly by fishing vessels from Europe ever since the modern European 'discovery' of America. At first there was little shore-based activity, except

[1] Freshwater fish: 1947 figures.

for the supply of ships' requirements, such as fresh water. Gradually the territories developed their own fishing fleets, and the
early growth of New England, the Maritime Provinces, and
Newfoundland owed much to their sea resources. With the growth
of local fishing ports, a smaller number of European vessels
crossed the Atlantic, though, as we have seen, numbers of vessels
from Portugal, Spain, France, and other countries still regularly
fish the Grand Bank. Since the recent Icelandic restrictions,
increasing numbers of British craft are fishing Greenland waters.

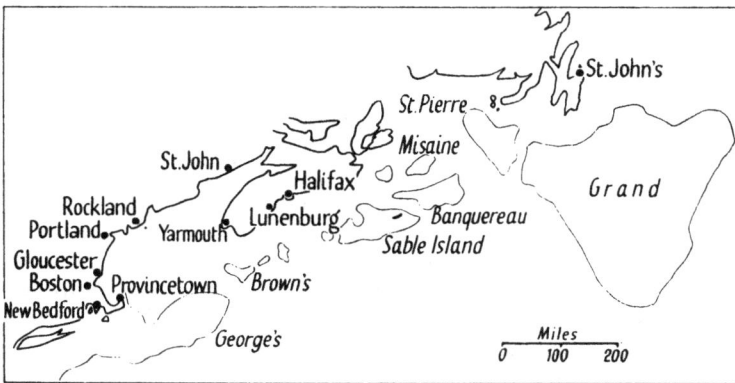

*Fig. 53.* New England, Nova Scotia, Newfoundland. Main offshore banks

This region is still the most important in the Americas, though
other regions have lately been developing at a faster rate. The
core of the region is the area of the Grand Bank, Sable Island
Bank, and Gulf of Maine (see Fig. 53). This has long been
heavily fished, and in some parts now appears to be over-fished.
Remoter areas in the Davis Strait and along the East Greenland
coast are still capable of further development. Nevertheless, the
region is essentially old and more or less stable, like the western
European shelf, with long-established fishing ports unlikely to
see any revolutionary expansion in the future. The region is,
however, bound to remain a major one in world status because
it has the largest area of shelf within easy reach of the most
densely populated part of the Americas.

A wide shelf stretches more or less continuously from south of
Cape Cod to Cape Breton Island. A short distance eastwards
are St Pierre Bank and the Grand Bank, while the southern Gulf
of St Lawrence also has a large area of shallow water. Labrador

has a fairly narrow shelf, but many fiords. Along the shelf of the west coast of Greenland, summer cod fishing is carried on well north of the Arctic Circle, by Portuguese dory-carriers and others.

Greenland itself is not in any sense the base for most of the vessels, although small settlements have harbours and provide fresh water and some emergency supplies. Holsteinsborg is the chief one, with a hospital and a fisheries research centre maintained by the Danish Government. Greenland now has a growing commercial fishing industry based on its own settlements, owning small modern craft, and exporting cured cod. There are now over a hundred curing plants on the west coast of Greenland, and the catch has risen from under 7,000 tons in 1938 to about 25,000 tons in 1949. With the present warming-up of northern waters, the limit of good cod fishing is extending more and more to the north.

At present, in the Davis Strait, the 32° mean annual water surface isotherm nearly reaches the Arctic Circle, which of course does not approach its northward extent in the Spitsbergen area. The Davis Strait is strongly affected by ice-capped Greenland and the partly ice-capped Baffin Island. The cold Labrador current flows from the north down its western side, but the West Greenland current carries the warming effect of the North Atlantic drift, from which it stems, northwards along the Greenland side, and is partly responsible for the fishing activity there. The east coast of Greenland has a narrower shelf, and fewer settlements. The cold East Greenland current moves along it from the north, and this coast is visited by fishing vessels much less than the west coast. Some commercial fishing does take place, however. It is chiefly used for long-lining for halibut by long-range vessels, including some from Britain. Interest in Greenland waters by British fishermen will undoubtedly increase now that their access to some of the better Icelandic and Norwegian grounds is barred by recent edicts of these countries.

The banks south of Newfoundland lie at the meeting of two currents, the Gulf Stream and Labrador current. Such meetings tend to cause local concentration of plankton, partly due to their transport to the area and partly to vertical movements which bring nutrients into the euphotic zone. Good plankton density naturally leads to good fish concentration. Species plentiful on the Grand Bank and the banks off the Maritimes and Maine, which have rather similar temperature conditions, are cod, haddock, rosefish, or ocean perch (*Sebastes marinus*), pollock

(*Pollachius virens*), and various flatfishes. Pelagic fish, particularly herring and mackerel, are also plentiful.

Newfoundland was the first part of the Americas to be developed on a large scale by European fishermen. Fleets called each year from France, Spain, Portugal, and England. By 1520 the total number of men in these fleets numbered some 15,000. Gradually the shore establishments expanded, partly to supply the fleet and partly to salt and dry the cod, which could be done better and more easily ashore than on board ship. Newfoundland became itself a large exporter of salt cod to the West Indies, Latin America, and southern Europe. For a very long period, fish dominated the economy of the island, and settlements were limited to the coast.

In this century industries based on timber and minerals have grown rapidly, and destroyed the old dominance, but fishing remains very important. There seems little doubt that it could be yet more important if greater enterprise were shown in the output of higher grade products than the traditional salt cod. The industrial populations of the Lake Peninsula and north-eastern U.S.A. are nearby, with a good market for fresh or frozen fish. Although the province's export of such fish is growing fairly rapidly, it is still relatively small. In 1948 exports of fresh or frozen fish, chiefly of cod or haddock fillets, steaks, and cutlets to the U.S.A., amounted to 14,400 tons, whereas exports of cured fish were over 79,300 tons. This cured fish chiefly took the form of dried cod to Puerto Rico, Italy, Portugal, and Greece, all traditional markets. Other exports were pickled herring, lobsters, salmon, fish meal, and fertilizer, and oil from whale, seal, and cod. Total exports were 110,000 tons processed weight, representing a high proportion of the total catch, in the round, of 296,500 tons.

This total catch represents the very high production rate of over 800 Kg. per head per year, the highest rate of any of the world's important fishing areas save Iceland. This figure reflects the continuing importance of fishing to the province's economy, yet this importance is falling in relative terms. While other sections of the economy of Newfoundland and its dependency Labrador are expanding, fishing is remaining static. After a slight increase in the immediate post-war years, fish production had fallen by 1951 to barely the same quantity as in 1938. There is a steady drift of fishermen to less arduous and better paid work in other industries such as paper-milling. The union with Canada has also opened up new fields of employment on the mainland.

Particularly has Banks fishing by Newfoundland vessels declined, although the Banks are still heavily fished by vessels from outside the island. In 1948 only about a seventh of the province's landings came from the Banks; the rest came from fishing in coastal waters, including that by large-scale fish-traps in the Labrador fiords to catch spawning cod. Old schooners with cut-down masts and auxiliary engines are all that are required for such coastal work. A small number of Newfoundland-manned trawlers operate from St John's to the Banks to catch fish for the American fillet trade. However, the days are over when the Newfoundlander was perhaps an archetype of the deep-sea fisherman. In 1900 there were over 300 sizeable Newfoundland vessels fishing the Banks alone. In 1948 there were about 125 deep-sea vessels, not by any means all of which worked the Banks, and another 125 vessels working the coastal Labrador fisheries. Altogether there were 30,000 fishermen remaining; still a substantial total. These fishermen, together with the ancillary workers, the supported families, and the part of the island's economy catering for their needs, must still account for about a third of the population of some 370,000, although the proportionate contribution to the province's total income is lower. Even before the war, fisheries were well surpassed by the paper and mineral industries.

Mammal 'fisheries' are a small but recently growing sector of the production. In 1948 they accounted for a fifteenth of the value of fisheries exports. Substantial numbers of whales are caught along the Labrador coast. The industry is dominated, as it is in most areas, by Norwegians. Sealing takes place along the coast of Labrador and Newfoundland by vessels from St John's and other ports, during a short regulated season in March and April. Sealing is, of course, only remotely a fishery, as the seals caught have 'hauled out' on the shores, and are extremely vulnerable. By law only 'bachelor' male seals, those without harems, are allowed to be killed. Breeding stocks are thus preserved. Despite the laws, shooting is at times reported to be irresponsible, thousands of seals being severely injured but not collected. The chief mammal products exported are whale oil, seal oil, and sealskins to the U.S.A., Europe, and the rest of Canada.

Fisheries based on the Maritimes and New England may now be considered. The Canadian mainland's eastern seaboard provinces have been falling in relative fishery importance in recent years, with the development of the Pacific coast. Today they produce a little under half of the Canadian mainland output by value. In 1947 (before Newfoundland's accession) Nova Scotia produced 21·5 per cent of the value of the Canadian output, New Brunswick 13·8 per cent, Quebec 4·3 per cent, and Prince Edward Island 2·4 per cent.

Nova Scotia has the important Sable Island Bank off its coast, and is within easy range also of the St Pierre Bank and Grand Bank to the east, and the Gulf of Maine banks to the south-west. It is also well situated for markets, with good main-line rail communication to the St Lawrence-Lake Peninsula cities and to the north-eastern industrial zone of the U.S.A. Halifax, more-over, is an ocean port well sited for export to Europe and else-where. The coastline has an abundance of natural harbours. From the first days of settlement, fishing has been an important industry, and in methods and products has broadly resembled that of Newfoundland.

In recent times, however, its fisheries have been more pro-gressive than those of Newfoundland. Helped by its land com-munications to American markets, it has concentrated to a lesser extent on the low-value cured fish, though this still has a sub-stantial output. The auxiliary schooners for dory fishing have diminished steadily in numbers, but their places have been taken by a considerable number of modern oil-driven draggers. The chief demersal species are cod, haddock, hake, and pollock. Also caught are herring, 'sardines' (which here are mainly young herring), and mackerel. There is also an important inshore fishery for lobsters (*Homarus americanus*), and quite important fisheries for scallops and oysters. Small fishing ports are closely spaced, particularly along the province's Atlantic coast, while Halifax itself is an important port for fishing as well as cargo.

New Brunswick is also an important fishing province, for much the same reasons as Nova Scotia. St John and other ports have easy access to the Gulf of Maine and Sable Island Bank, while the north coast has access to the considerable area of shallow water on the south side of the Gulf of St Lawrence. Prince Edward Island has a smaller output, though still substantial in proportion to its size. Quebec has a rather small output considering its long coastline around the gulf and estuary of the St Lawrence, but its centres of population are well away from these coasts. Neverthe-less, it has a good number of small fishing settlements, particularly on the Gaspé peninsula, where the inhabitants also obtain an appreciable income from holiday-makers from the industrial regions to the south-west.

New England, like the Maritime Provinces, is an old-established fishing region, and for similar basic reasons. In the last century, however, the economy of New England has undergone a markedly different development from that of the Maritimes. In its southern areas it has long been heavily industrialized. This has reduced the relative importance of fisheries in the regional economy, but

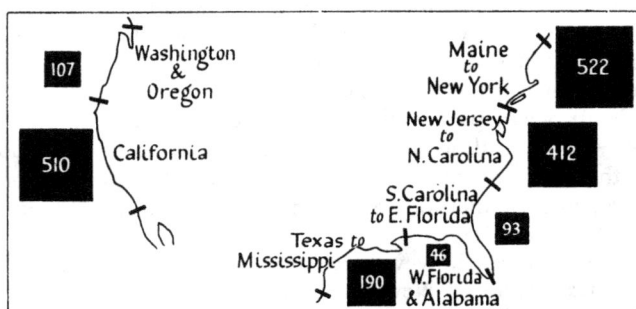

*Fig. 54.* Fisheries output (thousands of metric tons, 1949) by state groups of approximately similar coast front

not their absolute importance, for it has provided a large local market; a market, moreover, in which the New England fishermen are at an advantage as compared with the Canadians because they have no tariff to pay.

Whereas in pre-industrial days New England, like the Maritimes, exported salt cod to the West Indies and elsewhere, its exports of such products are now negligible. Of its landings of cod, haddock, and related species, well over a third is marketed fresh, and well over a third frozen. Curing by salting, drying, and so on, accounts for only about 1 per cent.

The bulk of the catches are by medium-sized oil-engined draggers, though there are a good number of smaller oil-engined boats and auxiliary sailing craft.

The chief demersal landings are of rosefish, haddock, cod, whiting (*Merluccius bilinearis*), pollock, and flatfish, mostly by otter trawl. Large quantities of herring and fair amounts of mackerel are caught by purse seines, and along the shore by weirs or traps. Shellfish are important, particularly lobsters along the Maine coast. Sea scallops (*Pecten magellanicus*), soft clams (*Mya arenaria*), hard clams (*Venus mercenaria*), and oysters (*Crassostrea virginica*) also form a substantial catch.

There is a large shore industry in New England engaged on filleting, quick-freezing, and other processing and packaging. Demersal landings are strongly centred on Boston, Gloucester (Mass.), and Portland (Maine). Boston in particular, with its well-developed facilities and command of a good rail network in a densely populated region, has points of resemblance to Hull. Areas of really dense and continuous population are not often encountered in North America, which is a major reason for the general absence of strong centralization of fishing ports. Even in the case of these large New England ports there is a contrast with the main British and German ports, for the average range and size of their vessels is a good deal less. Over four-fifths of the New England catch is from its own waters, and under a fifth from banks off Nova Scotia and Newfoundland.

TONNAGE LANDED

|  | *1950* | *1949* | *1938* |
|---|---|---|---|
| Maine | 162,000 | 134,000 | 30,500 |
| Massachusetts | 258,000 | 294,000 | 245,000 |
| Rhode Island | 17,000 | 15,000 | 6,300 |
| Connecticut | 9,000 | 11,000 | 5,400 |

New Hampshire, with its short coast, has a very small output. It can be seen that Massachusetts is still easily the most important state of the area, although its landings show no marked long-term expansion, unlike those of Maine.

*The Great Lakes.* These lakes, shared between the U.S.A. and Canada, form such a large body of water that they cannot be ignored even by a study primarily concerned with sea fisheries. Large numbers of craft are employed, Canada alone having 2,300 powered fishing boats on inland fisheries in 1950, the bulk of which were on the Great Lakes.

The chief Great Lakes commercial species include lake herring (*Leucichthys artedi*), chubs (*Leucichthys* species), blue pike (*Stizostedion vitreum glaucum*), yellow pike (*S. vitreum vitreum*), sauger (*S. canadense*), common whitefish (*Coregonus clupeaformis*), yellow perch (*Perca flavescens*), lake trout (*Cristivomer namaycush*), and pickerel (*Esox* species).

Lakes Erie and Michigan normally have the largest total output, and are near densely populated areas. The total Great Lakes catch by the U.S.A. varies between about 30,000 and

50,000 tons per year, while the Canadian figure is about half of this. Because of its shores on the Great Lakes, Ontario actually catches slightly more fish, by value, than Quebec, accounting for 4·4 per cent of the Canadian landings in 1947. Most freshwater species have a higher value-to-bulk ratio than the typical sea-fish, partly because they are scarcer on the market. A lower rate of catch per fisherman can therefore be sustained by these freshwater fisheries.

*The Warm Atlantic.* In the latitude of New York and New Jersey the character of the fisheries changes from that prevailing for a long distance northwards. The mean yearly sea surface isotherm of 55° meets the coast. South of it, warmer water species begin to figure markedly in the catches, while cold-water types like cod and haddock become insignificant. The belt of water shallower than 200 metres also becomes generally narrower, so there is less space on which to develop demersal fisheries.

This area has, however, the greatest pelagic fishery of the Americas, concerned with menhaden (*Brevoortia tyrannus*), a species allied to the herring. Nearly half a million tons of this fish were landed in 1950. This is more, for example, than the total fisheries catch of France in that year. As we have mentioned, menhaden is used for conversion into oils, animal food, fertilizers, and other by-products, not for human food. The vast catches can be taken conveniently because of the surface schooling habits of this fish which makes it an easy prey to the purse seine. The fishery stretches from New York to Florida, being particularly important in New Jersey, Delaware, Virginia, and North Carolina.

There are also pound-net fisheries, along the coasts and estuaries, for alewife (*Pomolobus* species), shad (*Alosa sapidissima*), and striped bass (*Roccus saxatilis*), which ascend the rivers in the summer, and for sea trout or weakfish (*Cynoscion* species), Atlantic croaker (*Micropogon undulatus*), butterfish (*Poronotus triacanthus*), and scup (*Calamus* or *Stenotomus* species). Otter trawls are used during the winter for croaker, scup, butterfish, flatfish, and others.

The most valuable fisheries in this region, however, are those for shellfish. Delaware Bay is important for hard clams, oysters, and blue crabs (*Callinectes sapidus*), taken with dredges, rakes, and tongs. Chesapeake Bay is still more important, the scene of the most intensive shellfishery in the world. Tonging and dredging for oysters is the dominant activity, while catching blue crabs by trot lines and dip nets also employs many men. There are many shore plants here engaged in packing shucked oysters and fresh-cooked crab meat. Crab fisheries are valuable also in the many bays and estuaries of North Carolina. From here southwards, shrimps (*Penaeus* and *Xyphopenaeus* species) are the most valuable of the landings. They are caught by otter trawling from motor boats.

This middle and southern Atlantic coast region, though not traditionally a major fishing area, now has a weight and value of catch exceeding that of New England. It must be remembered, however, that New England has only about a third of this region's coast, and so has considerably greater landings in proportion to coast front. This middle and southern region, with its relatively narrow shelf, concentrates mainly on short-range and shore fisheries.

TONNAGE LANDED

|  | *1950* | *1949* | *1938* |
|---|---|---|---|
| New York | 64,000 | 66,000 | 42,500 |
| New Jersey | 86,000 | 95,000 | 49,500 |
| Delaware | 72,500 | 75,000 | 8,000 |
| Maryland | 30,500 | 27,000 | 26,000 |
| Virginia | 143,000 | 125,000 | 108,000 |
| N. Carolina | 78,000 | 90,000 | 90,000 |
| S. Carolina | 6,800 | 4,500 | 3,600 |
| Georgia | 7,800 | 9,500 | 9,000 |
| Florida (E. coast) | 25,600 | 79,000 | 80,000 |
|  |  |  | approx. |

The great relative expansion of Delaware's production since before the war is accounted for by the development of its menhaden fishery. East Florida's menhaden fishery has been liable to large fluctuations, which mainly accounts for the sharp fall from 1949 to 1950.

*The Gulf of Mexico.* The United States part of the Gulf is now moderately fished, as the following table shows.

TONNAGE LANDED

|  | *1950* | *1949* | *1938* |
|---|---|---|---|
| Florida (W. coast) | 28,000 | 42,000 | 30,000 approx. |
| Alabama | 5,000 | 4,500 | 5,700 |
| Mississippi | 38,000 | 24,000 | 7,700 |
| Louisiana | 144,000 | 130,000 | 56,000 |
| Texas | 44,000 | 36,000 | 11,300 |

A wide shelf lies off the United States part of the Gulf. There has been marked recent development in the centre and west of its coastline, mainly in the menhaden and shrimp fisheries. Menhaden landings in the Gulf have risen from 5,400 tons in 1939 to 149,000 tons in 1950. They now dominate the catch in terms of weight, but shrimps (*Penaeus* and *Xyphopenaeus*) are by far the most valuable catch. Indeed, this area has the largest shrimp fishery in the world. The crustaceans are taken by motor craft with otter trawls, and are particularly important in Louisiana.

Other important landings are of mullet (*Mugil*), especially off the west coast of Florida, oysters and blue crabs, both mainly in Louisiana, red snapper (*Lutianus blackfordii*), Spanish mackerel (*Scomberomorus maculatus*), and sea trout. There has been quite a valuable sponge fishery on the west coast of Florida, the sponges being marketed at the Exchange at Tarpon Springs. They fetched $1,742,000 in initial sale value in 1947, but subsequently the output has fallen steeply. The chief Gulf processing industries are concerned with freezing shrimps, canning oysters and shrimps, and the manufacture of meal and oil from menhaden.

The Mexican part of the Gulf is far less important. The shelf is generally narrow, save for the wide Campeche Bank north of the Yucatan peninsula. The country is not economically and technically very progressive, although it has improved in recent years. There has, however, been marked development of the fisheries. Mexico's total production by her own fishermen was estimated at about 58,000 tons a year in 1952, as compared with 18,700 tons in 1938. The major part of the production by Mexican fishermen is from the Gulf of Mexico. The main base is Vera Cruz, which supplies the large market of Mexico City and the surrounding region of dense population. Species caught include red snapper, kingfish (*Genyonemus lineatus*), mullet, sea trout, and shrimp. The latter fishery has grown quickly on the Campeche Bank. Fresh or frozen shrimp form an important export to the U.S.A. The present state of Mexican fisheries is, however, not impressive. The annual consumption per head in 1947 was only about 1·6 Kg., though this was about four times the pre-war figure. Production rate in 1952 was about 2·5 Kg. The 15,000 fishermen averaged only 3·9 tons each, although this was higher than in some other Latin-American countries. In 1945 Mexico had only fifteen vessels of over 50 tons, but she had about 1,200 motor boats of under 50 tons, more than double

*Plate XIV.* TUNA VESSEL AT A FISH PIER IN SAN DIEGO

the number in 1941. In addition, there were about 3,700 boats without power.

The government has encouraged the local fishermen to form *co-operativas*, which now account for the bulk of the country's landings. The co-operatives handle the selling of the fish for their members. They are granted tax exemptions, and have the exclusive right to fish shrimp and some other species.

Mexico is the chief fish exporter in Latin America. In 1951 it exported 91,000 tons, and imported only 1,400 tons. These export figures include those of landings by American craft in Mexican ports for dispatch to the U.S.A. The country's fishing industry is of considerable value as a source of foreign currency, but plays small part in its nutrition. The chief market is the U.S.A., and the chief export produced by local fisheries is frozen or iced shrimp, amounting to 18,000 tons in 1950. In addition, there is a larger export of frozen tuna, but this is chiefly caught by American ships.

*The .Warm Pacific.* The Mexican Pacific area is dominated by tuna clippers from San Pedro and San Diego, California, which are allowed in Mexican waters by government permits. Most of their catch is landed at their home ports, but some is landed in Mexico for dispatch to the U.S.A. There are a few tuna-freezing plants on Mexico's west coast. There are also at the time of writing some thirteen shrimp-freezing plants and three sardine and mackerel canneries. The chief development concerning Mexican Pacific coast fishermen is the large growth of their shrimp trawling fleets operating about the·Lower Californian peninsula and in the Gulf of Tehuantepec. This shrimp output is nearly all for export northwards. Other developing fisheries are for sea bass, shark, and the mollusc abalone (*Halotis*).

While Mexico's exports of tuna, shrimp, and other fairly high-priced products to the U.S.A. will doubtless further increase, there is also scope for a great expansion of output of cheap fish for domestic use, in view of the present low rate of fish consumption and the generally low standard of the country's diet. Of particular importance in this respect are the great under-developed sardine or pilchard resources off the west coast of Lower California. Canned sardines form a cheap and easily kept product, well suited to a hot country with a low standard of living and poor communications. A canning industry has been started at Ensenada, and one may expect the government to encourage further development along the west coast.

The American part of this region, California, has undergone intensive development. This state, for a number of recent years, has had the greatest landings of any in the U.S.A., and indeed more than any province of Canada or country of Latin America. In addition to large fisheries in its own waters for sardine (now in an eclipse, it is to be hoped only temporarily), jack mackerel, mackerel, anchovy, and flatfish, it is the chief base for the great fishery for the tuna group which ranges from Washington State to Peru, and far to the west.

The warm Pacific waters of the Americas are essentially a pelagic area (see Fig. 55). The coast runs more or less parallel to lines of strong folding and faulting, so that the shelf is narrow. Water conditions are also very suitable for a great development of pelagic fish. The relatively cool California current moves southwards along the North American coast with an offshore component due primarily to the trade winds, so that there is upwelling of deeper nutrient-rich water. In South America the Peru current creates similar conditions. Plankton-rich waters are then borne far westwards on the North and South Equatorial currents, making a large area in which oceanic pelagic fishing is profitable. Due to these peculiarly favourable circumstances, its lack of shelf has not prevented California from becoming in normal recent years a fishing area of the first rank, landing about 610,000 tons in 1950, 510,000 tons in 1949, and 590,000 tons in 1938, or about double the landings of Newfoundland and Labrador.

The most important fish by weight in normal years has been sardine (*Sardinops caerulea*), caught by purse seines, lampara nets, and ring nets. An enormous quantity is used for low-priced canned food, and for conversion into oil and animal feeding stuff. However, since 1952, the catch has fallen catastrophically. By autumn 1954, some 130 processing plants had closed. The sardine had practically vanished from Californian waters. Considerable hardship has been caused to fishermen and other workers.

CALIFORNIAN LANDINGS OF SARDINE, IN TONS

| | |
|---|---|
| 1936 (peak year) | 660,000 |
| 1944 | 520,000 |
| 1947 | 115,000 |
| 1950 | 325,000 |
| 1952 | 5,000 |
| 1953 | 5,000 |

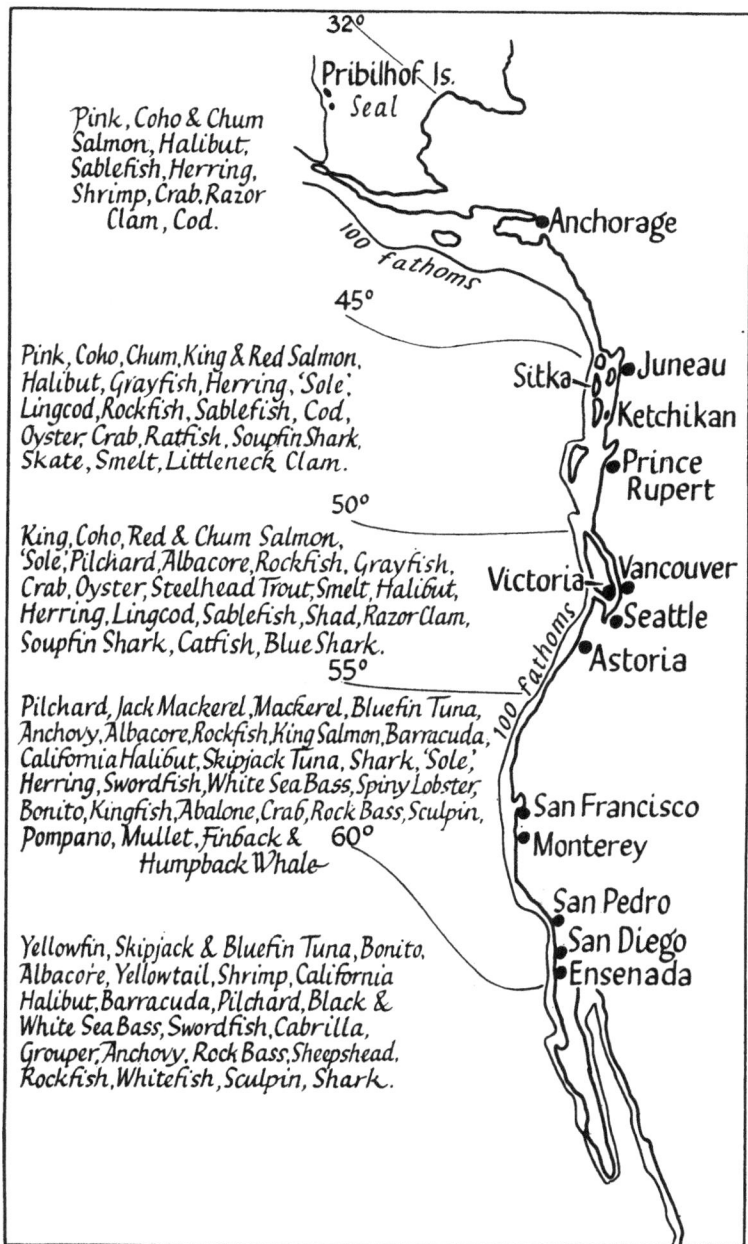

32°

Pribilhof Is.
• Seal

Pink, Coho & Chum
Salmon, Halibut,
Sablefish, Herring,
Shrimp, Crab, Razor
Clam, Cod.

100 fathoms

• Anchorage

45°

Pink, Coho, Chum, King & Red Salmon,
Halibut, Grayfish, Herring, 'Sole',
Lingcod, Rockfish, Sablefish, Cod,
Oyster, Crab, Ratfish, Soupfin Shark,
Skate, Smelt, Littleneck Clam.

Sitka — Juneau

Ketchikan

Prince Rupert

50°

King, Coho, Red & Chum Salmon,
'Sole', Pilchard, Albacore, Rockfish, Grayfish,
Crab, Oyster, Steelhead Trout, Smelt, Halibut,
Herring, Lingcod, Sablefish, Shad, Razor Clam,
Soupfin Shark, Catfish, Blue Shark.

Victoria — Vancouver

Seattle

55°

Astoria

Pilchard, Jack Mackerel, Mackerel, Bluefin Tuna,
Anchovy, Albacore, Rockfish, King Salmon, Barracuda,
California Halibut, Skipjack Tuna, Shark, 'Sole',
Herring, Swordfish, White Sea Bass, Spiny Lobster,
Bonito, Kingfish, Abalone, Crab, Rock Bass, Sculpin,
Pompano, Mullet, Finback &    60°
    Humpback Whale

100 fathoms

San Francisco

Monterey

San Pedro

San Diego

Ensenada

Yellowfin, Skipjack & Bluefin Tuna, Bonito,
Albacore, Yellowtail, Shrimp, California
Halibut, Barracuda, Pilchard, Black &
White Sea Bass, Swordfish, Cabrilla,
Grouper, Anchovy, Rock Bass, Sheepshead,
Rockfish, Whitefish, Sculpin, Shark.

*Fig. 55.* Pacific Coast
Latitudinal zones, with their chief commercial species.
Isotherms are of mean annual sea surface temperature.

Energetic government action has been taken to attempt to discover the cause of the disappearance and the present location of stocks. Systematic searches by several research vessels have not at the time of writing revealed any substantial quantity off the U.S.A., although proof has been obtained of the large size of the stocks off Mexico. The full explanation of the great fall in numbers off the American coast has not yet been attained. Presumably it is a complex in which such factors as over-fishing, current shifts leading to a fall in water temperature below the minimum for satisfactory spawning, and changes in the food available to larvae may all play a part.

The tuna group accounted in 1950 for over a quarter of the weight of total catch, representing nearly three-quarters of the total value. The yellow-fin tuna is easily the most important, obtained chiefly by hand lines and 'chumming' with live bait from the large tuna clippers ranging to the Galapagos and beyond. Purse-seining is also used by shorter-range vessels. The tuna craft supply a large canning industry in southern California.

Other important fish are jack mackerel (*Trachurus symmetricus*) and Pacific mackerel (*Pneumatophorus diego*), of which a good deal is canned, and flatfishes. King (chinook) salmon, chiefly taken by gill nets and troll lines, is an important catch in the northern waters of the state, and is canned, smoked, mild-cured, or frozen.

In order of importance, the major Californian fishing ports in normal years are San Pedro (near Los Angeles), San Diego, Monterey, and San Francisco.

*The Cool Pacific.* Because of the overlapping of the range of various species, we cannot draw a precise line between this region and the last. Northern California and Oregon are a transition zone in which the characteristic southern catches of tuna and pilchard decrease rapidly as one proceeds northwards, while the characteristic northern catches of salmon, halibut, and cod quickly increase. The mean annual surface isotherm of 55°, which we have taken as an approximate dividing line between the warm- and cool-water fisheries on the east coast, can again be used as a rough guide. It meets the Pacific coast in Oregon. However, because of statistical usage it is convenient to include the whole of Oregon within the cool region, which extends northwards to the Bering Sea.

The fishing industry of this region is dominated by the salmon. It forms the most important sector of the great salmon belt stretching along the Pacific coasts from California to Japan. Alaska is the chief area, and has in some recent years accounted for about 60 per cent of the whole Pacific canned salmon output, which itself forms the great bulk of world output.

As salmon are anadromous fish, spending most of their time in the sea, but ascending the rivers to breed, they can most conveniently be caught during their yearly spawning runs. Pacific salmon, unlike the Atlantic, die after one spawning. For good food condition the fish should be caught before entering fresh water, for after this they stop feeding and deteriorate. The river-mouths are thus the centres of the industry, equipped with pound nets, gill nets, and beach-hauled seines.

Because salmon are fairly quickly perishable, and are mainly caught in remote areas, processing is normally necessary. Only about a fifth of the output is sold fresh. By far the most important use is in canning, and cannery plants dot the coasts. There are also a few floating canneries. In addition, small amounts of salmon are frozen, smoked, mild-cured, kippered, dried, or pickled. Canneries are naturally situated at catching points beside river-mouths, or where they have easy communication by vessel with several rivers. They are also fed by craft fishing the inlets and open sea by purse seines or troll lines. The latter gear is mainly used in the open sea on the feeding grounds of the king and silver salmon, and this fishery is carried on for much of the year. Most boats, however, do not go very far from the coast. Ice is used when daily landings are not made. A good deal of the trolled output is used fresh or for curing. Trolling has taken about a fifth of Washington's salmon catch in recent years, but a much smaller part of Alaska's. The other sea method, purse-seining, is particularly important in the Puget Sound area. In Alaska, purse-seiners are limited in size by law to prevent over-fishing.

Alaska's industry is run mainly by large organizations which can establish and maintain canneries and fishing gear in remote places. There is less scope for the small independent fisherman. Nearly a third of the Alaska catch is by traps, otherwise called pound nets, although these are banned in the Bristol Bay area on the Bering Sea. Another third is by stationary gill nets, and most of the rest is by purse seines. Because of its stress on shore catching, the Alaskan salmon fishery is highly seasonal. The smallness of the local population means that thousands of workers must come seasonally by ships from Seattle, and in lesser numbers from San Francisco. These are the two main American financial, outfitting, and initial marketing centres of the industry.

Pacific salmon represented in 1950 about a ninth of the total value of American (with Alaskan) fisheries output, and about a fifth in 1947. In Canada in 1947 it formed over a quarter of the total value. United States exports of canned salmon have fallen to very small amounts since the war, as the prosperous home market can pay relatively high prices for it. Canada, however, exports a large though diminished amount: 14,600 tons in 1951, chiefly to the U.K., Belgium, and Italy. In addition, about 13,000 tons of fresh or frozen salmon were exported, chiefly to the U.S.A.

There are five Pacific salmon species. The king, chinook, or spring salmon (*Oncorhynchus tshawytscha*) is the largest in size, averaging over 20 lb., and the best in quality. A higher proportion of its catch is sold fresh or frozen than of the other species. Its greatest concentrations are at the Columbia River, where it has three distinct 'runs' during the warmer part of the year. The mature fish, returning to spawn, vary from four to six years of age.

Red, sock-eye, or blueback salmon (*O. nerka*), a smaller fish, is especially important at the Fraser River district. The catch is almost entirely canned. The silver or coho salmon (*O. kisutch*) is a lighter red colour and fetches a lower price. It is widespread, but not caught in large quantities, and is chiefly used fresh or cured. Pink or humpback salmon (*O. gorbuscha*) is the most abundant, and is relatively cheap. The flesh is pale, and the individual's weight averages only 4 lb., its life-cycle being only two years. South-east Alaska is its main area. Finally, the chum or keta salmon (*O. keta*), with light yellow flesh, is the least valuable. It runs late in the season, in some areas as late as November.

About a quarter of Oregon's catch is normally salmon. Other important products are tuna, particularly albacore, and sardines and crabs. Washington has a larger fishery, and over a third of it is normally salmon. Pacific halibut (*Hippoglossus stenolepis*) is also valuable. Essentially a fish of northern cool and cold seas, halibut shows the significant change in water conditions as one proceeds northwards. It is caught on long lines. Another important and growing demersal fishery is the otter trawling for other flatfish, and for ling cod (*Ophiodon elongatus*) and rockfish (*Sebastodes*). There has also developed a valuable fishery for sharks, for the manufacture of vitamin oils from the liver. Canned shellfish are an important Washington product; especially canned oysters, Dungeness crab (*Cancer magister*), and Pacific razor clam (*Siliqua patula*).

TONNAGE LANDED

|  | *1950* | *1949* | *1938* |
|---|---|---|---|
| Washington | 54,000 | 79,000 | 73,000 |
| Oregon | 26,500 | 28,000 | 32,500 |

British Columbia now accounts for about half the value of Canada's fishery output. Between 1935 and 1939 it averaged 44 per cent, while in 1947 it reached 47·3 per cent. Its salmon landings weighed about 67,000 tons in 1948, a drop from 1947. About three-fifths of the value of the province's total fisheries output is salmon. Gill nets, pound nets, and beach seines are used along the coast, the most important area of which is the Fraser River. Offshore, the world's largest salmon fleet operates with purse seines or troll lines. Other important fisheries are long-lining for halibut and purse-seining, from September to March, for the abundant herring, which is chiefly used for reduction to meal and oil.

The halibut fishery is a classic case of successful international sea fishery conservation measures. Severe over-fishing took place along the Pacific coast in the early part of this century, leading in 1924 to a convention between the U.S.A. and Canada, which established an International Fisheries Commission to investigate the habits of the fish. A winter closed season was initiated, which varies according to year and area. Quotas are set, and the season, beginning in May, ends when these are reached. Halibut is chiefly marketed fresh or frozen. Other fish of significance in British Columbia are the sablefish or black cod (*Anoplopoma fimbria*), caught with the halibut, and ling cod and pilchard. The latter is mainly reduced to meal and oil. Clams, crabs, oysters, and shrimps are also produced in significant amounts, while interest has recently grown in an albacore fishery.

Vancouver and Prince Rupert are the province's two main centres for landing, storage, and dispatch. They command the two main rail routes eastwards and southwards, and also ship the products by sea.

Alaska is far the greatest salmon-producing area. In 1938 its salmon landings were 267,000 tons; in 1950 (a poor year) they were 120,000 tons. The great value of this catch, however, is not fully reflected in the Alaskan economy. The industry is largely financed and controlled from Seattle and San Francisco, and a great many of its workers have their homes in these areas, to which they return in the winter. These are also the main centres for distribution within the U.S.A. Nevertheless, the fishing industry is still the dominant one in Alaska. In 1950 there were about 11,200 persons engaged in fishing, 2,100 in transporting fish, and 14,200 in processing and handling. The total population of Alaska appears to be about 130,000, though it is difficult to obtain clear estimates because of the presence of transient military and naval personnel.

As we have seen, the bulk of Alaskan salmon production is from shore installations. There are other important fisheries, which in contrast depend chiefly on vessels, though the true bases of the vessels are generally in Seattle and other ports to the south. These fisheries include long-lining for halibut and sable-fish, and purse-seining and gill-netting for herring. Most of the herring are reduced to poultry meal and oil, with small amounts cured or used for bait in other fisheries. The Alaska herring, like the halibut, is protected by a winter closed season, in this case from December to June. Shellfish are of some significance, mainly comprising shrimps, Dungeness crab, and the razor clam. Cod fishing is carried out in the Bering Sea by a few vessels, chiefly using long lines. The cod and other demersal fish resources of this sea are little used at present, because of their remoteness, but there seems little doubt that in course of time this will become a major world fishing area. At present the chief activities on the North American side are the salmon fisheries along the coast of Bristol Bay. Some Japanese vessels, however, fished waters close to the American side before the war and will doubtless do so again. Total Alaskan fish landings were 220,000 tons in 1950. Those of fish other than salmon were just on 100,000 tons, only about 7,000 tons above the 1938 figure.

A long-standing industry of the Bering Sea is the fur-seal fishery. The Pribilof Islands, in Alaskan territory, are a major breeding ground. Sealing in this region has been regulated since 1911 by an international treaty between U.S.A., the British Empire, Russia, and Japan, which put an end to a destructive over-exploitation. Only bachelor seals are allowed to be taken, and there is a limit on total numbers taken per season. In the Pribilof Islands production is limited to about 50,000 skins each year.

This region completes our consideration of North American fisheries. It will be seen that they form a valuable resource, generally well utilized. Methods of catching, processing, and distribution are usually efficient in technique and organization. Considerable further expansion, especially in the Pacific, is likely as increasing population provides the stimulus.

## REFERENCES

*Yearbooks of Fishery Statistics, 1947, 1948–9,* and *1950–1.* (F.A.O., Rome.)

*Fishery Statistics of the U.S.A., 1950.* (U.S. Department of the Interior, Washington, 1953. Also previous annual issues.)

*Commercial Fisheries Review.* (Monthly Periodical of the Fish and Wild Life Service, U.S. Department of the Interior, Washington.)

*Commercial Fisheries Abstracts.* (Monthly, Fish and Wild Life Service.)

*Bulletins of the Bureau of Fisheries.* (U.S. Department of Commerce, Washington.)

*California Fish and Game Review.* (Quarterly, California Division of Fish and Game, Sacramento.)

*Fisheries Statistics of Canada.* (Dominion Bureau of Statistics, Ottawa, annually.)

*Reports on the Fisheries of Canada.* (Ottawa, periodically.)

*Progress Reports of Pacific Coast Stations.* (Vancouver, periodically.)

*Canada Yearbooks.* (Dominion Bureau of Statistics, Ottawa, annually.)

*Regulation and Investigation of the Pacific Halibut Fishery in 1950.* (International Fisheries Commission, Seattle, 1951.)

There are several North American journals devoted to fisheries, including;

*Atlantic Fisherman.* (Goffstown, N.H., monthly.)

*Canadian Fisherman.* (Gardenvale, Quebec, monthly.)

*Commercial Fisherman.* (New Brunswick, N.J., monthly.)

*Commercial Fisherman.* (Vancouver, monthly.)

*Fishing Gazette.* (New York, monthly.)

*Pacific Fisherman.* (Seattle, monthly.)

*Pan-American Fisherman.* (San Diego, monthly.)

*Southern Fisherman.* (New Orleans, monthly.)

# CHAPTER XIV

# AFRICAN REGIONS

IN proportion to its coast frontage and population, Africa's production is unimpressive by comparison with Europe, North America, or Asia. It resembles South America in its low total production, which was estimated at about 1,500,000 tons in 1953, as compared with South America's 600,000. In its low population density, poor internal communications, and low average standard of living, Africa also has rather similar marketing conditions to much of South America, and similarly has a low *per capita* consumption.

Africa is the least endowed with shelf area of any continent. There is a small but productive shelf off South Africa, but elsewhere deep water is usually reached very near the coast. African fisheries are thus dominated by pelagic species. This continent is also entirely within warm waters, so that many commercially important groups of fish are excluded from its catches. Of the great temperate water group of cod and related fish, only the South African shelf has any substantial production; this being of Cape hake, or stockfish. The west coasts, however, contain rich zones of upwelling in both hemispheres, associated with the offshore Trades and the Canaries and Benguela currents, and here are found rapidly developing pelagic fisheries. Fig. 56 shows the distribution of the commercially dominant species in African waters.

Until recently there were few areas in which fishing was carried out efficiently, and even now the bulk of the continent uses backward methods. The importance of its fish resources as a means of raising the low protein standards of the diet of many areas has been realized by many governments, both colonial and independent, and active encouragement of fisheries modernization and expansion is taking place in many countries. Present production of some representative countries is shown by Fig. 57. It must be borne in mind that computation of output in many areas where subsistence fishing is important can only be approximate.

African fisheries may be divided into the following main regions:

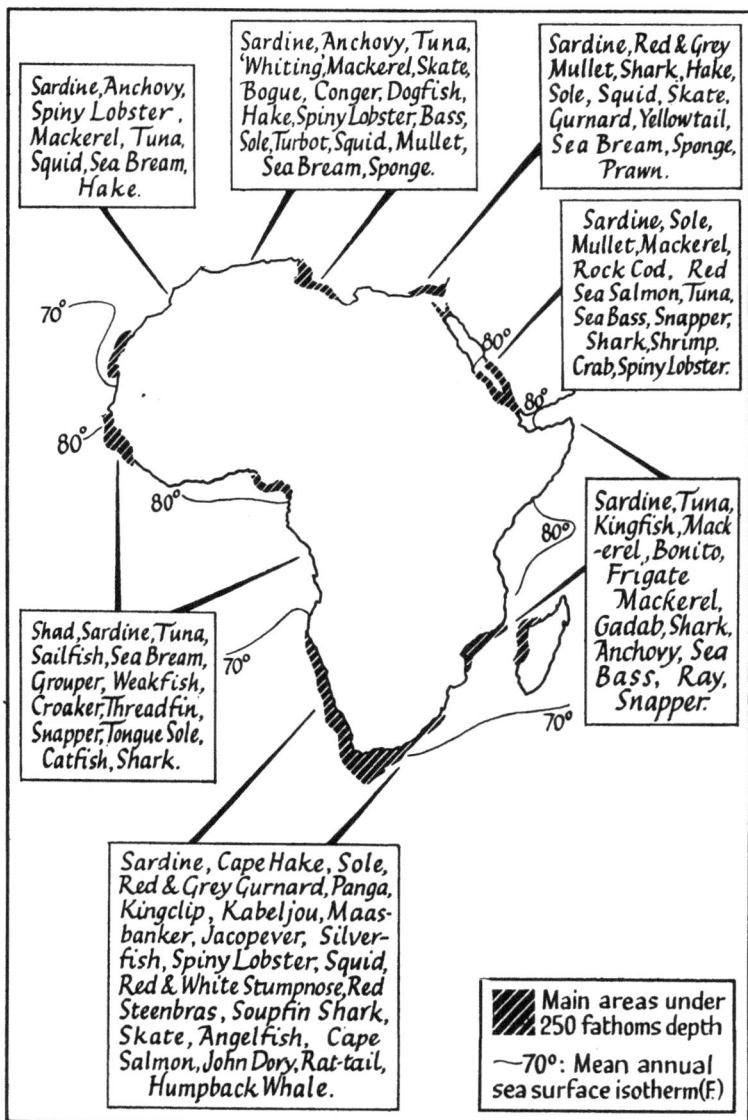

Sardine, Anchovy,
Spiny Lobster ,
Mackerel, Tuna,
Squid, Sea Bream,
Hake.

Sardine, Anchovy, Tuna,
'Whiting, Mackerel, Skate,
Bogue, Conger, Dogfish,
Hake, Spiny Lobster, Bass,
Sole, Turbot, Squid, Mullet,
Sea Bream, Sponge.

Sardine, Red & Grey
Mullet, Shark, Hake,
Sole, Squid, Skate,
Gurnard, Yellowtail,
Sea Bream, Sponge,
Prawn.

Sardine, Sole,
Mullet, Mackerel,
Rock Cod, Red
Sea Salmon, Tuna,
Sea Bass, Snapper,
Shark, Shrimp,
Crab, Spiny Lobster.

Sardine, Tuna,
Kingfish, Mack
-erel, Bonito,
Frigate
Mackerel,
Gadab, Shark,
Anchovy, Sea
Bass, Ray,
Snapper.

Shad, Sardine, Tuna,
Sailfish, Sea Bream,
Grouper, Weakfish,
Croaker, Threadfin,
Snapper, Tongue Sole,
Catfish, Shark.

Sardine, Cape Hake, Sole,
Red & Grey Gurnard, Panga,
Kingclip, Kabeljou, Maas-
banker, Jacopever, Silver-
fish, Spiny Lobster, Squid,
Red & White Stumpnose, Red
Steenbras, Soupfin Shark,
Skate, Angelfish, Cape
Salmon, John Dory, Rat-tail,
Humpback Whale.

Main areas under
250 fathoms depth

⌢70°: Mean annual
sea surface isotherm(F.)

*Fig. 56.* Broad distributional features of some commercial species in African
waters

The Mediterranean
The East Coast
The Southern Shelf and Benguela Current Zone
The Inner Tropical Atlantic Coast
The Canaries Current Zone

*The Mediterranean.* The African waters of the Mediterranean have long supported useful fisheries. The Phoenician settlements, for example, developed advanced and efficient techniques for catching tuna and other fish. While not an organically rich sea, for reasons already discussed, the Mediterranean has been well used because of the considerable populations living on its shores. This applies more to the European than the African coast, which has only one centre of dense population, the Lower Nile, although a coastal strip of moderate density extends westwards from the Gulf of Gabes to the Atlantic.

The bulk of Egypt's fishing industry is situated on the Mediterranean, though the Red Sea is of some importance, and a fair number of fishermen are employed in freshwater fisheries, notably on Lake Karoun, where there are about 200 fishermen with 400 rowing boats. The total number of sea and freshwater fishermen, and fisheries workers, in the country is about 50,000. Output was about 59,000 tons in 1951, a slight increase on 1947. After a sharp immediate post-war rise in recovery from the difficulties of the war period, production has not shown any marked buoyancy, although the government is now encouraging fisheries in various ways. The number of motorized small trawlers is increasing rapidly, having expanded from 160 in 1949 to 239 in 1950 in the Mediterranean ports. In all types of motor craft, Egypt now has over 300.

Pair-trawling by sailing or motor craft is important off the Nile delta. The soft mud of the grounds would bury a heavy otter trawl. The catch includes red mullet (*Mullus barbatus*), sea bream (such as *Sargus noct* and *Pagellus centrodontus*), gurnard (*Trigla corax*), grey mullet (such as *Mugil auratus*, *M. ramada*, and *M. saliens*), and skate. Shellfish are also important, particularly prawns and the blue-clawed swimming crab. This crab did not exist in the Mediterranean before the opening of the Suez Canal, but has since made its way from the Red Sea and flourished. A good deal of the delta grounds trawling is by the colony of Italian fishermen at Port Said. Other fisheries are seining from shore and boats for sardinella (a sardine-type fish),

*Plate XV.* SALMON TROLLER OF ASTORIA, ON THE COLUMBIA RIVER MOUTH. FISHING POLES NOT IN USE

red and grey mullet, common sole, prawns, crabs, and other fish, stake-netting, chiefly for mullet, and hand-dredging along the shores for cockles. As the densely populated delta, with large coastal towns like Alexandria, adjoins the main fishing grounds, disposal of the catch fresh offers no difficulties. There are good rail communications within the delta to Cairo and other cities, and well up the Nile Valley. Under the circumstances, the production rate of only 3 Kg. per head is decidedly low, even allowing for the low concentration of fish in Egyptian waters. Production per fisherman is little more than a ton a year.

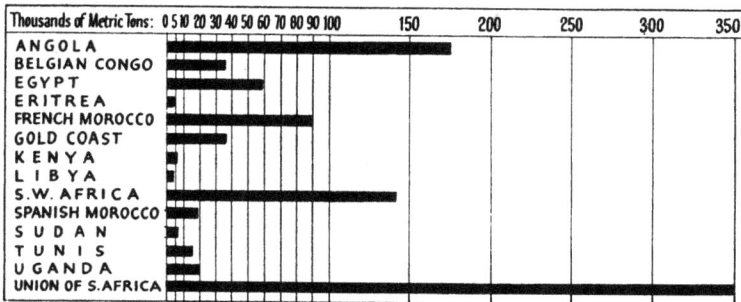

*Fig. 57.* Estimated production of sea and freshwater fish by certain African countries in 1951

Increasing mechanization to give longer ranges and more economically efficient fishing will undoubtedly expand the catches considerably, though the danger of over-fishing will not permit any spectacular expansion in Mediterranean waters. Doubtless bearing this in mind, the government is encouraging the development of the Red Sea line fisheries, and of fish culture in inland waters.

Egypt imports appreciable amounts of fish: about 17,000 tons in 1951, or over a quarter of her own production. Her consumption rate still remains low. Exports are small, being about 550 tons in 1951. They included £74,000 (Egyptian) worth of sponges.

Westwards from Egypt lies Libya, a very sparsely populated desert country with few natural harbours. The cultivated zones about Tripoli and Benghazi form a small market, but the chief purpose of developing Libyan waters would be to supply markets in Egypt, Italy, and other countries. There is undoubtebly scope for further expansion. The shelf is not very wide, save west of Tripoli, but there are considerable resources in pelagic fish, while the present production is only some 3,000 tons a year.

There is a coastal trap-net fishery for tuna, which is preserved in oil and by other methods at seven factories along the coast, for export to Italy. About 1,600 men, including 250 Italians, are employed in this industry as fishermen and factory workers. Some 1,100 tons of tuna were caught and processed in 1951. The same plants also salt part of the local sardine catch for export to Egypt. Another fishery of value is for sponges obtained in shallow water by divers using breathing equipment, operating to depths of 75 metres. Also used are dredges and hooked rods directly from boats. Yearly production during the last few years has varied between about 45 and 95 tons, the bulk, of course, for export. The quantity appears small, but sponges still fetch a high price, averaging over £4,000 a ton on export in recent years. Most of the sponge-fishing boats on the Libyan coast are Greek and Italian.

The widest shelf of the African Mediterranean is found in Tunisia off the Gulf of Gabes and the Gulf of Hammamet. The narrow Straits of Sicily confine the tuna close to the coasts during their annual migration. Considering these facts, and the substantial markets of Tunis, Sfax, and interior areas along the railways, the production is low. It was 11,700 tons in 1950, a small increase on pre-war figures, and represented a production rate of about 3½ Kg. The chief fisheries are by lampara nets for sardines and other small pelagic species, fishing by trap nets, and trawling for bottom fish. There is also appreciable production from fisheries on the coastal lakes. About half the tuna catch is canned. Recently successful experiments have been made locally with Californian live bait hand-lining, and this method may perhaps develop a fleet here.

Algeria, with roughly the same coast length but over twice the population, has a larger industry than Tunisia. Its shelf, however, is narrow. The number of trawling craft, 149 in 1949, had doubled in the previous decade. Trawler catches per unit of effort are markedly declining, and over-fishing of the small grounds appears to be taking place. The government has, therefore, prohibited trawling from June to October, but this restriction only applies to territorial waters.

Sardine fishing, mainly for canning, is the most important

fishery. There were 492 sardine boats in 1949, but the number is decreasing. There is also a substantial catch of anchovies for salting or brining in barrels.

Algeria landed about 28,000 tons in 1949, representing a production rate of about 3 Kg. Consumption rate is still lower, as substantial amounts are exported. In 1947 exports were 9,250 tons, chiefly of canned sardines and anchovies in brine to France. Imports are small, the chief item being cured cod.

In proportion to its coast length and population, Spanish Morocco has a more important fishery than Algeria. About 15,000 tons were landed in its two main ports of Ceuta and Melilla in 1945. Over half were sardines, chiefly caught by lampara and drift nets. There are two canning and some fifty salting plants on the Moroccan coast.

*The East Coast.* The Red Sea coast of Africa, although long, has too small a fishery output to warrant discussion as a separate region. While the northern end is not far distant from the densely populated part of Egypt, its ports lack rail communication with it, with the exception of Suez, which is therefore its main fishing centre. However, in 1950 Suez had only twenty motorized craft as compared with 239 in the Egyptian Mediterranean ports. Trawling is impracticable in many of the shallower coastal areas of the Red Sea because the nets are damaged by coral formations. Line fishing is thus the chief method for ground fish. The Sudan and the Eritrean coast have small, though increasing, productions.

In the Gulf of Aden fish are abundant, but here again a sparse population and poor communications have hampered development. There are large quantities of fish of the sardine type, and plentiful tuna and kingfish. The best possibilities lie in the development of an export trade in canned sardines and tuna. A cannery has been established in British Somaliland, while the government has been carrying out research. The main market for Gulf fish will not be in British Somaliland, with its population of only about three quarters of a million, but in the more densely populated countries of Kenya, Uganda, and Tanganyika. India and Pakistan may also prove valuable markets.

The tropical Indian Ocean coasts of Africa and Madagascar form an area of low fisheries production. With few exceptions the coasts are not densely populated. The chief fishing centres are therefore those, such as Mombasa and Dar-es-Salaam, that have good communications to the more populated interior

17

highlands. Zanzibar, a traditional entrepôt, is also a fishing centre. This town also imports a good deal of fish from the south coast of Arabia, some of it for dispatch to the East African mainland.

Fishing methods along the East African coast are backward, almost entirely run by native fishermen in canoes. The authorities have been making efforts to improve these by research and the technical education of the fishermen. A research station was opened in Zanzibar in 1953. A privately owned steam trawler with a British crew has also recently been operating from Dar-es-Salaam. These waters do not appear, however, to give a very good catch per unit of effort. They have only a narrow shelf. Their surface warmth and the small seasonal changes limit vertical mixing by seasonal overturn, while they also lack the continuous upwelling movements of parts of the Atlantic coasts of the continent. Nevertheless, there is scope for considerable expansion above the hitherto low levels of output, and energetic government action is bearing fruit. Kenya's output, for example, rose from about 3,000 tons in 1948 to 8,500 in 1952, and is still rising rapidly.

Recent government fisheries surveys of the resources of the shallow waters about the Seychelles and Mauritius gave very favourable results, and private companies are reported to be interested. Some of the catch is intended for export to East Africa and Madagascar.

*The Southern Shelf and Benguela Current Zone.* The Union of South Africa presents a marked contrast to East Africa. Its catch has grown rapidly and it is now far the largest in Africa, accounting for well over a third of the output of the continent. This region as a whole landed in 1951 over two-thirds of the continent's catch. The reasons for this are both physical and human. The area of the south coast is one of converging currents, where the warm Agulhas current meets the cool West Wind Drift and the Benguela current which stems from it. Convergence and vertical mixing lead to rich plankton concentration. The Benguela current moves northwards along the coast of Southwest Africa, taking a rich plankton which is increased by the upwelling in the offshore trade wind belt. These conditions give rise to a good concentration of demersal as well as pelagic fish, for there is a moderately wide shelf stretching between Port Elizabeth and Luderitz.

The human factors leading to the development are the advanced economic and technological state of the Union as compared with most of the rest of Africa. It has a European population of over two millions, from which it has drawn capital and skilled labour, and which provides a local market with a high *per capita* spending power. Inland transport is the best on the continent. For export to world markets it possesses large ports on well-used routes.

The Union's landings and exports rose moderately between 1938 and 1947, and then began to climb rapidly, as the following table (in tons) will show:

|  | *1938* | *1947* | *1949* | *1951* |
|---|---|---|---|---|
| Catches (excluding whales) | 64,000 | 115,000 | 201,000 | 350,000 |
| Exports | 10,340 | 15,200 | 30,100 | 50,000 |

This records consistent expansion which was still continuing, although with changing emphasis. The pilchard or sardine fishery (for *Sardinops ocellata*) has been growing rapidly, both in fleet strength and production; 250,000 tons were landed in 1951, as compared with 150,000 in 1950. These are mainly used for canning, while there were also ten factories operating in 1951 for their reduction to meal and oil. Trawling for Cape hake and other groundfish is not now expanding rapidly. There were forty-two large trawlers in 1951, as compared with thirty-seven in 1948. These are mostly steam trawlers, not common in the world outside European fisheries. Their chief base is Cape Town, while substantial trawler landings are also made at Port Elizabeth, East London, and Mossel Bay.

Another important fishery is for crayfish, or spiny lobster (*Jasus lalandii*). The majority are canned or frozen. There is a large export. The crayfish were in danger of over-fishing, so in 1947 the government imposed a yearly ceiling of 6,000,000 lb. on crayfish exports. Other species caught in quantity include snoek (*Thyrsites atun*), soles (*Austroglossus* species), maasbanker or horse mackerel (*Trachurus trachurus*), soupfin shark (*Eulamia limbata*) for liver oil, panga (*Pterogrymnus laniarus*), kabeljou (*Johnius hololepidotus*), silverfish (*Argyrozona argyrozona*), and kingklip (*Genypterus capensis*). Whaling is quite important.

In 1951 the Union had 763 motor or steam fishing craft and about 1,800 sail or hand-propelled boats. There were about 7,000 fishermen, who then had a yearly output per head of about 18 tons, rather more than that of the U.S.A. Production rate in 1951 for the country was about 30 Kg. per head per year, which is not only very high for Africa, but is about double of that of the U.S.A. Consumption rate is appreciably lower, because of the large exports and the large amounts of pilchard reduced to oil and meal. Precise calculation is rendered difficult. Nevertheless, it must now be quite a high figure.

The chief exports are canned pilchards to Malaya, Ceylon, Australia, the Pacific Islands, East and West Africa, and Israel; frozen crayfish tails to the U.S.A.; canned crayfish to France, Belgium, Britain, and U.S.A.; and cured hake and other fish to Australia, the Rhodesias, and the Congo. There is also a moderate amount of fresh or frozen fish exported to neighbouring countries to the north. Oils reduced from pilchards, and the valuable vitamin oils from the livers of sharks and other fish, form a valuable export, while whale oil exports approach those of fish oils in value. Finally, over a third of the total weight of fish product exports in 1951 was accounted for by fish meal. Imports of fish in 1951 were under a fifth of exports, and came chiefly from South-west Africa.

The long-term trend of the prosperous and energetic South African fishing industry will doubtless continue upwards. There are large areas in Africa, and for that matter in southern Asia, which form markets capable of marked expansion, and which South Africa is well placed to supply.

Northwards up the Benguela current coasts lie South-west Africa, politically linked to South Africa, and the Portuguese colony of Angola. Both of these territories have undergone great fisheries expansion in recent years. South-west Africa's catch had reached 140,000 tons by 1951. Angola had reached 135,000 tons in 1950, from 52,000 in 1947 and 26,000 in 1938.

South-west Africa, a country largely of desert and dry steppe, has a population of only about a third of a million, so the bulk of its large output is exported. Weight of exports has grown from a mere 1,000 tons in 1938 to 35,000 tons in 1951, representing a decidedly higher weight before processing. Important export items are oil and meal from pilchard. Most of the oil goes to the Union, some for re-export, while the meal goes chiefly to the U.S.A., the Union, and the Low Countries. Canned pilchards go chiefly to the Union and Britain. There is also a large export of canned crayfish to the U.S.A., the Union, and Europe, and of frozen crayfish tails to the U.S.A. A moderate amount of fresh fish is sent to the Union. Finally, there is a sporadic export of oil from humpback whales caught locally during their winter sojourn away from the Antarctic in this area of warmer water. The 1951 production rate of South-west Africa is over 400 Kg. per head, approaching that of Norway. Fishing plays a major part in its economy.

While discussing Commonwealth territories in this part of Africa, it may be mentioned that the British islands of St Helena, Ascension, and Tristan da Cunha have recently been surveyed with the intention of developing their fishery resources, particularly for the canning and export of crawfish. Tristan da Cunha is in production.

Angola resembles South-west Africa in some respects. Its total production is roughly the same, and it exports the bulk of it. Weight of exports in 1951 was 52,000 tons, as compared with 18,000 in 1938. The relatively low and scattered native population of about 4,000,000 does not appear to provide any large effective demand. Important items of export are cured fish to the Congo, Mozambique, and French Equatorial Africa, canned tuna to Portugal and Italy, and fish and whale oils to western Europe. The greatest item by weight is fish meal, amounting to three-fifths of the weight of fish products exports in 1951, and some two-fifths of the value. The motor fishing fleet numbered 179 in 1950, over triple that of 1948, and there were about 2,000 sailing or hand-propelled craft, including those on the rivers.

The fisheries region just discussed offers a classic example of how, with the application of enterprise and skill, the fish production of under-developed waters can be raised very quickly, far more quickly than can agricultural production in underdeveloped lands.

*The Inner Tropical Atlantic Coast.* This region contrasts with the last in its more densely populated lands and its poorer waters. Its countries have long been substantial·fish importers, and its fisheries are of low efficiency and productivity. There is no upwelling off these coasts, so that the organic production is less, while those resources that are available are not adequately exploited. The fisheries are dominantly in the hands of native fishermen using canoes. They are limited to inshore and river waters, and are most intensive in the Niger delta, which is now fished to the limit of its resources.

As so much of the fishing is for subsistence or immediate sale at the small and scattered fishing settlements, published output statistics are unlikely to be very accurate. Recent figures (metric tons) available for some countries are:

| | |
|---|---:|
| French West Africa (1952) | 60,000 |
| French Equatorial Africa (1951) | 40,000 |
| Gold Coast (1948) | 36,000 |
| Sierra Leone (1953) | 5,000 |
| Gambia (1947) | 1,000 |

Much of these outputs are from rivers, which can easily be exploited by the often quite dense populations along their shores. The Gold Coast production rate is about 8 Kg. per head per year, that of French West Africa only 4 Kg.

The use of large modern vessels for sea fishing off West Africa is hampered by the general lack of good natural harbours, so that the best solution would appear to be by the development of small motorized surf boats. This is the policy of the British Colonial Office. Sierra Leone is an exception, with good natural harbours at Freetown and elsewhere. Here there are possibilities for the use of large fishing vessels. An experimental sea fishery with a small trawler has already been conducted from Freetown. This town is also the centre of the British Government-sponsored West African Fisheries Research Institute. The shelf between Sierra Leone and Gambia is the only one of real width in West Africa. Two steam trawlers are also operating out of Lagos and Port Harcourt in Nigeria for West African Fisheries, a subsidiary of the Colonial Development Corporation. Their catch is sent inland in refrigerated lorries.

These Western-style operations are, however, still of minor importance as compared with the traditional native fisheries. Fixed gill nets, beach seines, hand-cast nets, staked net traps, and basket traps are common methods, particularly for the abundant 'bonga', or shad. Also used are drift nets, ring nets, hand lines, long lines, and troll lines, while spears are used in some areas for rays and barracuda. Some forms of net have interchangeable uses, for example, as drift nets or ring nets. Boats are mostly dugout canoes driven by sails, paddles, or both. Fleets often leave with the land winds after midnight, and return with the sea breeze next afternoon. Catches are partly sold fresh in the immediate vicinity of the landing beach, or preserved by part-cooking or smoking, followed by sun-drying. Salting is not very common, presumably because of its relatively high price from the point of view of the native fishermen. The drying is often inefficient, and the dried fish reaches inland markets in none too good a state. Local Europeans commonly refer to it as 'stink-fish'.

Important species caught at various points in the seas and estuaries of this region by local fishermen are sardine types, shad (related to herring, and rather deeper in body), tuna, sailfish, sea bream, groupers, Sciaenidae such as weakfish and croaker, ,threadfins (Polynemidae), snappers (Lutjanidae), tongue soles (Cynoglossidae), catfishes (Siluroidae), and sharks. There is also some shark-fishing by European concerns in Sierra Leone and Gambia for the production of liver vitamin oil.

The Gold Coast appears to have the most intensively pursued sea fisheries. Nigerians, on the other hand, have rather neglected their sea coast because of the good fishing opportunities in the Niger delta, but the British Government set up a Fisheries Department in the country a few years ago, which, among other things, is demonstrating to local fishermen the possibilities of sea fishing.

Approximate figures are available as to the numbers of fishermen and craft in some areas, although they do not differentiate between marine and freshwater fishing. In 1947 the Gold Coast had 50,000 fishermen and 800 dugout canoes. Many of the fishermen operated from shore without boats. Production per fisherman is well under a ton a year. Senegal, in French West Africa, had 20,000 fishermen and 200 dugout canoes. Liberia had only about 1,200 fishermen, but as many as 525 canoes. Sierra Leone had about 5,000 canoes, although figures are not available of the number of fishermen. It is clear, however, that throughout this inner tropical region production per fisherman is generally very low.

Nigeria and the Gold Coast, the two main centres of fairly dense population, have long been substantial importers of fish. Their imports, after having shrunk during the war and immediate post-war years, have now regained their previous volume, despite the steep rise in fish prices on the world market. Nigeria imported 10,000 tons, and the Gold Coast 8,600 tons, in 1951. The chief items were dried cod from Norway, Newfoundland, and other northern countries; dried shad and other local fish from French Togoland, Sierra Leone, and other nearby territories; and canned sardines and other fish from such countries as Portugal and South Africa. The existence of these imports shows that there would be little difficulty in disposing of an increased local catch. It is likely, however, that Nigeria, with its large population of over 24,000,000, much of it inland, will always remain a substantial importer.

There is still plenty of room for improvement in the protein standards of the diet of most areas of tropical Africa. Cheap species of fish, properly treated for preservation in the hot and often humid conditions, can contribute a great deal to the solution of the problem. Smoked fish do not keep well in this climate, but canned or well dehydrated fish are satisfactory.

*The Canaries Current Zone.* Between Senegal and Morocco lies the desert belt of very sparse population. Fisheries by the coastal inhabitants are therefore unimportant. However, the seas throughout the Canaries Current Zone are rich because of the plankton nourished by the upwelling waters in their zone of offshore trade winds. There are abundant sardine, anchovy, mackerel, and tuna. The southern part of this zone is too far from Europe to be very intensively fished, though it will doubtless attract increasing attention. Vessels from the Canaries and Cape Verde Islands regularly fish these waters, and these island groups have an appreciable export of fish.

In the northern part of the Canaries Current Zone, on the other hand, there is a major fishery in French Morocco, which has grown rapidly in recent years. Output reached a peak of 123,000 tons in 1950, as compared with 50,000 tons in 1947 and 30,000 tons in 1938. The bulk of the production, as with Angola and South-west Africa, is exported. The weight of exports in 1950 was 80,000 tons, compared with 18,000 tons in 1938. Production and exports have since fallen from the 1950 peak, landing in 1951 being 91,000 tons.

French Morocco has several advantages over the rest of this zone. It has a moderately dense coastal population and several well-established ports, while it is the nearest part to the European market. French enterprise and capital have recently been energetic in many branches of the Moroccan economy: the invasion of the last war has tended to stimulate investment outside metropolitan France.

About two-thirds of the weight of exports is of canned sardines, chiefly to France, with fair quantities to Britain, western Germany, other western European countries, and other French colonies. Some fresh or frozen sardines are sent chiefly to France and Algeria, and some cured sardines and anchovy to the same countries. Tuna, mainly canned, are also a valuable export, while canned or frozen crawfish have appreciable exports.

Finally, about a fifth of the weight of exports is of meal and oil, to western Europe and the U.S.A.

The country has probably not yet reached the maximum possible long-term output. Further development may depend more on human than physical factors, especially on the state of political and economic relations between France and Morocco.

The question of the future political status of many of the colonies and protectorates of Africa is indeed of great importance in the assessment of fisheries potentialities. Large-scale modern fisheries such as those of the Union of South Africa cannot develop without plenty of capital, whose providers must be reasonably sure of continuing political and economic stability in the region of their investment. They cannot be sure of these in the present transitional phase affecting much of Africa.

There can be little doubt that, in most of the continent, economic activities will tend to be increasingly in the hands of local individuals and governments. With increasing political independence they will need to obtain more of their capital and organizers, whether private or governmental, from within their own territories. In tropical Africa, therefore, we may generally expect a gradual expansion and modernization of fisheries, with small-scale fishermen remaining for some time as the basic units, rather than a major revolution to produce fisheries with large vessels and business units.

## REFERENCES

*Reports of the Fisheries and Marine Biological Survey Division.* (Division of Fisheries, Pretoria, annually.)

'Otter Trawl Fisheries of South Africa.' Peter Scott. (*Geographical Review,* New York, Oct. 1949.)

*The Fish and Fisheries of the Gold Coast.* F. R. Irvine. (Crown Agents for the Colonies, London, 1947.)

*Report on the Sea Fisheries of Sierre Leone, 1945.* G. A. Steven. (Freetown.)

*Pêche sur les Côtes D'Afrique Occidentale.* E. Postel. (Dakar, 1950.)

*Review of Kenya Fisheries, 1950.* H. Copley. (Nairobi.)

*Marine Fish Stocks of Somalia.* (F.A.O. Fisheries Bulletin, July/Aug. 1953.)

*Mediterranean Fisheries.* (F.A.O. Fisheries Bulletin, May/Aug. 1952.)

*Production of Fish in the Colonial Empire.* C. F. Hickling. (Colonial Office, London, 1949 and 1954.)

*Report on the Mauritius-Seychelles Fisheries Survey.* J. F. G. Wheeler and F. D. Ommanney, (H.M.S.O., London, 1953.)

# CHAPTER XV

# SOUTH AND CENTRAL AMERICAN REGIONS

THE South American catch, estimated at about 600,000 tons per year, is the lowest of any continent, save very sparsely populated Australia. With an ice-free coast length of approximately that of North America it has just over a sixth its production. With South America we will also discuss here Central America and the West Indies, which have more in common with it than with North America, though statistically they are now usually included in North America for continental production totals. All the countries south of the United States have from the point of view of human geography much in common with South America, but we have discussed Mexico with North America for reasons already indicated. Central American and West Indian production is also low, totalling some 40,000 tons.

The reasons for the generally low Latin-American figures are several, and are primarily human, for the potential output is much higher than the actual one. The continent is rather sparsely populated with about seven inhabitants per square kilometre, but the food needs of its people are by no means fully met, save perhaps in Argentina, Uruguay, and the more developed parts of some other countries such as Brazil and Chile. South America is, however, better placed than Asia for providing increased flesh foods from the land, with considerable areas of tropical and temperate grasslands capable of carrying increased densities of livestock. Nevertheless, fisheries output will undoubtedly increase considerably in the future. Traditionally, Latin American interests have been in agriculture and to a lesser extent mining. The people of the tropical areas of the continent have not been particularly energetic in developing their resources, and the sea is no exception, although river and short-range sea fishing has long been carried on. Further development depends on supplies of capital and technical information, which are being encouraged or provided by various governments, while the F.A.O. is also assisting with technical advice. Fig. 58 shows the relative fisheries importance of the mainland countries.

*Fig. 58.* Relative fisheries output of South American seaboard countries in 1950 (save for Ecuador and Guianas, whose outputs are 1949 F.A.O. estimates. They have subsequently developed markedly.)

The Second World War provided an incentive to increased production, as the chief sources of fish imports such as Norway and Newfoundland were either cut off or seriously impeded in their exports by the war. Latin America's population was meanwhile increasing rapidly: 22·32 per cent in the decade 1937 to 1947. During this decade total food production has been estimated to have increased by barely 20 per cent. The inevitably higher prices for foodstuffs stimulated fish production, and the increase for some countries is shown below, for years for which statistics are available.

PRODUCTION IN TONS

|  | *1938* | *1939* | *1947* | *1949* | *1952* |
|---|---|---|---|---|---|
| Brazil | — | 103,300 | 139,700 | 152,600 | 174,600 |
| Chile | 30,600 | — | 60,100 | 76,200 | 118,300 |
| Peru | — | 4,800 | 36,600 | 60,800 | 113,000 |
| Venezuela | 21,700 | — | 76,200 | 75,400 | — |

The increase in Peru is particularly striking, and to this must be added the great increase in fish caught off Peru by United States vessels and taken directly back to their home ports. By all reports this clear upward trend in South America is continuing, though there are certain exceptions.

For more detailed study we may divide the area into five regions:

> The Caribbean
> The Tropical Atlantic Waters
> Southern Temperate Waters
> The Tropical Pacific Waters

*The Caribbean.* This sea is traversed by the Caribbean current, a continuation of the South Equatorial current, and consequently it has very warm water, the mean temperature of the surface water for the year being everywhere above 80° F. As is to be expected in such water, the variety of fish species is very great, but the total stock does not generally reach a high concentration. The waters are not organically rich over much of the area. There is no cool winter to provide nutrient supply from deeper waters by overturn, nor is there any strong offshore current of water leading to upwelling. Again, the narrowness of the islands and the isthmus means that there are no large rivers discharging land-derived organic matter and nutrients, save along the coast of South America. This is one reason why Venezuela, which occupies the bulk of the mainland coast of the Caribbean, has about double the total output of all the West Indies and Central American countries, though these have a considerably greater total coastline and population.

In shelf area the Caribbean is not very well provided. It is surrounded mainly by belts of strong folding, so that coast plains generally are narrow, and depths increase rapidly away from the shores. Exceptions are found around the Orinoco delta, the Gulf of Venezuela, and parts of the south coast of Cuba, all of these being fishing areas of significance. The largest area of shallow water, the Mosquito Bank off Nicaragua and Honduras, does not appear to be well fished, presumably because the main centres of population of these countries are in the healthier uplands of the west, rather than on the east coast.

Despite the physical environment, which is not favourable to large fishery production, there is no reason to suppose that

Caribbean production could not be increased considerably above its present figure. Many of the islands, such as Cuba, Hispaniola, and Jamaica, have quite high densities for almost purely agricultural countries, while some of the smaller islands, such as Barbados, have much higher densities. Food is becoming a pressing problem in many areas, as recent demonstrations have shown. Continuance of the islands' position as a major world producing area of sugar-cane for export may depend on satisfactory supplies of foodstuffs which do not compete for land with the sugar-cane; and fish is one of the best of these. Human and economic obstacles to increased production can be overcome by the dissemination of information about modern fishing methods, the supply of capital on easy terms to fishermen for such purposes as motorization of craft, and the development of rapid distribution systems to inland markets. In the British West Indies, for example, a government-sponsored fishery survey has been carried out, and fishery officers subsequently appointed to advise local fishermen on methods of increasing output. What can be done by vigorous government encouragement has been shown by Venezuela, which greatly expanded its fisheries in recent years, under the stimulus of loans by government agencies to fishermen for motorization of craft, and government assistance in marketing. Computed production of countries having all or part of their coastline on the Caribbean, or closely adjacent waters, is tabulated below in tons, for 1951 or the nearest available year.

| British Honduras | 500 | Haiti | 2,000 |
|---|---|---|---|
| Bahamas | 1,400 | Honduras | 100 |
| Barbados (1938) | 500 | Martinique and | |
| Jamaica | 5,500 | Guadeloupe (1938) | 400 |
| Leeward Is. | 2,100 | Netherlands, W. Indies | 200 |
| Windward Is. | 5,600 | Nicaragua | 200 |
| Colombia | 16,000 | Panama | 900 |
| Costa Rica | 2,500 | Puerto Rico | 2,100 |
| Cuba | 9,800 | Venezuela | 75,000 |
| Dominican Rep. | 500 | Virgin Is. | 100 |
| Guatemala | 250 | | |

Yearly production rates per head are, with the exception of Venezuela (at 17 Kg. in 1951), usually very low. For example,

Cuba's is about 2 Kg., while for Honduras it is under 0·1 Kg. Output per fisherman is low; too low even for local conditions of relatively sparse fish concentrations and small capital. The British West Indies production has been estimated by the Colonial Office at less than a ton per fisherman per year. Craft are generally simple, small, and unpowered, with short range. For example, in 1946 Dominica had a total of 834 fishing craft, of which 642 were dugout canoes of less than 20 ft. length, 89 were dugout canoes of over 20 ft., and 96 were planked open rowboats, mostly under 20 ft. There were but 6 motor boats and 1 decked sailing boat. In the same year Trinidad (with Tobago) had 1,805 boats, of which only 47 were dugouts, while 1,321 were planked open sail or rowboats of less than 20 ft. long, and 297 were more than 20 ft. There were also 29 decked sailing craft and 111 motor boats, by far the highest number of motor craft of any Caribbean island, yet representing only 6 per cent of the total number of fishing vessels. Clearly there is much scope for improvement here.

Species caught are characteristic warm-water types, in most areas representing a wide selection, without any one species bulking especially large. The figures for Venezuela, given below, are broadly representative.

TONNAGE OF VENEZUELAN LANDINGS OF CERTAIN SPECIES, 1945

| | |
|---|---:|
| *Perches, Croakers, Breams, and Allies* | 19,150 |
| Weakfish (*Plagioscion squamosissimus*) | 10,500 |
| Grunt (*Haemulon flavolineatum*) | 3,000 |
| Snappers (*Lutianus* species and *Rhomboplites* aurorubens) | 1,610 |
| Groupers (*Epinephelus* species) | 980 |
| *Sardines, Anchovies, and Allies* | 8,670 |
| Sardine (*Sardinella anchovia*, and others) | 6,540 |
| Anchovies (*Anchoa parva* and *Anchovia nigra*) | 670 |
| *Mackerels and Allies* | 7,680 |
| Spanish mackerel (*Scomberomorus maculatus*) | 4,760 |
| Other *Scomberomorus* species | 1,500 |
| Cutlass fish (*Trichiurus lepturus*) | 960 |
| Swordfish (*Xiphias gladius*) | 55 |
| Bonito (*Sarda sarda*) | 49 |
| *Jacks, Pompanos, and Allies* | 5,140 |
| Common jack (*Caranx hippos*) | 2,180 |
| Pompano (*Selene vomer*) | 1,730 |
| Big-eyed scad (*Trachurops crumenophthalma*) | 650 |

TONNAGE OF VENEZUELAN LANDINGS OF CERTAIN SPECIES, 1945

| | |
|---|---|
| *Mullets and Barracudas* | 3,910 |
| Mullets (*Mugil* species) | 3,410 |
| Great Barracuda (*Sphyraena barracuda*) | 500 |
| *Elasmobranchii* | 2,060 |
| Dog shark (*Mustelus canis*) | 1,780 |
| *Crustaceans* | 75 |
| Spiny lobster (*Panulirus argus*) | 51 |
| Shrimp (*Penaeus* species) | 24 |
| *Other Marine Fishes* | approx. 2,400 |
| *Freshwater Fish* | |
| Characinidae | 3,400 |

Foreign trade of the Caribbean countries in fish is relatively small. Imports exceed exports in most areas, as is to be expected. The chief imports are the cheap forms of cured fish. By 1949, these cured fish imports had recovered from war-time dislocations, and in many areas exceeded pre-war figures. Thus the Dominican Republic imported 2,700 tons in that year, as against 1,900 in 1938; Haiti imported 3,900 as against 2,400, and Cuba 12,100 compared with 9,000. In the case of Venezuela, however, whose own production had risen considerably during the war, fish imports were well below pre-war.

As broadly representative of the foreign trade in fish of the Caribbean islands we may take Cuba, the largest in population. In 1949 it imported 15,722 tons and exported only 1,169. The main import was salted cod and related fish, supplied mainly by the Maritime Provinces of Canada and by Norway, and to a lesser extent by Newfoundland, Britain, and New England. Canned sardines were the next most important group, the U.S.A. being far the greatest supplier, followed by Portugal, Canada, and French Morocco. Cured herring was another important import, chiefly from Norway and Canada, and to a smaller extent the U.S.A. Other imports included canned bonito and tuna from Spain, Portugal, and U.S.A., canned mackerel from U.S.A., and canned anchovies from Portugal. Canned cuttlefish from Portugal and U.S.A., and cod-liver oil, chiefly from Norway, were in significant amounts. The great predominance of cured and canned fish can be seen: only 32 tons of fish, and a small quantity of shellfish, were imported fresh or frozen. Sufficiently fast and cheap transport routes and marketing arrangements have not yet been developed for such imports. Cuba's small quantity of exports mainly consisted of fresh spiny lobsters to the U.S.A. Shark-liver oil, which fetched a very high price during and just after the war for vitamin manufacture in the U.S.A. and elsewhere, has slumped heavily in price, and production

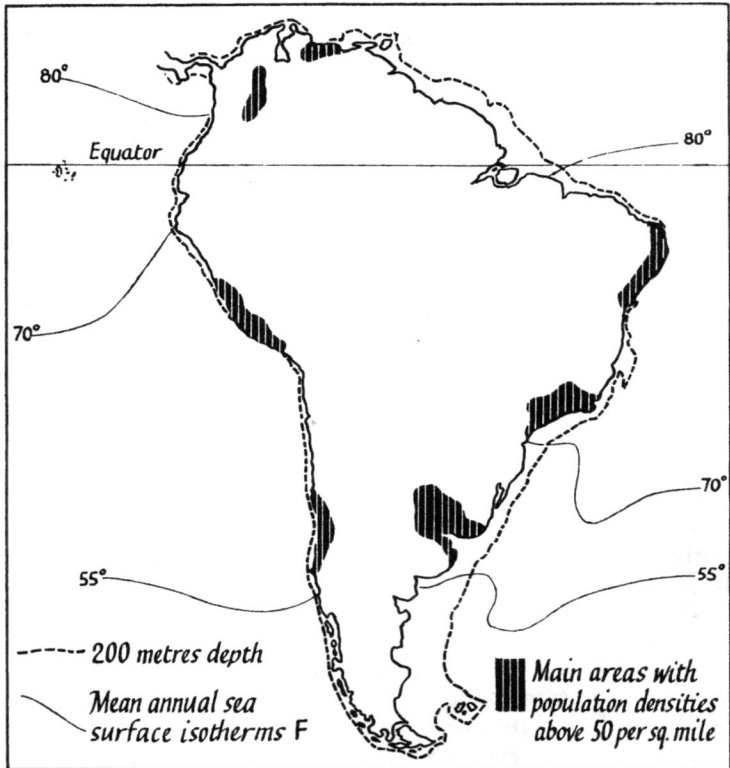

80°

Equator

80°

70°

70°

55°

55°

------ *200 metres depth*

*Mean annual sea
surface isotherms* **F**

▮▮▮ *Main areas with
population densities
above 50 per sq. mile*

*Fig. 59.* South America: some sea conditions, and the chief markets

has therefore also fallen in quantity. The value of this export in 1949 was under a tenth of its 1947 figure.

Fishing settlements in the Caribbean countries are generally dispersed widely along the coastlines, supplying only their immediate neighbourhoods. There are some exceptions; for example, fresh fish landed at Barranquilla, Cartagena, and

Santa Marta are flown some 400 miles by Colombian Airlines to Bogota. In general, however, improved transport, processing, refrigeration, and other facilities need to be developed by private enterprise or the governments concerned in order to tap the considerable potential markets. This is gradually taking place, and local production should then respond. That there is great scope for expansion of demand can be seen from the following table:

APPROXIMATE FISH CONSUMPTION PER HEAD PER YEAR (1947)

IN KILOGRAMS

| Colombia | 0·6 | Guatemala | 0·2 |
|---|---|---|---|
| Costa Rica | 1·4 | Haiti | 1·2 |
| Cuba | 4·2 | Honduras | 0·1 |
| Dominican Rep. | 1·4 | Panama | 2·2 |

Alone of the major Caribbean countries Venezuela has a substantial consumption, at 16½ Kg. in 1947. This was nearly three times its pre-war level.

*The Tropical Atlantic.* This includes the bulk of Brazil, while in the north it merges with the Caribbean region in the Guianas area. The mean annual water surface isotherm of 75° is carried as far south as the southern tropic by the warm Brazil current, a branch of the South Equatorial current deflected southward by the 'bulge' of Brazil. The composition of the fish stocks therefore does not differ greatly from that of the Caribbean. In shelf area Brazil has a moderate endowment, particularly off the Amazon delta. This area, combined with its great length of coast and rivers, and population of some 52,500,000 (1950), makes it natural for the country to achieve the highest total fishery output in South America. This was computed at 153,000 tons in 1950, representing a rate of only about 3 Kg. per head per year. It has about 68,000 commercial fishermen with an output of only some 2 tons per head per year. Brazil's output increased 40 per cent between 1939 and 1949. There is a considerable output from fresh water, because of the many large rivers, and a substantial proportion of this freshwater catch is probably not fully recorded because of the scattered and near-subsistence nature of some of the interior river settlements. The official figures for production by states are given overleaf.

18

CATCHES IN TONS

| | 1946 | 1950 |
|---|---|---|
| Guaporé | 80 | 96 |
| Acre | 283 | 308 |
| Amazonas | 2,951 | 5,487 |
| Rio Branco | 31 | 29 |
| Pará | 6,271 | 9,021 |
| Amapá | 225 | 313 |
| Maranhão | 10,053 | 34,284 |
| Piauí | 291 | 679 |
| Ceará | 3,116 | 3,541 |
| Rio Grande do Norte | 4,436 | 3,535 |
| Paraiba | 559 | 1,037 |
| Pernambuco | 785 | 1,124 |
| Alagoas | 1,428 | 1,218 |
| Serigipe | 773 | 994 |
| Bahia | 3,988 | 4,484 |
| Minas Geraes | 1,050 | 1,467 |
| Espírito Santo | 2,331 | 1,324 |
| Rio de Janeiro | 30,438 | 28,136 |
| Distrito Federal | 13,546 | 9,843 |
| São Paulo | 15,429 | 12,612 |
| Paraná | 687 | 826 |
| Santa Catarina | 4,493 | 10,056 |
| Rio Grande do Sul | 17,972 | 21,771 |
| Mato Grosso | 1,094 | 797 |
| Goiás | 100 | 125 |
| *National Total* | 122,410 | 153,107 |

The average consumption per head per year is only about 3·3 Kg., so there is much room for expansion of demand. Imports, chiefly of cured fish, are relatively low in proportion to population, and were 26,100 tons in 1950, as compared with 16,600 tons in 1938. Both home production and imports have thus risen markedly. Imports are almost entirely of cured cod in most years. Norway is by far the greatest supplier, followed by Britain, Canada, Iceland, and U.S.A. Brazilian exports are negligible.

The government regulates the conduct of fish markets in towns, while fishermen are required by law to join the *colonia* or fishermen's association of their port. These associations are concerned with the social welfare and technical education of fishermen, and are affiliated to the General Confederation of

Brazilian Fishermen, with headquarters in Rio de Janiero. As a move to assist modernization and expansion of the industry, the Credit Bank of the Fishing Industry advances money to fishermen, canners, and others. It obtains its capital from a 3 per cent tax on fish at landing points, but does not appear to have sufficient at its disposal for the expansion intended. Nevertheless, the interest of the government has doubtless been one of the factors in the substantial recent increase of output.

The Guiana colonies, with their small population, have low total outputs, recent estimates being about 10,000 tons for British Guiana, which gives the colony quite a high production rate, 3,000 for French Guiana, and 1,000 for Surinam. These should be capable of considerable increase if needed. The substantial rivers of these colonies provide plenty of freshwater fish and also bring down a great deal of organic material and nutrients to assist the development of fish resources in the shelves off their mouths. The shelf off the Guianas is decidedly wider than that off Venezuela. Some quite sizeable craft from Georgetown operate on it (Plate XVI). Ultimately this area may become an important supplier for less favoured and more densely populated countries of the Caribbean.

*Southern Temperate Waters.* These form the section of South American fisheries capable of the greatest expansion, and may eventually become important exporters elsewhere in the continent and even farther afield. Of the three countries concerned—Uruguay, Argentina, and Chile—Argentina has by far the greatest area of shelf, an area which ranks with the North Sea and other traditionally important regions. In temperature the sea here broadly resembles the western European shelf, though the currents are not analogous. The mean annual surface water isotherms are pushed northwards along the coast by the cool Falkland current, branching off from the West Wind Drift as it rounds Cape Horn. Mean annual surface temperature at the latitude of the Plate is thus only 60°, while the 45° isotherm reaches the coast just north of the Straits of Magellan, no farther polewards than 52°S. In Europe the sea isotherm of the same temperature reaches north of the Arctic Circle at one point. Despite its lower latitudes, then, the Argentinian shelf approximates to the temperature conditions of the western European shelf. Its seasonal range, however, is less, and thus might tend to lower the organic production by reducing the winter overturn and replenishment of surface nutrients.

Uruguay, in the warmest part of the area, has a fauna transitional between the tropical and temperate regions. Weakfish (important in the Caribbean) and croaker (*Micropogon opercularis*) are the two species of greatest landing, but some warm temperate fish such as menhaden are caught. These southern varieties do not necessarily correspond precisely to their northern hemisphere counterparts, but are recognizably similar.

Farther south, off the Argentinian and Chilean coasts, a form of hake (*Merluccius gayi*) becomes plentiful. Types of herring (*Clupea maculata*), sardines, and anchovy are also plentiful. The coast of Chile has fairly cool water much farther north than has the east coast, because of the wide Peru current carrying much water from higher latitudes, and because of the upwelling consequent upon the offshore trade winds in the north. While, because of the Andean folding, southern Chile has a much narrower shelf than has Argentina, it is nevertheless appreciable, and well sheltered by numerous islands. There are also many fiords, so that the coast somewhat resembles British Columbia or Norway. This submergent coastline should aid the development of fishing by providing many harbours and sheltered anchorages. Inland transport is of course difficult in such mountainous country, but the bulk of the catch will presumably be shipped coastwise to Valparaiso or abroad, in similar fashion to the sea movement of much of the catch of Norway, British Columbia, and Alaska. Northern Chile, on the other hand, has few natural harbours and practically no shelf, as the sea-bed slopes rapidly to the very deep Peru-Chile Trench. However, the upwelling of deep water makes it one of the richest areas of pelagic fish in the world.

In total production, Uruguay is small, with about 4,000 tons, representing a production rate of little more than $1\frac{1}{2}$ Kg. per head per year. This figure has barely advanced on pre-war outputs. Imports in 1947 were a mere 350 tons, well below the pre-war average. Uruguayan annual fish consumption, at about 1·7 Kg. per head in 1947, had fallen from 1·9 in immediate pre-war years. It would therefore appear that Uruguay, with its relatively sparse population and high output of meat, does not yet feel impelled to turn to the resources of the sea. With probably the highest standard of living in real terms of any country in Latin America, it is largely free of the problems of nutrition facing other countries on the continent. The small Uruguayan fishing industry nevertheless vies with that of Chile

*Plate XVI.* FISHING KETCH OF GEORGETOWN, BRITISH GUIANA, MAKING FOR
BANKS OVER 100 MILES TO THE NORTH-EAST

as the most efficient of Latin America; of 150 fishing craft, 44 had engines in 1949, while the 400 fishermen had a yearly average production per head of 9·5 tons, over four times that of Brazil. Part of the country's output is by a State organization, the Servicio Oceanografico y ed Pesca, which also carries out research.

Argentina's catch was about 65,000 tons in 1950, not greatly above the 1938 catch of 55,300 tons, and below the 1948 peak of 71,200 tons. Nevertheless a long-term increase is to be expected, which may gather momentum. The government has been attempting by propaganda to increase the consumption of fish. Statements have been publicized that the high meat intake of the Argentines is conducive to high blood pressure and other ailments. Be that as it may, there is no doubt that the country has recently had difficulties in maintaining its meat exports at levels sufficient to pay for the large imports of capital goods needed to sustain the industrial expansion programme. Substitution of easily produced fish for a larger part of the still large meat diet would therefore assist the country.

The production rate is only 4 Kg. per head per year, very low for a sparsely populated country with good sea resources, and only to be explained by the perhaps even more accessible land resources; though the period of rapid and easy development of the better lands has now closed. Consumption rate for 1947 was about 3·8 Kg. per head, against 4·5 before the war. Imports have been falling steadily from 10,100 tons in 1938 to a mere 300 in 1949, partly due to shortage of foreign currency and to government restrictions.

As in Uruguay, part of the output is by a State organization, the fisheries section of the Flota Mercante del Estado, which operates several trawlers, based on Buenos Aires, to a fair range out on the continental shelf. The hake and other demersal fish caught by these are distributed fresh, chiefly within Buenos Aires. There is also an important canning and salting industry, with about ninety plants in Mar del Plata. The chief products here are canned mackerel and anchovy. A substantial contribution to the country's output is made by freshwater fisheries, chiefly from the rivers entering the River Plate. Yearly freshwater production is some 15,000 tons, nearly a quarter of the total. The chief freshwater fish is the sábalo, most of its catch being processed into oil and animal feeding·stuff.

There were about 7,500 commercial fishermen in Argentina

in 1947, having an average yearly production of 8·7 tons per head. There were about 4,000 fishing craft, of which only 350 or so had engines. In a relatively wealthy country such as Argentina there is a good deal of investment capital available internally, both from private sources and the Banco de Crédito Industrial. Thus there seems no reason why the industry should not quickly achieve a much higher degree of mechanization, if the attempt to stimulate demand for fish succeeds.

Chilean conditions contrast with those in Argentina. Here there is no such great output of meat as a competing foodstuff, and the Chilean diet has long included a fair amount of fish. Consumption rate for 1947 was 10½ Kg. per head, nearly three times that of Argentina. This consumption was a marked increase on the 7·2 Kg. per head average for the immediate pre-war years, and the upward trend is continuing. Chile has begun to realize the great value of her sea resources. It is natural that she should be more maritime-minded than Argentina, for she has a very high ratio of coastline to area, and all her large markets are close to the sea. Economic conditions due to the war stimulated output, and catches soared from 30,600 tons in 1938 to 60,100 in 1947, 93,000 in 1951, and 118,300 in 1952. The last figure represents a production rate of over 20 Kg. per head per year.

Exports are significant, but not yet large, though they will undoubtedly increase. In 1950 they were 1,330 tons, compared with 220 in 1938. They are composed of canned or frozen tuna to the U.S.A., dried hake and other fish to Brazil and other South American countries, and fertilizer and feeding-stuff produced from fish. Imports have fallen heavily since before the war, and are now negligible.

The efficiency of the industry is the highest on the continent. Output per fisherman for 1949 averaged 10 tons. The country has the greatest number of powered boats of any South American country; these were 959 in 1949, of which the great majority were motor boats of under 10 tons. There were also some 3,300 unpowered craft, mainly rowboats, so there is still much room for further mechanization.

The northern waters in the upwelling zone are very rich in sardine and anchovy, and production of these could be increased greatly above the present figure. Development of markets in other South American countries for the cheap dried and salted form of these fish could substantially raise the diet standards of the poorer areas and classes of the continent. Tuna also are plentiful off the northern coast and far out into the Pacific. This is a relatively high-cost fish in terms of catching and processing effort, and the chief outlet for expanding production will probably continue to be the U.S.A. Off the southern part of the coast, hake is the dominant commercial species, and output of this could also be further increased. There is also a large output of mussels from inshore waters.

TONNAGE COMPOSITION OF THE CHILEAN CATCH IN 1946

| | |
|---|---:|
| *Molluscs* | 20,200 |
| Mussels (*Mytilus* species) | 15,080 |
| Sea snail (*Concholepas concholepas*) | 1,200 |
| *Hake* | 15,170 |
| *Cusk eels (Genypterus species)* | 7,670 |
| *Tuna and Mackerel Group* | 5,660 |
| Swordfish (*Xiphias gladius*) | 2,170 |
| Snake mackerel (*Thyrsites atun* and *Thyrsitops lepidopoides*) | 2,160 |
| Tunas | 920 |
| Bonito (*Sarda chilensis*) | 410 |
| *Herring and Allies* | 4,300 |
| Sardines (*Sardinops sagax* and *Clupea fuegensis*) | 3,350 |
| Herring (*Clupea maculata*) | 540 |
| Anchovies (*Engraulis ringens*) | 410 |
| *Perches, Croakers, Breams, and Allies* | 3,980 |
| Rock cod (*Notothenia* species) | 2,030 |
| Croaker (*Cilus montti*) | 1,180 |
| Grunt (*Isacia conceptionis*) | 430 |
| *Flatfish* (Lenguado: *Paralichthys adspersus* and *P. woolmani*) | 340 |
| All other fish | approx. 3,600 |

*Tropical Pacific Waters.* These form the only fishing region of South America important for exports. In addition to exports from the countries themselves, there is a considerable catch in these waters by American vessels, taken directly back to the U.S.A. for landing. The southern part, off Peru and northern Chile, is a very rich pelagic area; one of upwelling where the South-east Trades blow along or offshore and the Peru current water is swung away from the coast. Upwelling also takes place in a belt along the Equator stretching far across the Pacific to Asian waters. This is due to surface divergence of waters, as the Trades deflect water to their right in the northern hemisphere and to their left in the southern hemisphere. While rich in pelagic fish, these tropical Pacific waters offer little in the way of demersal fishing. The coast is parallel to axes of strong folding a little way inland. The continental shelf is thus very narrow, and flanked seawards by very deep water, such as the Milne Edwards Deep off Peru, reaching over 6,100 metres, and the Guatemala Trench, reaching over 6,200 metres in depth.

Peru has recently undergone the most rapid fishing expansion of any country in the Americas. In 1939 her catch was 4,800 tons. By 1947 this was 36,600; by 1952 it was 118,300. Large amounts are now exported. In 1938 exports were a mere 23 tons; in 1950 they were 21,600. There has also been a substantial increase in domestic fish consumption, from about 0·9 Kg. per head in pre-war years to 7 Kg. in 1950. This figure is still under half of Venezuela's, so there is much room for further development.

There are now more than twenty-five canneries for bonito and tuna spread along the coast. Unlike those of some of the countries of South America, the industry appears to be dominantly the product of private enterprise, though the government assists the industry in various ways, such as the recent establishment of a research laboratory at Callao, primarily concerned with the development of processing methods.

With a population of over 8,000,000, the country's production rate was about 10 Kg. per head in 1950, well below Venezuela or Chile. Despite its rapid expansion, the fishing industry is still not a major sector of Peruvian economy. The exports, however, form a valuable source of dollars, as by far the greater part consists of canned or frozen tuna and related fish for the U.S.A. market. Canned tuna, furthermore, has a high value-to-weight ratio. Most of the remainder of the exports consists of fish meal and fertilizer to the U.S.A. Imports of fish into Peru are now very small. In 1949 they were 290 tons, as compared with 1,630 in 1938.

The tuna group dominates the Peruvian catch. In order of importance in an average year, the chief species of this group caught are bonito, swordfish, yellowfin tuna, and skipjack tuna; bonito is easily the most important. Other species of significance are mackerel, pompano, drums (particularly *Sciaena deliciosa*), sea bass (*Paralabrax callaensis*), and sharks.

Despite the growing importance of fishing and the considerable amount of mechanization involved in processing part of the landings, the catching side of the industry does not yet appear to be particularly efficient. In 1949 the 7,670 fishermen averaged

5·9 tons per head. Of the 2,808 fishing craft in 1948, only 544 were motor boats. The relatively high prices obtained in the American market should steadily furnish the industry with the capital for further modernization.

Ecuador reflects on a smaller scale the same process that has taken place in Peru, though precise figures are not obtainable of output. In 1949 production was about 5,000 tons, as compared with about 1,800 tons in 1938. Domestic consumption remained very low. Some 400 tons of frozen tuna were shipped to U.S.A. in 1950. The industry is backward. In 1949 the 2,900 fishermen had an average production of only 1·7 tons per head, while of the 1,750 craft, only four were powered. In addition to that of the local industry, there is a substantial yearly output of about 15,000 to 20,000 tons of the tuna group caught by U.S.A. tuna clippers in the Galapagos Islands.

Colombian Pacific waters are less prolific than the cooler upwelling waters to the south. Also, for historical reasons of early accessibility to Europe, the bulk of the coastal population lives on the Caribbean. The country's Pacific coast production, though small, is increasing. However, it does not yet share appreciably in the tropical Pacific region's tuna exports to the U.S.A. The state paternalism common in fisheries has developed here. A government-sponsored fishing and trading organization, the Colombian Marine Fishing Industry, is engaged in developing fisheries on both coasts, but the greatest relative development appears to be on the Pacific. A Swedish firm has been placed under contract to provide modern craft and equipment, and establish canneries.

The Pacific coasts of the Central American countries have still only a small production. These countries have relatively small populations with very low consumption rates. Poor inland communications often limit the effective market. Two areas only have fishing industries of any size based on them: Costa Rica and the Canal Zone, their chief concern being the production of frozen tuna for the U.S.A. Exports of this to the U.S.A. in 1950 were 4,360 tons from Costa Rica and 2,680 tons from the Canal Zone. Costa Rica also has one tuna canning plant. In addition, there is a good deal of fishing off the Central American Pacific coast by American tuna clippers which take their catch straight back to their home ports. Local production by Central American countries, particularly of tuna and sardine, could be increased greatly.

## REFERENCES

*F.A.O. Yearbooks of Fisheries Statistics, 1947, 1948–9,* and *1950–1.*

*Anuário Estatistico do Brasil, 1953.* (Conselho Nacional de Estatistica, Rio de Janeiro.)

*Better Utilisation of Fisheries Resources in Latin America.* (F.A.O. Fisheries Bulletin, May/June 1951.)

*Fisheries in the Caribbean.* (Anglo-American Caribbean Commission, published at Washington, 1952.)

# CHAPTER XVI

# AUSTRALASIA AND THE PACIFIC ISLANDS

THIS extensive area makes but a small contribution to the world's catch. In 1951 its estimated catch was under 150,000 tons, less than 1 per cent of the world total. The chief reason for this is the sparse human population. The Australian continent, with only 8,000,000 people, and an important producer and exporter of meat, has never been under any pressure to use the resources of its seas. .New Zealand, though of somewhat denser population, is in the same position. In the tropical Pacific islands, on the other hand, fish is an important proportion of the diet, but the small population on the limited land area of the islands does not attain a high total catch.

As a source of variety in the diet, fish are in a certain demand in Australia and New Zealand. With increasing population, fish production shows a gradual expansion. In fish and shellfish, Australia caught about 45,700 tons in 1952, compared with 33,500 tons in 1939, while between the same years New Zealand's catch rose from 28,700 to 35,300.

Australia imports a moderate amount of fish. However, its fish exports (including mammal products) have increased considerably since the war to roughly the same weight as imports. In 1950 production rate (excluding mammal products) was about 5 Kg. per head, and consumption rate about 6 Kg. Both are low figures for an advanced country. Nevertheless, it is likely that Australia's demand for fish will rise more rapidly in the future as it becomes more industrialized. Long-term government policy now appears to be to encourage a decentralized form of industrialism, with an increase of factory workers in proportion to the population and a relative decrease in agricultural workers. This process, which is taking place in most of the once dominantly primary producing and exporting 'new' countries, seems inevitable even without official backing.

Australia already has a high proportion of urban dwellers for a country of her economic pattern. It is likely that this proportion will be further increased by the post-war wave of European immigrants, who tend to gravitate to the towns. Ultimately, therefore, Australia's abundance of meat for home consumption and export must cease. If this traditional export is to be maintained, an increasing amount of fish must be eaten.

There seems little doubt that the seas about Australia could produce enough to meet any such increasing demand for many years. They are not organically rich, but have ample resources in relation to any foreseeable expansion of Australia's population in the next century.

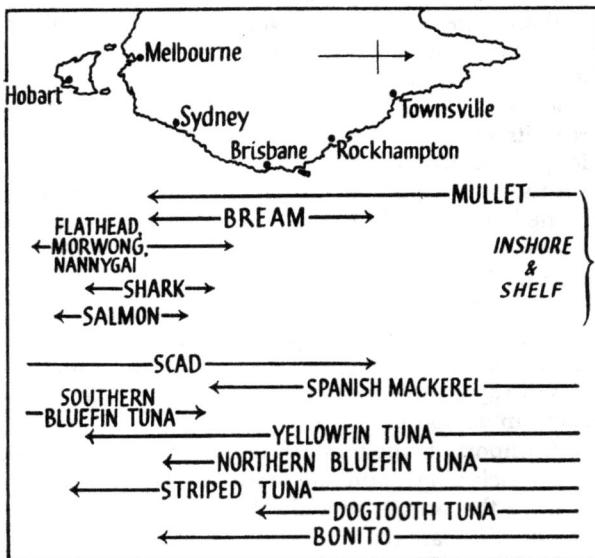

*Fig. 60.* Approximate latitudinal range of commercial catches of certain species in East Australia

The most populous regions of Australia are not very well placed in regard to the potentially best fishing grounds. Off New South Wales the shelf is very narrow. Bass Strait and the Great Australian Bight have a good area of shallow water, but these areas are too continuously warm, with too little seasonal temperature range to have any marked enrichment by overturn. The middle of Bass Strait has a surface temperature of 15°C. in February and 12°C in August. Nor is there any upwelling water on this side of the continent, with the winds and the East Australian current moving towards the coast. The average richness in nutrients of the surface waters off South-east Australia has been found in fisheries investigations to be about a third of that off California, in similar latitudes, and about a quarter of that of the sub-Antarctic waters to the south.

Off Western Australia the West Australian current moves northward from the rich Southern Ocean, and there is upwelling due to the wind and surface current divergence from the coast. Here the waters are doubtless richer, though their potentialities have never been tested on a large scale because of their remoteness from any major consuming centres. Off Queensland lies the moderately wide shelf behind the Great Barrier Reef, and there is a fair amount of short-range fishing here. Finally, along the north of the continent is a really large shelf stretching to New Guinea. Even in relatively poor waters this great area, substantially greater than the West European shelf, must be capable of a large total output. At present its output is very low, for it is bounded by very sparsely populated coasts to the south and primitive New Guinea to the north. The main consuming centres of Australia are thousands of miles away, while the nearest area of dense population, Java, is some 600 miles away from the nearest part of the shelf, and in any case has a rather low purchasing power for the financing of a long-range fishery. Development of the North Australian shelf, however, will doubtless proceed as less remote waters become over-fished and the population pressure of South-east Asia increases.

As is typical of warm-water areas, Australian waters have a very large number of species present, though the total quantity of fish is not particularly great. Only a small number of these species enter in quantity into commercial catches. In New South Wales waters the nannygai (*Centroberyx affinis*), morwong (*Nemadactylus* species), and flathead (*Neoplatycephalus* and *Platycephalus* spp.) are the most important. These demersal fish are obtained chiefly by a small number of sizeable trawlers. There has also lately developed a troll fishery for the southern bluefin tuna (*Thunnus maccoyii*), mainly along the south part of the New South Wales coast, although fishing for it also takes place round Shark Bay in Western Australia. Victorian landings include quantities of flathead, barracouta (*Leionura atun*, a member of the tuna group, and not to be confused with the barracuda), shark, and crayfish.

In Tasmania the barracouta, shark, and flathead are again important, together with crayfish and scallops. Other fish of significance in South-east Australian seas or estuaries are mackerel

(*Scomber australasicus*), Australian 'salmon' (*Arripis trutta*), mullet (e.g. *Mugil dobula*), trumpeter (*Pelates sexlineatus*), bream (*Acanthopagrus australis*), crested flounder (*Lophonectes gallus*), red cod (*Physiculus bachus*), silver trevally (*Usacaranx georgianus*), gar-fish (*Reporhamphus* species), 'whiting' (*Sillaginodes* and *Sillago* species), Australian pilchard (*Sardinops neopilchardus*), scad (*Trachurus novae-zelandiae*), and oysters and prawns. The fisheries of South Australia are concerned particularly with crayfish, sharks, and Australian anchovy (*Austranchovia australis*). Crayfish

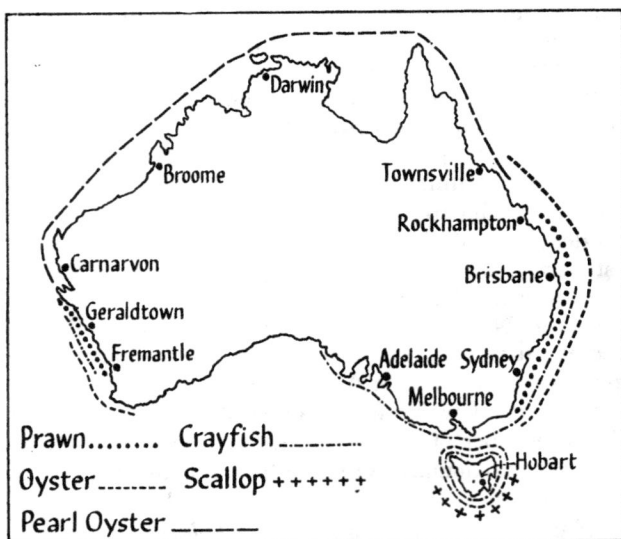

*Fig. 61.* Coastal extent of chief shellfisheries

are also important in Western Australia, and there is a small amount of trawling, chiefly for nannygai and flathead. In Queensland there are fisheries for mackerel, barred Spanish mackerel (*Scomberomorus commerson*), mullet, prawns, oysters, and pearl oysters. Some features of the catches of commercial species about the continent are shown in Figs. 60 and 61. It must be borne in mind, of course, that fishery boundaries are inevitably somewhat flexible.

New South Wales is easily the chief producing state by virtue of its substantial market in Sydney and other populous areas. The following data on the various states are for 1949:

| | Weight landed, as percentage of whole country (excluding Northern Territory) | Number of Fishermen |
|---|---|---|
| New South Wales | 36 | 2,700 |
| Tasmania | 17 | 1,650 |
| Victoria | 14·5 | 2,470 |
| Western Australia | 13·5 | 1,560 |
| Queensland | 11 | 5,800 |
| South Australia | 8 | 3,230 |

It will be seen that there is a considerable difference in productivity per fisherman in terms of weight, though the differences are rather less in terms of value. A relatively high proportion of Australian fishing is inshore or in estuaries or rivers. Large numbers of small boats are used, in many areas in the ratio of one boat to one or two men. The average productivity of the country's fishermen is only about 3 tons per head per year, very low for an otherwise technically advanced country. However, the average value-to-weight ratio of fish is higher in Australia than in most countries, as it falls more into the class of a semi-luxury than a regular necessity. A good number of the fishermen also have other part-time work.

Exports (including mammal products) in the year ending in June 1952 were 14,400 tons, compared with 8,650 tons in 1950–1, and only 3,950 in 1938–9. Expansion is thus rapid, but the chief item in the increase is whale oil. There is a moderate-sized whaling industry off Western Australia, concerned with the humpback whales which emigrate there in winter from the Antarctic. In 1951 there were six catcher craft, which caught 1,224 whales. To protect the stock, the Australian Whaling Commission sets a limit for the maximum catch each year. Output has fluctuated considerably. In 1951, a good year, Australia produced 9,500 tons of whale oil, about 2 per cent of the world total. A good deal of this was exported.

Other export items include frozen crawfish, chiefly to the U.S.A., trochus shells, and canned pilchards and other fish to British New Guinea, the Dutch West Indies, and other colonies. The long-established pearl fishery along the northern coasts is, however, not now a major source of fisheries exports. Exports of pearl oyster shells in 1951–2 were about a quarter of the 1938–9 figure, though the value at £370,000 was rather more, because of the steep rise in world prices. This represented about

a tenth of the total value of Australian fishery exports (£3,544,000).
Pearls themselves were a negligible export, valued at only £17,000.

Imports into Australia were 16,500 tons in 1949–50. Items of
importance were fresh and frozen fish from New Zealand, cured
fish from South Africa, canned herring, and other fish from
Britain and Norway, canned salmon from Siberia and Canada,
and cod-liver oil from Britain. The import trade of various types
of fish from South Africa is developing considerably.

Australian fisheries, it will be seen, at present make only a
minor contribution to the country's economy, either as food or as
exports. Turning to New Zealand, we find that the role of
fisheries is still minor, yet relatively more important. New
Zealand production rate in 1950 was about 17 Kg. per head,
or three times that of Australia. This is understandable in a
relatively small island country. New Zealand's seas are also
organically richer than the average Australian waters. The
West Wind Drift passes close to the southern coast and sends
some water northwards up both east and west coasts. In proportion to its land area, the country has a fair amount of shelf,
especially in Cook Strait and southwards from South Island.
The north coast of North Island has a moderate belt of shelf,
with a good deal of really shallow and sheltered water in the
Hauraki Gulf, on which lies Auckland.

In approximate order of importance by weight in New Zealand's
landings are snapper (*Pagrosomus auratus*), oysters, tarakihi
(*Dactylopagrus macropterus*), groper (*Polyprion oxygeneios*), blue 'cod'
(*Parapercis colias*), gurnard (*Chelidonichthys kumu*), crayfish (*Jasus*
species), sole (*Peltorhampus novae-zeelandiae*), flounder (*Rhombosolea
plebeia*), mussel (*Mytilus canaliculus*), barracouta, trevally (*Caranx
platessa*), ling (*Genypterus blacodes*, unrelated to the European ling),
and elephant fish (*Callorhynchus milii*). Demersal fish form the
bulk of the catch. About 55 per cent of the landings in a recent
year were obtained by trawling, and about 15 per cent by
Danish seining. Other methods of significance are long lines,
hand lines, set lines, and trolling. In 1949 the country had
1,535 fishing craft. The numbers of the chief types are listed
below:

| | |
|---|---|
| Motor trawlers | 172 |
| Steam trawlers | 8 |
| Danish seining motor vessels | 36 |
| Motor boats for set-netting and line-fishing | 797 |
| Shell-fisheries boats | 425 |

These classes have shown considerable increases in recent years, with the exception of Danish seiners and steam trawlers, which have fallen somewhat in numbers. Motor trawlers have increased from seventy-nine in 1938.

A feature of the country's fisheries is that a great deal of the work is by part-time fishermen, who may also do farming or other work, as is common, for example, in Norway. This tendency is particularly noticeable in the shell-fisheries. Being concerned with inshore or short-range work, needing only small craft with low overhead costs, they lend themselves well to part-time work. Thus in 1949 there were 247 part-time crayfishing boats and only 159 working full-time. Before the war there were in the country more part-time fishermen than full-time, but since the war the numbers have been roughly equal, and totalling about 1,600 men. This small fishing force has over six times the output per head of Australia's, which also has considerable numbers of part-time fishermen. The New Zealand figure of about 20 tons per fisherman per year is near that of U.S.A. While the New Zealanders are technically efficient, they are also helped by the fact that their waters are generally still under-fished, so that catches per unit of effort are high.

The industry is quite strongly centralized, four ports accounting for some 56 per cent of the weight of catch in recent years. Auckland, with about 30 per cent of the national landings, is the most important. Good grounds lie immediately off its area of relatively dense population. Wellington lands about 11 per cent of the total, Port Chalmers, close to Dunedin, about 9 per cent, and Napier about 6 per cent.

Foreign trade in fish is small, with exports slightly more important than imports. There has also been an export of seaweed products in the post-war period. This reached a peak of £83,000 in 1948. New Zealand's coasts have fair supplies of the types of seaweed most in world demand for the production of gels used in a wide range of goods from ice-cream to munitions. Nevertheless, the falling exports tend to show that the more accessible stocks have been over-exploited, for there has been no marked fall in the world prices of these seaweeds. The processed seaweed, of course, fetches a good price. The value of the 1951 exports had, however, fallen to £19,000, while in the following year it fell to only £10,000, whereas Japanese exports were expanding rapidly during this period.

More important in value is the export of whale oil. New

19

Zealand has a small production of whale oil, about 760 tons in 1951, from whales caught in local waters. The bulk of this is exported, the 732 tons in 1951 fetching £48,000. In fish exports proper, the chief items are fresh and frozen blue cod, tarakihi, and snapper to Australia. Fresh and frozen fish exports weighed 3,500 tons in 1951. Canned and other processed fish are unimportant in exports, but form the bulk of the imports, in which the chief items are canned salmon, of late mainly from Japan, and canned herring and sardines from Britain and Norway. Imports in 1951 totalled 2,800 tons. With edible exports and imports small and roughly balancing, the country's consumption rate is identical with the production rate, about 17 Kg. per head in 1950. This is a high figure for a relatively newly developed, dominantly agricultural country, with a large surplus of meat for export. New Zealanders clearly demand both quantity and variety in their food, so that the fish consumption rate is much greater than those of some broadly comparable countries such as Australia and Argentina.

The future will doubtless see the rising trend of production continued, as the home market steadily expands. There should be no danger of over-fishing in most of the near demersal grounds for some time to come, and there are other grounds not far distant, about the Auckland, Macquarie, Campbell, Antipodes, Bounty, and Chatham groups of islands. There is also the possibility of a considerable increase in pelagic fishing, particularly in long-range tuna fishing. Canned tuna could form a valuable export to the U.S.A. and elsewhere.

The final area with which we have to deal, the Pacific Islands, form an amorphous unit, yet they have sufficient in common, from the physical and human points of view, to be treated together. They are all tropical or sub-tropical, many are coral atolls, and with few exceptions they are still in a relatively primitive economic state. Although they are all colonies or protectorates, their remoteness from Europe and the U.S.A. has spared most of them from any drastic economic revolution turning the people rapidly from a secure subsistence peasantry into a hired and insecure proletariat, as has occurred in many other such areas. Only a few islands of strategic position or on world trade routes have as yet been strongly westernized, though, with their increasing accessibility by air, outside influences on the islands will gain in force.

At present, however, production in many islands remains

mainly for immediate local consumption. Farming and fishing for subsistence or local sale are the two key occupations. At present the highly dispersed nature of the fisheries makes an accurate check of total landings impracticable. At any rate, the average *per capita* consumption of fish must be quite high. The intimate contact of the inhabitants of small islands with the sea has long made them proficient fishermen. Their methods, however, retain the simplicity and small-scale operation appropriate to small communities. Spearing, harpooning, and shooting with bow and arrow are still important methods, particularly in Melanesia. Sharks are even caught by a form of lassoo. In Polynesia, rod and line fishing is important for bonito. The rod has a number of lines, each with a lure. Other methods in use in various islands include long lines, basket traps, stake nets, stonework pounds, drift nets, and beach-hauled seines. Fish-poisoning by bundles of certain roots is practised in Fiji and some other islands.

The sheltered waters of the lagoons found in many coral islands form an ideal fishing ground, in which fishing can be done from the shore and in small canoes. In these quiet waters traps of relatively flimsy construction can be operated successfully. The islanders also fish the open sea, using large dugout canoes. These often have outriggers, for stability. This is particularly necessary for sailing canoes. Some sailing canoes are double hulled. Craft are sometimes built of planking, or are of composite dugout and planked construction. Size may be considerable; the Samoan bonito-canoe, for example, being up to 50 ft. in length.

Exports of fish from the area are insignificant, save for tuna from Hawaii to the U.S.A. There are, of course, tuna vessels from Japan and other bordering lands operating in various parts of the area, but they normally return direct to their home bases with their catch. The Pacific Islands are a fish-importing area, though the main consumers of imported fish are naturally the trading centres themselves. Japan is once again becoming an important supplier. In 1950 it sent to Hawaii alone 500 tons of canned fish and shellfish, 190 tons of frozen fish, and 130 tons of cured fish. In that year South Africa sent the Pacific Islands about 500 tons of canned fish. Australia and some other countries also send moderate quantities of fish, chiefly canned. The total weight of imports, however, is small in proportion to the islands' own output.

The most economically important island group, the Hawaiian,

has a population of over half a million. Its landings in 1950 were recorded as 7,200 tons, giving a production rate of about 13 Kg. per head, very similar to that of the U.S.A. itself, though not particularly impressive for a territory of small islands.

There is a substantial European and Asiatic population in Hawaii, and the group is, of course, an important American naval and air base, and an exporter of various plantation crops, such as pineapple. The commercial life of the chief islands is largely organized in Western fashion, and this has particularly affected the fishing industry. Hawaii has become a base for long-range tuna clippers. The tuna group provides over half the weight of catch. The skipjack tuna is far the most important, but the swordfish, yellowfin tuna, big-eyed tuna, albacore, and bonito are also of importance. Other fish landed in substantial quantities by commercial and subsistence fishermen include big-eyed scad, amberjack (*Seriola*), mackerel, crevalle (*Caranx*), mullet, and various snappers.

The mid-Pacific is an area rich in pelagic fish, particularly along the equatorial upwelling belt. If it possessed a larger human population, these resources would be used more intensively, but at present the cost of transport and preservation of catches sent to the distant markets on each side of the Pacific limits full exploitation. However, the economic range of vessels is constantly increasing, and it is already profitable to travel great distances in the search for tuna. A steady increase in the use of the mid-Pacific by craft from Japan, U.S.A., Australia, New Zealand, and some island bases like Hawaii is therefore to be expected.

## REFERENCES

*Yearbooks of Fishery Statistics, 1947, 1948–9,* and *1950–1.* (F.A.O., Rome.)
*Fish and Fisheries of Australia.* T. C. Roughley. (Angus & Robertson, Sydney, 1951.)
*Australian Fisheries.* Ed. I. G. MacInnes. (Halstead Press, Sydney, 1950.)
*Australian Journal of Marine and Freshwater Research.* (Commonwealth Scientific and Industrial Research Organization. Melbourne, periodically.)
*Fisheries News Letter.* (Commonwealth Director of Fisheries, Sydney, monthly.)
*Report on Fisheries for the Year Ended 31st March, 1950,* and subsequent annual reports. (Government Printer, Wellington.)

# CHAPTER XVII

# THE SOUTHERN OCEAN WHALING REGION

THIS study is concerned essentially with fish and shellfish. Sea mammals, such as whales and seals, are not strictly the object of fisheries, though their catching industries are often referred to as fisheries. Many countries include sea mammals with fish for statistical purposes of total catch, foreign trading, and so on. Although their techniques of catching, and the types of organization and equipment involved, are often markedly different from those of true fisheries, a sharp distinction cannot be made. In the foregoing regional studies reference to whaling and sealing has been required when they have made a significant contribution to a country's output of sea products. Whaling is an industry which frequently involves operations at very long range from the home bases. By far the most important catching area is the Southern Ocean, and it is felt that a brief study of certain features of it may be of value here.

The circumpolar belt between 50° S. and the edge of the pack-ice was first exploited in 1904, and now accounts for about 80 per cent of the world output of whale oil, the main product of the industry. The bulk of the production is now from pelagic whaling, that is, from factory ships which can move about the seas following the concentrations of whales. They come out from their home ports in Norway, Britain, and elsewhere, and take their cargoes back at the end of the season. Nevertheless, land stations on islands in the area of the Falkland Islands Dependency are still of importance. They lack the advantages of mobility, but offer more room for plant and equipment. In addition, there are various harbours, such as Deception Island in the South Shetlands, which offer shelter, fresh water, and sometimes other facilities to whaling vessels This area south of South America, with its many islands and lesser remoteness from Europe than the other side of the Antarctic, was the first intensively used part of the whaling belt.

South American countries themselves, however, play small part in whaling. Argentina and Chile together accounted for about a fortieth of the world's output of whale oils in 1951.

The most important countries using the Southern Ocean for whaling are listed below, with their production (from all regions) of oil in 1951, in tons.

| | |
|---|---|
| Norway | 195,600 |
| U.K. | 83,300 |
| South Africa | 42,700 |
| Japan | 34,600 |
| U.S.S.R. | 31,000 |
| World total production | 503,000 |

The true bases for whaling in this region are thus mainly in the northern hemisphere.

As we have seen, the sub-Antarctic belt is an area of upwelling of water rich in nutrients collected on its long journey southwards. This gives rise to a dense phytoplankton, which in turn feeds much zooplankton, particularly the small euphausid crustaceans known to whalers as 'krill'. The whalebone whales derive their nourishment from great quantities of such plankton obtained by the bony filters in their mouths. This is an efficient food sequence, as there is no intermediary stage of other creatures between the plankton and the whale, so that the end-product available to man is a much higher proportion than usual of the initial organic production. One should qualify this by saying that at present full use is not made by man of his opportunities, for the whale meat, which represents nearly a half of the creature's weight, is little eaten. Only Japan has a large consumption of whale meat, and attempts to introduce it into Britain and other countries have not been very successful.

By far the most valuable commercial products are the oils obtained by boiling the blubber (the fatty covering layer), and from some other parts, such as the head cavity of the sperm whale. These oils are used in the manufacture of foodstuffs, soap, lubricants, and for dressing leather, 'batching' jute, 'quenching' steel, and other purposes.

Antarctic output of animal feeding-stuffs made from the meat and bone at present amounts to under a tenth of the output of oil, by weight. Other products include fertilizer from dried blood and from the residue after the blubber has been boiled. Whalebone, from the baleen plates in the mouth, once important in dressmaking, now has but a small market.

In the history of whaling some species have been important and then hunted almost to extinction so that further catching became unprofitable. Sometimes areas and species have partly recovered after a resting period. The chief whales now hunted in the Southern Ocean are the blue, fin, and humpback. The average adult blue whale is about 80 or 90 ft. long, while the fin whale is about 70, and the humpback is only 40, but carrying plenty of fat.

Modern factory ships are large, averaging about 14,000 tons. The stern has a wide opening and a ramp up which the dead whale is hauled by winch on to the deck where it is dismembered. The vessel has steam saws, grinding machines, boilers, storage tanks, and other equipment, and is a self-contained factory capable of handling over a dozen whales a day. Each factory ship is mother to a number of catchers, small fast vessels of about 400 tons, and over 15 knots. These search for and catch the whales with the harpoon guns on their bows. It is to be hoped that there will be a general adoption of the recently developed electric harpoon, which stuns or kills the whale immediately. The existing harpoon, which explodes inside the whale, is unsure. The whale, being a mammal, is presumably highly sensitive to pain, and its death struggle is frequently long. Some whales are not killed until several harpoons have been exploded in them. The carcasses are then injected with air from a nozzle to make them float, and they are towed back to the factory ship, or in some cases a shore factory. The total crew of a factory ship and catchers will be 400 men or more, and the number tends to increase with greater complexity of equipment. A British expedition of 1954 carried helicopters for spotting, while an earlier expedition carried scouting amphibian aircraft.

Increasing efficiency, however, leads to the danger of 'overfishing' this last major world stock of whales. The average annual production from the Southern Ocean in the pre-war decade was about 1·3 million tons of whales, representing 400,000 tons of whale oil. The greatest season was that of 1930-1, of 600,000 tons of oil. This overloaded the market, and subsequently voluntary restrictions on total catch were made by the chief whaling companies. Then, in 1946, the International Convention for the Regulation of Whaling was signed in Washington by the representatives of the governments of the chief whaling countries. Their annual total catch in the Southern Ocean is now limited. It is 15,500 blue whale units for 1954-5. One blue whale equals two fin whales, two and a half humpbacks, or six of the small sei whales.) This represents about two-thirds of the pre-war catches. When this number has been caught, the season ends. It now lasts up to four months, from early December. Whaling in the rest of the world is still not fully limited, and increased steadily from 1945 to a post-war peak in 1950-1.

Professor Ruud, the Norwegian whaling authority, considers it likely that the recent rate of catch in the Southern Ocean is still too high, and is particularly concerned about blue whale stocks. The following figures show the numbers of whales caught in 1950-1 and 1933-4. In both cases there were nineteen floating factories in operation, though in the earlier season they were smaller and had little more than half the number of catcher vessels.

|  | *1933-4* | *1950-1* |
|---|---|---|
| Blue whales | 16,813 | 6,966 |
| Fin whales | 5,472 | 17,474 |
| Humpbacks | 780 | 1,630 |
| Total blue whale units (including other species) | 19,861 | 16,416 |

The catch-per-catcher's day's work fell substantially. The proportionately heavy fall in the blue whale catches, together with the fact that about a third of their number caught are immature, tends to show that blue whales need independent protection regulation.

Norway has dominated the Southern Ocean whaling industry, making a good deal of the total catch in its own vessels, while Norwegian gunners and seamen are prominent in the expeditions of Britain and some other countries. Much of the modern technique is due to Norwegians like Svend Foyn, who developed the harpoon gun, and C. A. Larsen, the captain who was responsible for much of the pioneer work in opening up the South Georgia and Ross Sea areas. Whaling is an important source of foreign currency to Norway, both in exports of her own products and in the wages of her foreign-employed men. The U.S.A. imports large quantities of whale and sperm oil; some 20,700 tons in 1951, valued at nearly six million dollars. Of this the great bulk came from Norway. While it seems likely that Norway's own expeditions will remain large, it is probable that, with the passage of time, foreign ships will gradually replace Norwegians by their own men.

## REFERENCES

*Norsk Hvalfangst-Tidende* (Norwegian Whaling Gazette). In Norwegian and English. (Sandefjord, monthly.)

*Whaling in Antarctica.* A. G. Bennett. (Henry Holt & Co., New York, 1932.)

*Air Whaler.* John Grierson. (Sampson, Low, Marston & Co., London, 1949.)

*Giant Fishes, Whales and Dolphins.* J. R. Norman and F. G. Fraser. (Putnam, London, 1937.)

*Whales and Modern Whaling.* J. T. Jenkins. (Witherby, London, 1932.)

*The Adventure of Whaling.* Frank Crisp. (Macmillan, London, 1954.)

*The Great Whale Game.* Georges Blond. (Weidenfeld and Nicolson, London, 1954.)

*International Whaling Statistics.* Sandefjord, annually.)

CHAPTER XVIII

CHANGING ASPECTS OF FISHERIES

IT has frequently been pointed out in the preceding chapters that the fishing industry has on the whole a conservative attitude to innovation. In the last three-quarters of a century or so, the change from sail to power has, of course, been revolutionary, but there are many parts of the world where it has still hardly begun, while even in advanced countries the transformation may have taken half a century fully to penetrate the industry. Changes are, however, now being accomplished in less and less time, and it is likely that the next few decades will be of crucial importance to many still backward areas.

The value of the seas has now undoubtedly gripped the imagination of statesmen and officials in southern Asia and South America. There is much export of information on technique from advanced to backward countries, often under the sponsorship of the Food and Agriculture Organization of the United Nations. Estimates of potential increase in production of the various regions vary considerably, but there is no doubt that many under-fished areas can more than double their production. Such changes must affect the whole pattern of international trade. Major exporters such as Canada, Norway, and Iceland may find increasing resistance in world markets, particularly for the cheaper forms of fish. On the other hand, international trade in certain shellfish and other high-grade fish may increase. Much depends on general political and economic factors, and their influence on tariffs and quotas. At all events, fishermen in countries with large actual or potential home markets may feel more sanguine about their future prosperity than can those whose markets may be affected by decisions which it is beyond their power to influence.

In considering the fishing industry as a whole in competition with its major substitute, meat, few grounds for pessimism can be found. In most countries the costs of production and the prices of fish have advanced less than that of meat, by comparison with pre-war figures. In Britain, for example, the average rise in retail prices for fresh fish between mid-1939 and mid-1953 was 179 per cent. This compares with 267 per cent for fresh meat,

474 per cent for cereal products, and 400 per cent for fresh eggs. Fish can therefore easily hold its own competitively. There seems no reason to expect that meat will become relatively much less expensive, although a downward trend from excessive levels seems likely in temperate cereals. Expansion of meat production, however, is much less easy than that of fish on under-exploited grounds. In the areas where food needs are rising fastest, in monsoon Asia, there is small likelihood of much increase in food livestock because of existing pressure on suitable land. In India, religious and conventional obstacles, though weakening, are also important. Fisheries, both sea and freshwater, will play a vital part in raising the standards of nutrition of such areas.

Fish farming, or aquiculture, in ponds and also in the paddy-fields themselves, will be a substantial contributor to increasing production. It has long been important, of course, especially in China and Japan, but there is no doubt that yields of existing ponds could be increased, and much swampy wasteland turned into new ponds. Use of fertilizers to increase the production of plants and phytoplankton at the base of the food chain in such ponds can further improve output. Again, freshwater fish farming has the advantage, in countries with poor transport, of providing cheap fresh fish to markets far inland. Such freshwater cultivation is, however, unlikely to cut down the total demand for sea-fish, but will complement sea supplies in growing markets. On good land, normal arable cultivation remains the best use, with fish as a secondary interest in cases where the crop requires irrigation or drainage canals.

Fish farming in the sea is also occasionally discussed at the present time. This is not likely to develop anything like as rapidly as its freshwater counterpart. Farming any animal essentially involves some or all of the following operations:

1. Restricting or controlling its movement.
2. Selecting from local stocks, or introducing from elsewhere, the best parents to breed from.
3. Influencing the time, place, and other circumstances of breeding.
4. Protecting it, and particularly the young, from predators, weather, disease, or other hazards, when necessary.
5. Killing it at the economically most suitable time; usually, for a meat animal, soon after the end of its period of rapid youthful growth.

6. Killing or driving off unwanted species that compete with it for food.
7. Killing those of its own species which are growing too slowly to make economic use of the food or accommodation.
8. Increasing the natural food supply by fertilizing, or bringing food from elsewhere.

In freshwater aquiculture, all these measures are possible, though it is not always necessary or profitable to practise all of them. In the sea, the volume of water involved is so vast that none of them can be done with any sureness of gain. Fertilizing nearly enclosed sea inlets has been done in some places, and will often increase the phytoplankton and fish production appreciably when there is little or no loss of the enriched water by tidal or other currents. The cost of fertilizing the water, sometimes largely for the benefit of unwanted creatures, may be considerable. Nevertheless, the technique may develop as an economic proposition in some areas.

Oyster farming is, of course, the best example of sea farming, as practised in estuaries and partly closed lagoons in France, U.S.A., and elsewhere. Suitable places for the settlement and growth of the young are provided. Predators and competitors are removed, and the oysters taken when they have reached the desired stage of growth. It will be noted that these are virtually immobile creatures, and this is what makes their farming easily possible in waters communicating with the open seas. Farming of fish proper is a very different matter. Hatching and release of fry after they have grown beyond the most vulnerable stage is a process that may benefit the fisheries of a given locality, when the fish are of low mobility, like most flatfish. It is doubtful whether much could be done on a world-wide scale. A large production of the young of one species may increase its stocks in the seas, but only at the expense of other stocks, for basic production in the sea is not increased. To do this appreciably, fertilization on a vast and at present uneconomic scale would be necessary. Much of the fertilizer would be carried by currents beyond the euphotic zones of the continental shelves, to make a negligible impression on the great volume of oceanic water.

Man's deliberate attempts to influence sea production are thus at present limited. Agreements to restrict over-fishing are, of course, important. They are usually designed to protect spawning grounds, or young fish, or the total stock of fish. Breeding and protection of young creatures, and destruction of predators and competitors, are limited to relatively small areas, but may develop in importance in certain regions of favourable conditions.

Measures against over-fishing, however, are bound to grow in importance as more and more areas become intensively fished. For control on the European shelf there is the Permanent Commission, representing eleven nations (but not the U.S.S.R), set up under the International Fisheries Convention of 1946. These members have agreed on a number of provisions, which came into force in April 1954, and placed minimum limits on the mesh size of nets, and on the size of fish which may be sold. Among other such agreements in the world are the U.S.-Canadian agreement, limiting the season for Pacific halibut fishing, and the international agreement limiting whaling catches in the Southern Ocean. Other intensively fished regions in the northern hemisphere are ripe for further international agreements. At any rate, a technique of relatively amicable international discussion and agreement in such matters now seems to have been achieved, though complete enforcement of regulations will never be easy.

In addition to international agreements, there have long been local regulations made singly by countries or provinces, applying only to waters near their coasts. The recent action by Iceland in extending her territorial waters and banning trawlers in them has provoked much resentment among British fishermen. Ultimately it may become normal practice for nations wishing to take new measures for local fishery conservation to consult with foreign governments whose ships are likely to be affected, to try to achieve mutually satisfactory arrangements. It is beyond our scope here to discuss the vexed matters of the Icelandic and other disputes arising from national claims to extend their territorial waters. A claim by Peru, Chile, and Ecuador for limits no less than two hundred miles offshore has been made at the time of writing. Clearly some internationally agreed system of principles governing territorial limits will ultimately have to be formulated. Increased awareness by many countries of the value of the fishery resources, and possibly also of the sea-bed mineral resources, of their neighbouring seas, lends urgency to the subject.

Catching technique is now making rapid advances. At first, new inventions or developments are confined to a few countries, but the time taken for them to spread into general use among advanced countries is constantly shortening. These improvements are good in so far as they cut costs, so that fish can be sold more cheaply to the final consumer. Nevertheless, they often need cautious use. In areas already intensively fished they increase the danger of over-fishing. Again, as new, highly equipped vessels have an ever-mounting cost, there is the possibility that in any time of slump their owners may find themselves hard pressed to meet their interest charges and other overheads.

Much depends on the circumstances of each fishery. The economically optimum degree of mechanization varies greatly, but, broadly speaking, it becomes higher as wage-rates increase, as range of operation extends, and as capital becomes more easily available.

Certain devices are now gaining widespread use. We may mention particularly echo sounding and the mid-water or floating trawl. By mid-1952, of large fishing vessels, nearly 90 per cent of the British, 70 per cent of the Norwegian, 60 per cent of the Dutch, and about 45 per cent of the Icelandic were fitted with echo sounders. Apart from its value as a navigational aid, the recording echo sounder has become a standard method of finding and estimating the depth of shoals of fish, particularly herring. Time wasted in searching for fish is thus reduced, and with it the costs of production.

The echo-sounding technique has in turn created a demand for a trawl that can be hauled through mid-water to catch shoals which cannot be caught by surface drift nets or purse seines, or by normal bottom trawls. Such a trawl, whose depth can be adjusted by alterations in speed or the length of the towing warp, is, in conjunction with the echo sounder, a powerful instrument for catching schooling pelagic fish such as herring and pilchard. Various patterns of this trawl, some requiring one, and others two, towing vessels, are now in common use in Icelandic and Scandinavian waters, and will undoubtedly spread elsewhere as the technique is perfected.

Asdic, or echo sounding which can obtain horizontal bearings, is another aid likely to develop considerably as an aid to locating schools. Scouting by radio-equipped aircraft is again of considerable potentialities. It has been tried experimentally in various fisheries. The American tuna fishery, for instance, now has a fair number of its vessels carrying light float-planes. Their cost of operation has been more than offset by the increased catches. Helicopters are a promising type, as they can take off and land directly on to a small vessel, instead of having to be launched and picked up from the sea. At present, however, they are too expensive.

The cost of aircraft can be reduced greatly when a fleet shares the use of one or more as a co-operative venture. Such has been the case for several years in the summer Icelandic herring fishery. Two land-based 'planes are used, searching up to 100 miles from the coast.

Apart from direct aids to fishing, there have recently come into common use, in the larger vessels of advanced countries, many complex aids to general navigation and communication, such as radar, radio navigators, radio beacon receivers, direction finders, and increasingly efficient radio-telephone and radio-telegraph equipment. These, of course, require new skills in the crew, and, in the case of long-range trawlers and other large ships, the carrying of a specialist radio operator. In short-range vessels they are to be welcomed as improving the crew's safety, but they may do little to reduce the cost of production of fish. In long-range vessels, however, the more accurate navigation and reduced hazards in operating near the ice may increase the effective fishing time on a trip, and so reduce costs.

Devices which have not yet reached the stage of development when they are in use on a wide commercial scale include electro-fishing and equipment for automatic gutting and heading of fish on board a vessel. The latter might cut down labour requirements, and also save the crews a tiresome repetitive task, particularly unpleasant on the exposed deck in cold weather. Electro-fishing, or the use of electrically charged plates or cables to direct fish towards a net or funnel, has been tried experimentally in fresh water in several countries, and in sea water by Russia. There is no doubt that the direction in which fish swim can be strongly influenced by such methods, but the economic value of the method is still open to doubt. Whereas it enables large and cumbersome nets to be dispensed with, the cost and fuel consumption of the equipment may be too high for application to most kinds of fishing.

Increasing use is probable in some fisheries of vessels equipped to process the fish partly or wholly to the state in which it can be retailed. Although the system requires larger vessels and more crew, it has the advantage of permitting longer stays away from port and greater effective fishing time. If the fish are turned into a preserved form, as when they are canned, there is no need for the ship to return to port because of the danger of spoilage before her holds are full. Again, as the unwanted parts of the fish are removed and thrown away, or reduced to by-products, the effective capacity of the hold is increased.

Deep-freezing of fish immediately after capture, as opposed to mere packing in ice chips in lightly refrigerated holds, is a method of treatment capable of more development. The fish may then be kept at low temperature throughout the land transport and selling stages until they finally reach the consumer. They will therefore keep their freshness better and longer than the ice-cooled fish at present normally landed. Such a system is, however, more expensive, as it makes considerable power demands on the vessel, and requires suitable chains of cold stores ashore.

An interesting vessel embodying several recent developments made her first voyage in the summer of 1954. She is the 2,605-ton *Fairtry*, owned by Messrs. Salvesen of Leith, and is the world's largest trawler, with a length of 245 ft. and a moulded breadth of 44 ft. The trawl net is hauled up a stern slipway in a technique reminiscent of whaling, in which the firm has large interests. The ship has a factory deck which includes a heading machine, and skinning and filleting machines. There are two sets of quick freezers, and a conveyor system carries fish to the fully refrigerated holds. Man-handling of the fish is largely avoided. Residues are converted to fish meal, and there is also the normal cod-liver oil plant.

The ship is designed for voyages of as long as three months, and crew accommodation is therefore on a good scale. She has a hold capacity of 550 tons of fillets, representing about 1,100 to 1,200 tons of fish, which also provide about 110 tons of fish meal. The fillets, some of them already in consumer-size packages, are landed in a really fresh condition, and kept at low temperatures until they reach the consumer. Initial voyages have been successful, and the undertaking may influence developments elsewhere in the world to enable remote grounds to be opened up for the supply of fresh fish to distant consuming centres. The ease with which crews can be recruited and held for work involving regular absences from home of up to three months will be revealed by experience.

Great complexity of treatment of fish on board vessels may also increase the use of the mother-factory-ship system. In this, a large vessel contains the processing equipment and storage space, and is fed by a number of fishing vessels. It may act also as a fuel and equipment base and recreational centre for catcher crews. The system has advantages when fishing is carried out far from the home base, in seas without suitable ports. To date, its use has not been widespread, partly because of the difficulty of transferring fish in rough seas, but there are examples in the fishing by the Japanese and Russians in the Sea of Okhotsk and Bering Sea.

We may now turn from the catching side to the land distribution side of the industry. In advanced countries there is reasonable speed of transport by rail or road, but over much of the world inland transport facilities are poor. This is one of the main factors limiting the effective market for fish, especially fresh fish. Much further development of rail transport is unlikely because of the high capital costs involved, but road and possibly air distribution channels should extend greatly in the coming decades. Full refrigeration equipment in storage centres, shops, and rail and road vehicles should also become a standard installation.

In spite of the cost of such facilities, there appears to be room for reduction in the present somewhat high percentage distribution costs. For example, the price of plaice to the consumer in southern England in mid-1953 was about 2s. a lb., or 28s. a stone. The price paid on landing at the dock was between 5s. and 8s. a stone. Detailed consideration of this matter is outside the scope of this book, yet it has a bearing on the wider geographical aspects of the industry, as reduction in distributional costs is important to the development of the sea resources in many areas of the world.

In the last analysis, all questions of new catching, processing, and distributing techniques depend on the state of demand in relation to supply, as indicated by prices. The well-being and expansion of an industry depend on the receipt of a return sufficient to encourage new investment. When prices of the products are rising as fast as, or faster than, costs, the industry is normally in an optimistic frame of mind, and expansion occurs if there are no physical obstacles. New techniques may be adopted, although in some cases too easy profits may not encourage the taking of risks with new devices when the old methods are already very profitable. In the post-war period many industries have, of course, been in this rather too fortunate position. It is usually when prices are no longer rising as fast as costs, although reserves are high, that the attention of an industry is focused on devices for cutting costs. This seems to be the phase that many sections of production are now entering, and it should lead particularly to further installation of labour-saving equipment in the advanced high wage countries.

The overall demand situation for sea products should remain healthy, for reasons we have discussed. In addition to human food demand, there may well be an increasing demand for animal foodstuffs, vitamin and other oils, and also organic raw material, both animal and vegetable, for purely industrial uses, such as the manufacture of certain types of plastic.

Large mid-water trawls, together with echo sounding and other devices, may reveal and exploit economic concentrations of pelagic fish, and possibly of other creatures, in areas of the tropical and southern temperate seas little used at present. Where these are distant from the main markets of dense population, much of the catches may profitably be turned into meal or oil, possibly in factory ships. Demand for these products has been rising at a faster rate than that for most fish products for human consumption. Fish meal is now an essential element in the farm economies of many countries. It provides strong competition to feeding-stuffs of vegetable origin, although it cannot completely replace them. In Britain, for example, the wholesale price of herring meal increased by about 250 per cent between 1938 and 1951, whereas the average wholesale price of fresh herring only increased by about 185 per cent.

The seas are still by no means fully used. The true assessment of their possibilities can only be found by actual development. That this will attract increasing efforts in the near future there can be no doubt. Mankind can no longer afford to neglect such major resources.

# APPENDIX

## RECENT CATCHES OF COUNTRIES NOW PRODUCING OVER 5,000 TONS ANNUALLY

CATCHES are in metric tons, and are of full weight at time of capture. They refer to marine and freshwater fish, shellfish, and other non-mammalian products. The source is F.A.O., from data supplied by governments whose methods of computation are not uniform, although these differences do not in most cases affect these results substantially. Figures are for 1953, unless otherwise indicated. An asterisk indicates an F.A.O. estimate. There are a small number of countries for which no information is available.

### AFRICA

| | |
|---|---|
| Algeria (1952) | 29,700 |
| Angola | 222,400 |
| Belgian Congo (1952) | 48,200 |
| Egypt (1952) | 53,800 |
| French Equatorial Africa (1951)* | 40,000 |
| French Morocco | 128,000 |
| French Togoland | 10,000 |
| French West Africa | 70,000 |
| Gold Coast (1948) | 36,000 |
| Kenya | 18,700 |
| Nigeria | 42,000 |
| Rhodesias & Nyasaland | 27,000 |
| Sierra Leone* | 5,000 |
| S.W. Africa | 274,800 |
| Spanish Morocco approx. | 20,000 |
| Sudan (1947) | 5,000 |
| Tanganyika | 50,000 |
| Tunisia | 11,500 |
| Uganda | 23,400 |
| Union of S. Africa | 353,400 |

### NORTH AMERICA

| | |
|---|---|
| Canada (exc. Newfoundland) | 661,400 |
| Newfoundland | 263,300 |
| Greenland | 25,000 |
| Mexico | 67,300 |
| St Pierre & Miquelon | 7,600 |
| U.S.A. & Alaska | 2,385,200 |

### SOUTH AMERICA AND WEST INDIES

| | |
|---|---|
| Argentina (1952) | 78,700 |
| Barbados | 6,500 |
| Brazil (1952) | 174,600 |
| British Guiana | 10,000 |
| Chile | 107,200 |
| Colombia (1951) | 16,000 |
| Cuba (1951) | 10,000 |
| Ecuador (1951) | 10,000 |
| Peru (1952) | 113,000 |
| Venezuela (1951) | 75,000 |
| Windward Islands (1947) | 5,600 |

20*

ASIA

| | |
|---|---|
| Aden (1952)* | 50,000 |
| Cambodia | 90,400 |
| North Borneo (1952) | 5,600 |
| Sarawak (1952)* | 5,600 |
| Burma* approx. | 100,000 |
| Ceylon | 25,500 |
| China* approx. | 3,000,000 |
| Formosa | 130,070 |
| Hong Kong | 35,800 |
| India (1952) | 752,000 |
| Indonesia | 616,900 |
| Iran (1952)* | 30,000 |
| Iraq (1951) | 7,000 |
| Israel | 7,700 |
| Japan | 4,576,500 |
| N. Korea approx. | 300,000 |
| S. Korea (1951) | 276,900 |
| Fed. of Malaya | 164,400 |
| Singapore | 15,300 |
| Maldive Islands | 20,000 |
| Pakistan (1952) | 126,700 |
| Philippines | 311,900 |
| Thailand | 205,000 |
| Turkey | 102,500 |

EUROPE

| | |
|---|---|
| Belgium | 74,400 |
| Denmark | 343,800 |
| Faeroes | 88,800 |
| Finland | 62,100 |
| France | 490,000 |
| W. Germany | 730,400 |
| E. Germany (1951)* approx. | 50,000 |
| Greece | 46,000 |
| Iceland | 424,700 |
| Eire | 19,000 |
| Italy | 213,600 |
| Holland | 343,300 |
| Norway | 1,505,500 |
| Poland (1951) | 72,000 |
| Portugal | 392,400 |
| Spain | 625,000 |
| Sweden | 210,000 |
| U.K. | 1,121,600 |
| Yugoslavia | 24,400 |

OCEANIA

| | |
|---|---|
| Australia | 51,600 |
| Hawaii (1952) | 6,300 |
| New Zealand (1952) | 35,300 |

U.S.S.R.* approx. 2,500,000

# INDEX

*The page numbers given may concern textual or diagrammatic references. The more important page numbers are italicized.*

For Product Safety Concerns and Information please contact our EU
representative GPSR@taylorandfrancis.com
Taylor & Francis Verlag GmbH, Kaufingerstraße 24, 80331 München, Germany